MANTRAS FOR HAPPINESS

Prof.(Dr.)Jai Paul Dudeja

ISBN 979-888546198-6

This book is a humble dedication to my grandmother (my father's mother) who was an embodiment of contentment, compassion and happiness.

Contents

PREFACE

Dear Readers,

I am extremely happy to see this book titled, **"Mantras for Happiness"** in your hands. It is my firm belief that you have chosen to read this book with a specific aim in mind, and I assure you that you will not be disappointed.

This book is divided into **22 chapters.**

Chapter 1 explains the reason that prompted me to write this book. **Chapter 2** gives a definition of 'Happiness' and explains its difference with satisfaction, pleasure etc. **Chapter 3** deals with 'Right to Happiness'. **Chapter 4** explains the conceptof 'Gross National Happiness (GNH)'. **Chapters 5 to 9** discuss the concept of 'Happiness' in Hinduism, Buddhism, Jainism, Sufism, and Christianity, respectively. **Chapter 10** talks about 'Happiness Within'. **Chapter 11** asserts that 'Happiness is a Choice' for us. **Chapters 12-15** discuss how to achieve Happiness in Family, at Workplace, in Society, and in Digital Age, respectively. **Chapter 16** asserts that Happiness is contagious. **Chapter 17** describes what are the molecules or hormones in happy persons. **Chapter 18** emphasizes that the happy persons live longer and healthier. **Chapter 19** asserts that if you want to be happy, practice compassion, and vice versa. This is a two-way process and H.H. Dalai Lama also believes in the same philosophy. **Chapter 20,** titled 'Mantras for Happiness' justifies the title of this book and mentions various techniques to achieve a state of happiness. **Chapter 21** discusses an important topic about how to measure happiness at individual as well at collective level. Finally, **Chapter 22** describes various physical, mental and spiritual benefits of happiness.

The author sincerely believes that a book of this nature will be useful for all the readers across the globe who wish to be happy and are looking for techniques to achieve this state.

I would gratefully and open heartedly love to receive any encouraging/ critical comments as well as feedback from my dear readers at my Email ID: drjpdudeja@gmail.com

Sincerely

Prof.(Dr.)Jai Paul Dudeja

2021

ACKNOWLEDGEMENTS

The seeds of my interest in 'search for happiness' were sown more than sixty years ago by my revered parents, **Late (Dr.)Shanti Sawrup Dudeja and Late (Mrs.)Jai Devi Dudeja.** I, therefore, bow to them, wherever they are in the other world.

I have greatly benefitted in going through the books and articles referred in the 'Bibliography' of this Book. I gratefully acknowledge these authors for enhancing my understanding on the subject matter of this book.

Last but not the least, my greatest admiration is reserved for **Mrs. Rita Dudeja, my wife**, my best friend and my constant source of inspiration, for all my ventures and endeavours like this and many others.

Prof.(Dr.)Jai Paul Dudeja

2021

CHAPTER ONE

MY STORY AS A CHILD PRODIGY AND A TROUBLED YOUTH

What prompted me to write this book? In this chapter I shall give two accounts about my past: one, myself as a child prodigy and another about my troubled youth. So, here it goes.

1.1 As a Childhood Prodigy

This story was narrated to me by my elders in the family (including my parents) and my elder brother who has been living in Australia for the last 35 years.

The elders in my family could not migrate from Pakistan to India in or around the time of partition in Aug 1947. It was because my father was involved in the freedom struggle led by Arya Samaj Movement (a Hindu movement led by Lala Lajpat Rai). Our family finally could come to India in or around June 1948, with very few possessions to carry with. All the houses vacated by those people who had migrated from India to Pakistan (mainly Muslims) were occupied by the new returnees to India and, therefore, we had no option but to settle in a refugee camp in a small village Kachroli, near Panipat (District Karnal in Punjab, India, in those days), where I was born in June 1948. I was very weak and undernourished child, and my parents were not sure whether I would survive or not. The administration of that Refugee camp used to provide about 200 ml of family per day per family. It was one of the most difficult decision for my family as to which member of the family should be given that meagre quantity of milk. Ultimately the choice fell on my brother who was about two years elder to me (and now settled in Australia). He used to get that milk for his survival, and I was left on God's mercy to live on.

From the refugee camp, we soon shifted to a small village named 'Bega' (that time in united Punjab and now in Haryana).

My father was an Unani Vaidya (a doctor practicing the Unani system of medicine), which he had learnt from my Grandfather. He opened a small shop at a rent of Rs. 1/- per month and we lived in a house at a rent of Rs. 4/- per month. Both these amounts were not small in those days. So, to further support our family, my mother used to do sundry jobs, like stitching shirt-buttons on thick papers and selling used clothes and utensils which we could bring from Pakistan. Although my mother had a formal education up to the fifth standard only, yet she was quite good in Arithmetic. As a 3-year-old child, I used to listen to her attentively doing these calculations and negotiations with the buyers of our old stuff. Please note that I had not gone to school by then.

We were financially very poor to support a family of eight at that time. One day, my father took me along to a grocery shop to buy monthly rations for the family, like wheat, pulses, ghee (clarified butter), spices, etc. Those were the days when the new currency (rupees and paisa) was not existing. For weights, instead of kg, it used to be sair, paav, and chhataank etc. Instead of the new rupee and paisa, it was the old rupee, annas, and paisa. Doing calculations was far tougher those days than it is now, and that too in the absence of any calculators. My father might have ordered for 12-13 items, each having a different weight and a different rate. The shopkeeper wrote this list on a piece of paper before calculating the total amount to be paid by my father.

Once the shopkeeper read out the list of all the items along with their rates and quantity and was about to calculate the total amount, I (a three-year-old child) told the total amount in 3-4 seconds. My father and the shopkeeper were taken aback. The shopkeeper wrote this (result) separately on another paper and then did his calculations independently, which might have taken him 10-15 minutes. The two figures (one told by me and another calculated by the shopkeeper) came out to be the same. Just to satisfy his curiosity, he asked me 5-6 different questions like this, and each time I gave the correct answer within a couple of seconds.

Within an hour or so, this 'miracle' displayed by me spread like a wildfire in the entire village. Within days, it spread to neighboring villages, then to Sonipat (that time Tehsil), then to Rohtak (District at that time) and maybe to Delhi thereafter.

I was too small to understand the significance of a visual scene when, one day, my father was holding the two legs of my frail body with one of his strong hands, up in the air and he was crying loudly. Subsequently, my elders informed me that some reporters from an Urdu newspaper in Delhi had visited my village. They wanted to seek my father's permission to take me along to Delhi and probably bear all my expenses. My father never wanted to part with me. This made him cry.

I continued displaying this miracle to the educated people of my village (very few) until I turned five and took admission in the first grade in that village. We used to sit on the floor on the mats in the school. One day, a school inspector visited our school. It seems he had heard about me. With a pen and a paper in his hand, he asked me some tough questions about Arithmetic. For example, how many paisas are there in 7278 rupees 3 annas and 2 paisas. [The answer would be equal to (7278 x 16x4) + (3x4)+ 2 = 465792+12+2=465806]. Every time I gave the correct answer in about 3-seconds and thereafter he verified my answers with pencil and paper. He was so happy with me that he took out a one-rupee coin (a big amount in those days) and gave it to me. This news also spread in my village and the neighboring villages. Not only me, even my father was treated as a hero for giving birth to me.

Just for fun, my teachers and the seniors in the school would frequently approach me asking to solve problems in arithmetic. I would give the correct answer within a couple of seconds each time. So, very soon I became famous (not popular) in the school.

1.2 Adverse effects of Public Praise

There were very few patients visiting the one-room clinic of my father in that village; so not much income in his practice. I used to sit in that clinic most of the time and listening to my father talking about me with the visiting patients and their companions. He often used loads of words of praise about me. Like "my son is a God's special child. He is uniquely gifted. Probably he remembers his previous birth. I am very proud to him as my son. He is the best in the world at this age...." His patients would quietly listen to these comments. I was also a party to these listeners. I now believe that these patients would also compare me with their own 'less-privileged children'. But neither my father cared about this nor me. Very soon I also thought that, as declared by my father. I was the best kid in the world. This brought an inflated ego in me.

This attitude soon made me unpopular among my 'friends and batch-mates'. I would not tolerated a single word of criticism against me from these 'jealous' or even normal people. This resulted in my isolation from my them but my opinion about myself remained the same as the 'best kid in the world'. I thought that I should not care about those jealous people, without realizing the origin of this. Consequently, I gradually got cut-off and drifted to my 'isolation chamber'.

1.3 My Troubled Youth

In my small village, mixing freely with persons of opposite sex was not only discouraged, it was considered a taboo, particularly by the elders in our village. So I got no experience of interacting with girls in my youth, except my sisters in the family. These restrictions had an impact on me when I was growing in age in my school, college and university life. I used to watch other friends (boys) 'with envy' in freely mixing, chatting with the girls but I could never pick up the courage to talk to any girl. In passing, let me inform that my height is half-an-inch less than five feet, and I had the perception that most of the girls did not want to talk to shorties like me. This was multiplied by my restricted life in my village.

This problem got aggravated when I used to see 'beautiful girls' in the campus. I would enter into a 'world of fantasy' about these girls. They would often appear in my dreams. Needless to say, that it was 'one-way' attraction/affection/love from my side with other side not even knowing about it. Consequently I became 'withdrawn' from the world of girls.

But the above-mentioned problem was compensated to some extent by (i) my excellent performance in academics on a regular basis, (ii) my oratory skills as 'award winning debater/speaker', (iii) my wring skills as an author/editor, and (iv) my skills as a poet, and (v) my dramatical skills as an 'award winning actor'. Were these consciously/ sub-consciously meant to impress these girls or impress myself. I am not sure.

It took me 5-6 decades to reflect on the impact of these incidents in my life mentioned in this chapter. I contemplated on it and finally decided to author this book in order to share my thoughts with my dear readers. The one and only one aim of authoring this book is to share the "Mantras or secrets of happiness' with you all.

CHAPTER TWO

HAPPINESS: INTRODUCTION

Who doesn't want to be happy? The obvious answer is: everybody wants. Every year on 31st December, when the clock strikes 00:00 Hours in the middle of night, we start wishing 'Happy New Year' to our nears and dears, if they are awake at that time. On your birthday, many of your friends and family members wish you a 'Happy Birthday'. Similarly you reciprocate the same sentiments to others on their birthdays. On the occasions of festivals and on the 'wedding anniversaries' you greet them again with happy messages. The common word/sentiment in all the above sentences is 'Happy'. So, in a nutshell, everybody wants not only himself/herself to be happy, he/she also wants others to be happy. This concept (of happiness) will be discussed in detail in this book.

2.1 What is Mantra?

The word mantra comes from the ancient Sanskrit language. 'Man' means mind, and 'tra' means release. Any thought, idea or technique, which removes the blindness of mind, or trains the mind, is known as mantra. So, Mantras for Happiness are those techniques which lead to a happy state of mind.

2.2 What is Happiness?

The word 'happiness' is used in various ways. In the widest sense it is an umbrella term for all that is good. In this meaning it is often used interchangeably with terms like 'well-being' or 'quality of life' and denotes both individual and social welfare. The term 'happiness' is used in the context of mental or emotional states, including positive or pleasant emotions ranging from contentment to intense joy. It is also used in the context of life satisfaction, subjective well-being, eudaimonia (state of feeling well), flourishing and well-being. Research on happiness has been conducted in a wide variety of scientific disciplines, including gerontology, social psychology and positive psychology, clinical and medical research and happiness economics. Happiness is the overall appreciation of one's life as-a-whole. Overall happiness is the degree to which an individual judges the overall quality of his/her own life-as-a-whole favourably. In other words: how much one likes the life one leads.

Philosophy of happiness is often discussed in conjunction with ethics. Traditional societies often linked happiness with morality, which was concerned with the performance in a certain kind of role in a certain kind of social life. Happiness, sometimes, is no longer defined in relation to social life, but in terms of individual psychology. Happiness, however, remains a difficult term for moral philosophy. Throughout the history of moral philosophy, there has been an oscillation between attempts to define morality in terms of consequences leading to happiness and attempts to define morality in terms that have nothing to do with happiness at all. People in countries with high cultural religiosity tend to relate their life satisfaction less to their emotional experiences than people in more secular countries.

According to Aristotle , happiness is "the end of all ends." Positive psychology involves the instrumentalization of happiness as a technique. Happiness becomes a means to an end, as well as the end of the means. Happiness becomes, then, a way of maximizing your potential of getting what you want, as well as being what you want to get.

In general, happiness is understood as the positive emotions we have in regards to the pleasurable activities we take part in through our daily lives. Pleasure, comfort, gratitude, hope, and inspiration are examples of positive emotions that increase our happiness and move us to flourish. In scientific literature, happiness is referred to as hedonic, the presence of positive emotions and the absence of negative emotions.

"Happiness does not come automatically. It is not a gift that good fortune bestows upon us and a reversal of fortune takes back. It depends on us alone. One does not become happy overnight, but with patient labour, day-after-day. Happiness is constructed, and that requires effort and time. In order to become happy, we have to learn how to change ourselves."

-Luca and Francesco Cavalli-Sforza

2.2.1 Ingredients of Happiness

There are several theories of happiness in the literature that attempt to identify basic psychological elements that happiness consists of. The most notable theories include: subjective well-being, objective happiness (psychological well-being, eudemonic well-being, authentic happiness/ the well-being, social-psychological prosperity/flourishing, or the onion theory of happiness.

The subjective well-being theory argues that a happy individual experiences an abundance of positive feelings and few negative feelings – a balance that serves as the basis for the evaluation of life as very satisfactory. The objective happiness theory argues that broad cognitive evaluations of well-being ("Am I a happy person?") are usually biased; thus, only the quality of immediate experience (in terms of good vs bad as the indicator of utility) is a valid measure of well-being. The psychological well-being theory argues that a happy individual is characterized by several positive psychological characteristics such as autonomy, environmental mastery, or personal growth . The eudemonic well-being theory argues that a happy individual is, above all, intensely engaged in self-exploration, self-expression, and the development of their best potential with positive emotions as an additional consequence or a by-product of these pursuits. Social-psychological prosperity theory lists elements of positive functioning across diverse domains that are constitutive to a very happy life (flourishing) such as having rewarding relationships, contributing to happiness of others, or being engaged in daily activities. Happiness theories or authentic happiness theory that evolved into the well-being theory have distinguished components ("routes to happiness") that constitute the full life: pleasure and positive emotions (the pleasant life), engagement or flow (the good life), and meaning (meaningful life). Included in this are the components of achievements (conceptualized as the pursuit of them rather than their actual accomplishment) and social relationships. Happiness is described with a three-layer structure in the onion theory with the positive attractor (the will to live) as the core, the mid-layer of general subjective wellbeing, and the outer layer of current effective experience and satisfaction with specific life domains that reflects objective life events and circumstances.

2.2.2 Individual Differences in Happiness

Large scale cross-cultural studies indicated that most individuals consider themselves rather happy. There are however meaningful differences in happiness that result from several factors. Research has established that individual differences of various components of happiness result mostly from: (a) genetic influences that sustain a level of well-being characteristic for a specific person (i.e., the happiness set-point), (b) intentional activity (e.g., how individuals regulate their positive emotions), and, to a lesser extent, (c) life events (e.g., marriage) and circumstances (e.g., income). Life events can cause positive and negative temporal (childbirth or widowhood, respectively) or lasting changes in well-being (marriage or disability). Personality is the main determinant of well-being due to its constant interaction with several aspects of human functioning such as life events and circumstances, emotional experience, and cognitive processing. Several personality traits have been related to happiness, e.g., extroverts experience more life satisfaction, whereas individuals high on neuroticism experience less life satisfaction. Happiness-related personality traits evolve over time, e.g., individuals become more extroverted and more emotionally stable. Noteworthy, the influence of personality on happiness can be modified via intentional behavioural efforts. For instance, when less extroverted individuals intentionally try to initiate behaviours that are typical for extroverts, they temporarily improve their well-being. Various aspects of happiness (i.e., life satisfaction or positive emotions) can be successfully enhanced intentionally via happiness interventions or positive psychological interventions. These interventions are inspired by cognitive therapy methods and increase happiness through exercises that enhance positive emotions (e.g., gratitude), cognitions (e.g., optimism), or behaviours (e.g., kind acts).

2.3 Difference between Happiness and Pleasure

Happiness is often equated with a maximization of pleasure, and some imagine that true happiness would consist of an interrupted succession of pleasurable experience. There is no reason to deprive ourselves of the enjoyment of a magnificent landscape, of swimming in the sea or of the scent of a rose, but we must understand that the experience of pleasure is dependent upon circumstance, on a specific location or moment in time. It is unstable by nature, and the sensation it evokes can soon become neutral or even unpleasant. In other words, pleasure is externally motivated and fleeting, while happiness is internally generated and constant. Happiness is not necessarily dependent on any external or internal pleasurable stimuli.

2.4 Difference between Happiness and Success

"Success is getting what you want; happiness is: wanting what you get."- Ingrid Bergman.

Success is meeting the deadlines. Happiness is working toward your goals. Success is focusing on accumulating wealth. Happiness is focusing on improving your life. Success is promotion above your peers. Happiness is being respected by your peers. “When I look back on all these worries,

I remember the story of the old man who said on his deathbed that he had had a lot of trouble in his life, most of which had never happened.” -Winston Churchill.

Success is finding a life partner. Happiness is keeping your partner for life. Success is keeping the knowledge you glean to yourself. Happiness is sharing your expertise freely.

One of my Facebook friends recently wrote on her post,

“Success is father, and happiness is mother. Father wants his children to be successful but mother always wishes her children to be happy.”

2.5 Difference between Happiness and Satisfaction

Happiness' is defined as both a state of mind and an emotion. Man can choose to be happy. It is relevant to note that even people who are poor can be happy despite the fact that not all their needs are met, even the most basic ones. 'Satisfaction,' on the other hand, is the state wherein your desires are met. You will find it in the possession and enjoyment of things that you desire. In effect, it, too, is a state of mind wherein you find contentment knowing that your demands and desires are made possible.

Meeting the desires of your heart and the demands of your needs will not necessarily make you happy despite the fact that you will never want for anything when you are satisfied. Everything actually depends on your beliefs. If you see poverty as a blessing rather than a curse and be content with what you have, then your chances of being happy are greater than the person who sees material things as a necessity in life.

2.6 Difference Between Happiness and Peace of Mind

Majority of people are confused about the difference between happiness and peace of mind. If the average person is asked what they want in life their answer will be happy. Far fewer people respond that they want inner peace. These two states of mind are certainly closely related, and yet they are different and independent. Here we will take a look at the differences between happiness and peace of mind.

2.6.1 What Is Peace Of Mind?

To be at peace requires complete acceptance of how things are without any desire for anything to be different. This is one reason why peace of mind is different from happiness. Happiness is often the pursuit of worthwhile desires and ambitions, whereas peace of mind is the ability to let go of those ambitions and desires. The achievement of peace is the ability to simply accept things as they are.

The common perception is that peace represents dullness. This is a misunderstanding as this state is one of calmness rather than dullness. In fact, this state can put you in a good place to then experience more happiness. Often, when someone is always over-analysing the situation or going over past events, it creates stress. If they're always thinking about the future, this too can lead to discontent.

The human condition often creates discomfort in order to motivate a person into an action that will make things better. Some examples of this are if you get hungry, then you can experience discomfort until you've eaten. If you need to use the restroom, then you will feel discomfort until you're able to do so. In the same way, discontent can drive a person to create a better situation for their own life or the life of their family.

But this discomfort gets twisted and leads a person to no longer being able to be at peace. It is only when they can return to the ability to simply accept things as they are that they can feel at peace. When someone is at peace they are better able to experience happiness.

2.6.2 What Is Happiness?

This is a feeling that comes largely from a person's satisfaction with their current circumstances. If a person is living a fulfilling life and they are reasonably happy with the progress they're making then they will generally feel a sense of happiness. When someone is failing to have the kind of life that they want or find fulfilling, then they will have a sense of unhappiness.

In general, the feeling of happiness will come and go as a person achieves or experiences things that they are happy about. The important factor about this feeling is that you can choose it under any and all circumstances. When a person changes how they view happiness, they have more control over it and can keep the feeling alive longer. An example of this would be the difference between someone who looks at a difficult situation as a challenge and another person who looks at it as a burden.

In a study done at Harvard University, it was found that those who could focus more often on the here-and-now were far more at peace and experienced more happiness than those who thought more often of the past and the future.

2.7 Happiness versus Positive Psychology

2.7.1 What is Positive Psychology?

The term "Positive Psychology" was originally coined by the psychologist Abraham Maslow in the 1950's. He used the term somewhat loosely to call for a more balanced view of human nature, that is, to draw attention to human potentialities as well as psychological afflictions. In 2002, Martin Seligman popularized the expression 'Positive Psychology' through his influential work "Authentic Happiness," defining it as the study of positive emotions and the "strengths that enable individuals and communities to thrive."

2.7.2 What is the Science of Happiness?

The Science of Happiness, the scientific study of "what makes happy people happy," was launched by Mihaly Czikszentmihalyi in the late 1980's. Czikszentmihalyi pioneered the "Experience Sampling Method" to discover what he called the "psychology of optimal experience," and specifically, the experience of Flow.

2.7.3 How is Positive Psychology related to the Science of Happiness?

Positive Psychology could be regarded as a subset within the broader field we call the Science of Happiness, which extends to the natural as well as the social sciences. For example, Positive Psychology is largely focused on the study of positive emotions and "signature strengths," yet the Science of Happiness extends, for example, to such areas as the impact of exercise on psychological well-being, or the effect of social media on happiness.

2.8 Difference Between Happiness and Joy

The difference between joy and happiness lives in the mind and heart.

- Joy is a little word. Happiness is a bigger word.
- Joy is in the heart. Happiness is on the face.
- Joy is of the soul. Happiness is of the moment.
- Joy transcends. Happiness reacts.
- Joy embraces peace and contentment, waiting to be discovered.

- Joy runs deep and overflows, while happiness hugs hello.
- Joy is a practice and a behaviour. It's deliberate and intentional. Happiness comes and goes along its way.
- Joy is profound and Scriptural. "Don't worry, rejoice." Happiness is a balm: "Don't worry, be happy."
- Joy is an inner feeling. Happiness is an outward expression.
- Joy endures hardship and trials and connects with meaning and purpose.

A person pursues happiness but chooses joy.

2.8.1 Happiness versus Joy

For every person who says joy is an underlying truth that good or bad circumstances can't dictate, and that happiness is rooted in circumstance, there will be others who think the opposite, that joy is just a state of mind, the outcome of a mind seeking happiness and focused on pleasure, pleasing thoughts and pleasant experiences.

Despite the different perspectives, the idea that holds greater sway today is that experiencing happiness depends on external factors. Happiness happens to us. Even though we may seek it, desire it, pursue it, etc., feeling happiness is not a choice we make. Joy, on the other hand, is a choice purposefully made.

Happiness doesn't bring joy, and joy isn't the byproduct of happiness. Joy is something grander than happiness. Joy is a fruit of the Spirit, and when we find joy it's infused with comfort and wrapped in peace. It's an attitude of the heart and spirit.

Regardless of one's faith, joy is present inside everyone as an untapped reservoir of potential.

It's possible to experience joy in difficult times. It's possible to know joy or feel joy in spite of grief or uncertainty. Joy doesn't need a smile in order to exist.

Although joy does feel better with a happy smile, joy can share space with other emotions — sadness, fear, anger ... even unhappiness. Happiness can't.

Happiness isn't present in darkness and difficulty. It can't be present when its antithesis rules. But once discovered, joy undergirds our spirits and brings to life peace and contentment, even in the face of unhappiness.

Joy blooms through connection. It's what God wants for us. Often the connection is with other people, but it can also be with pets, creation, creativity, etc.

Joy is present, in the moment. Every moment. Happiness is ephemeral and temporary. It's mostly just passing through.

When happiness is present, it's larger than life. It feels good, and nothing feels better or seems worthy of attention. But happiness is also fickle. It can be present for weeks on end and gone in an instant. True joy is constant.

The true definition of joy goes beyond the limited explanation presented in a dictionary — "a feeling a great pleasure and happiness." True joy is a limitless, life-defining, transformative reservoir waiting to be tapped into. It requires the utmost surrender and, like love, is a choice to be made. Joy is not simply a feeling that happens.

Joy is also not great happiness or even extreme happiness. It is not elation, jubilation or exhilaration — emotions that may be present with joy, that may seem like an expression of joy, but which don't define joy. In its truest expression, joy transforms difficult times into blessings and turns heartache into gratitude. Joy brings meaning to life. It brings life to life.

2.8.2 Understanding the Difference between Happiness and Joy

Understanding the differences between happiness and joy has a greater purpose than being fodder for an intellectual debate. The distinctions between happiness and joy have many real-world applications. One practical application pertains to children living in extreme poverty.

Poverty is often synonymous with despair. A heavy word, but also a word with a bark worse than its bite. Despair is like happiness in that it's temporary, although it never feels that way. Despair is a product of circumstance, and it can't hold a candle to joy. Joy can overcome anything and everything in this world if it's allowed. If it's chosen.

In choosing joy, there is hope. With joy, hardship offers growth and opportunity. With joy, self-esteem and self-respect are indestructible.

"You turned my wailing into dancing; you removed my sackcloth and clothed me with joy."

— Psalm 30:11

2.9 In Pursuit of Happiness

A man always wants more, not less, happiness than he has already. He errs, however, when he thinks he can increase his happiness by adding to his possessions rather than expanding his awareness. Any effort to increase his happiness without at the same time expanding his sensitivity to the world around him, and his sense of identity with it, will be self-defeating. Whenever a person acts selfishly, he deprives himself of the force or vitality and capacity to perceive his essential unity with all life. He becomes, as a result, petty and mean. The expansion of happiness necessarily entails the expansion of awareness, not the expansion of property. For happiness is not a thing, and cannot be found in mere things. It is a quality of consciousness: something that one is aware with, rather than of.

Reason therefore suggests, and inner experience confirms that happiness is an intrinsic quality of human nature. We enjoy things only to the extent that we satisfy the thought in our own minds that things are enjoyable. In fact, it is never things themselves that we enjoy at all, but only a deeper reality within our own being. The clearest proof that things are not enjoyable in themselves may be seen in the fact that different people can have such very different ideas as to what gives them happiness. The theory of non-dualism is emphatic in its conviction that man is endowed with an innate quality of being (sat), consciousness (chit) and unalloyed happiness (ananda): he has only to look within to realise experientially that the jiva is an embodiment of the macrosmic existence.

The desire to attain happiness is actually symptomatic of the desire for self-discovery, for self-fulfilment. By the same token, the desire to avoid suffering is essentially a desire to eschew 'non-happiness' as foreign to our nature. We suffer only when something withholds from us that degree of happiness which we feel rightfully ours.

2.10 Seven Levels of Happiness

2.10.1 First level of happiness – Artificial Happiness

Artificial happiness means that where ignorance prevails and where happiness actually does not even exist. Where it does not even occur to one that a fake object is being considered to be an authentic one and our entire life is spent thinking it to be true. What does a person do in this artificial happiness?

2.10.2 Second level of happiness – Second hand happiness

The second hand happiness is derived by using others or having fun at the expense of others. In this type a person likes to enjoy by teasing, taunting, bullying or troubling others. He feels good about it. He likes to make fun of others; it gives him a kind of pleasure. It is just like some friends get together to harass one person and they enjoy it. In every school or college, such scenes of ragging are common. This is second hand happiness. Back home you find that brothers and sisters often tease, taunt, and quarrel with each other. And when the dispute grows out of proportion, they patch up by asking for forgiveness from each other, and then throw parties and enjoy themselves. This is the way people nowadays try to find some pleasure and happiness in their lives. When man does not know what is real happiness, he indulges in such kind of happiness. In every kind of happiness that we get, we should ask ourselves as to what type of happiness is ours.

2.10.3 Third level of happiness – Stimulation Happiness

The third level of happiness is known as stimulation happiness; this happiness is aroused by excitement. For instance a person attending a social gathering or a celebration finds much hustle and bustle happening around. This creates excitement and stimulation.

2.10.4 Fourth level of happiness – Formula Happiness

This kind of happiness is created by applying a formula. The meaning of formula is that by combining two things one formula emerges. Linking two types of pleasures, a formula for happiness is created. When we combine two elements it makes a formula such as x+y=z. Students are taught such formulae in schools. Each and every person has devised some formula in his life so as to feel some happiness. If everything goes well as per his formula, he is very happy. For many, the formula is "Sunday morning newspaper + A cigarette + Coffee." For some, the formula is "Saturday night party + A new date every time." For children, the formula could be "A whole day of play + A movie to end the day." For ladies, it could be "Gift + Gold = Happiness."

2.10.5 Fifth level of happiness – Happiness through Service

This is the first amongst the higher levels of happiness, where an individual derives happiness out of serving others. Some people render service by being instrumental for others in achieving happiness. After recovering from their own maladies and disorders, and after coming out of their own anxieties, they start serving the destitute, the deprived, the aged, and work for the welfare of the society. They get contentment and happiness due to such service.

2.10.6 Sixth level of happiness – Divine happiness

At this level of happiness, a person experiences joy due to his devotion to God. Here there is no place for entertainment type of devotion – a lot many things other than worship are being done today in the name of devotion. One such particular occasion is called as Jagran (a religious ceremony carried out in some parts of India). During Jagran, people sing devotional songs and eat and drink throughout the night. And then some people make a pledge : "If this particular desire of ours gets fulfilled, we promise to hold this event at our place next year..." This kind of devotion is either just a kind of entertainment or a business transaction with God. This is the same as is customary in business deals – "You do me a favour, and in return I will do something for you." This type of worship is just a business type of worship; which has got nothing to do with devotion or real happiness. Joy achieved from business type devotion or wavering devotion is not in reality the happiness that is derived through divine veneration. Happiness through worship is gained through intense divine ardour, which is totally different from business or wavering type of devotion. Wavering devotion means the faith that falters when your wishes are not granted by praying to the deities. Consequently, all faith is lost. Then someone advises saying, "There is another deity, let us try that one now." This way business devotion is ever persistent. This kind of worship is not at all divine veneration, as there is no awareness of the divine. There is no understanding of what is God. It is just entertainment kind of worship, or devotion that is adulterated with hypocrisy and deceitfulness, or business type of devotion, or wavering faith, or worshipping God for the purpose of atonement. True happiness cannot be derived from such types of devotion. If devotion is done to attain real happiness, only then it is divine devotion.

Happiness acquired from divine devotion is the sixth level of happiness. At this level, man is in love with the Creator. He sings the praises of God and admires everything created by God. Everything that happens in his life is fully acceptable to him. He says, "If God desires to keep me in this state, then I am happy as I am." He believes, "If this is what God desires, then I have no objection to it. If God is making me cry, then I shall cry with happiness..." It is a very beautiful state born out of surrendering. There is a level of understanding and spiritual growth out of which this happiness emanates. One is always in a feeling of gratitude and devotion at this level.

Those who know what is divine devotion, they can understand the ultimate happiness. Divine devotion is unconditional. In this type of devotion, our faith, our love for God does not diminish even if our desires are not fulfilled. But if our desire does get fulfilled, then that is a bonus. We are not worshiping in order to get bonus (material gains). We are worshipping for the sake of devotion, for the love of God that has awakened, for the Divinity within, which we have recognized. If divine devotion gets aroused in our hearts, we are bound to get this happiness. Many who are on the path of devotion are working towards it but due to lack of understanding, it results in worshipping blindly, therefore there should not be blind worship. Those who are following the path of devotion should also realize as to what understanding should be combined with it so that their devotion can become divine devotion, and devotion itself should become the ultimate goal. In this kind of veneration, God loves those who love Him.

2.10.7 Seventh level of happiness – Eternal Bliss

This kind of happiness differs from all other kinds of joys. This happiness is attained when a person is free from all false beliefs and misconceptions, and he knows the answer to, "Who am I?" He attains this happiness after he has realized his true self (self-realization). This happiness arises out of the experience of the Self or the sense of being. It is causeless, unremitting, pure joy that never diminishes and never ends. It is permanent happiness. Each one of us bears the eternal bliss within, but we are not aware of it. Yet everyone does get a glimpse of this joy. When you are in deep sleep and neither the mind is awake nor dreaming, nor are you aware of the body, then you are in connection with that eternal state. So every night when you are in deep sleep, where do you think you are - amidst absolute bliss, aren't you? In the morning when you wake up, you say, "I had wonderful sleep." What did you feel in sleep that makes you say so? Where and in which blissful state were you in that deep sleep? And certainly you were in a state of ecstasy. Each and every person in this universe loves going to sleep. Some even take pills in order to get sleep. All the miseries and sorrows, all the aches and pains of the body simply vanish in deep sleep. So what is it that happens during sleep? If we are able to get that 'something' in the wakeful state which happens in deep slumber, then we can get the taste of true happiness.

CHAPTER THREE

RIGHT TO HAPPINESS

3.1 UN's Resolution on 'Right to Happiness'

In 2011, the UN General Assembly adopted a resolution which recognized happiness as a "fundamental human goal" and called for "a more inclusive, equitable and balanced approach to economic growth that promotes the happiness and well-being of all peoples".

In 2012 the first ever UN conference on Happiness took place and the UN General Assembly adopted a resolution which decreed that the International Day of Happiness would be observed every year on 20 March. It was celebrated for the first time in 2013.

According to this 'Resolution' UN recommended to the Governments to:

a. Consider using a broader concept of well-being, going beyond GDP and economic growth, adopting a new economic paradigm that encapsulates the social, economic and environmental aspects of sustainable development.

b. Use carefully constructed regular, large-scale data on happiness and wellbeing as a more appropriate indicator for improving macroeconomic policymaking and informing service delivery.

c. Initiate broad consultations, involving all stakeholders, to identify and prioritize the well-being indicators that carry the potential for a shared view of the ways that social progress can be achieved and sustained over time.

d. Instruct national statistical offices to consider expanding the well-being content of their national statistical systems. A system of evaluation could take shape over time where policies might be judged by the changes in happiness that they produced per unit of net public expenditure.

e. Ensure the minimum conditions for happiness for the majority of people in low-income countries, as well as excluded groups in middle- and high-income countries, such as (i) access to food and basic services (ii) basic human rights and social protection and (iii) reduced inequalities, before pursuing broader well-being goals.

Advocate for the future work of the Bhutan international expert working group to be linked to the existing initiatives of the Secretary-General, the human development index of UNDP, the follow-up mechanisms to the United Nations Conference on Sustainable Development, and academic and civil society initiatives in related areas

3.2 International Day of Happiness

As stated above, the International Day of Happiness is celebrated throughout the world on 20 March. It was established by the United Nations General Assembly on 28 June 2012.

The International Day of Happiness aims to make people around the world realize the importance of happiness within their lives.

In 2015, the United Nations launched 17 Sustainable Development Goals to make people's lives happier. Its main development goals are to eradicate poverty, reduce inequality and protect our planet.

Before the International Day of Happiness was established, together with Luis Gallardo, President of the World Happiness Foundation, Jayme Illien founded "Happytalism." Illien ran a campaign at the United Nations from 2006 to 2012 to encourage and advance the primacy of happiness, well-being, and democracy.

In 2011, Jayme Illien proposed the idea of the International Day of

Happiness at the United Nations General Assembly. He wanted the United Nations General Assembly to promote Happiness economics around the world by improving the economic development of all countries. The idea was adopted by the United Nations General Assembly. On 19 July 2011, the United Nations General Assembly passed UN resolution 65/ 309, 'Happiness Toward A Holistic Approach To Growth', an initiative of then-Prime Minister Jigme Thinley of Bhutan, a country that has famously pursued the target of ""Gross National Happiness"" since the 1970s.

3.2.1 Ten steps proposed by UN to meet the goal of global happiness in 2021

1. Do things at makes you happy.
2. Tell Everyone.
3. Participate in and celebrate the World Happiness Contest.
4. Give and spread happiness to others.
5. To celebrate.
6. Share the things that make you happy on social media.
7. Promote the resolution.
8. We will advance the United Nations global goals for sustainable development.
9. Enjoy nature.
10. Adopt hedonism.

3.2.2 Seven main missions in 2021

1. Happiness as a fundamental human right and goal for all.
2. Happiness as a universal aspiration in the lives of all.
3. Happiness as a way of living, being, and serving communities and society.
4. Happiness as a north star for individuals, communities, governments, and society.
5. Happiness path toward achieving the sustainable development goals.
6. Happiness as a "new paradigm‘ for human development.
7. Worldwide celebration of the international day of happiness that is democratic, diverse, organic, and inclusive.

3.3 Is Happiness really a Human Right?

But is happiness really a human right? And is happiness a goal we should actively pursue? The answers are "no" and "it depends."

First, consider the analogy between psychological wellbeing — including happiness — and physical wellbeing, or health. The World Health Organization endorses a "right to health," but the details make it clear that it isn't health, per se, that is a right, but rather the means to achieve the best health possible. The WHO constitution recognizes "...the highest attainable standard of health as a fundamental right of every human being," with the right to health including "access to timely, acceptable, and affordable health care of appropriate quality." Similarly, the Declaration of Independence doesn't recognize happiness as a right, but rather the pursuit of happiness.

So it may be that the best way to understand a "right to happiness" is as a right to pursue happiness. Happiness just doesn't seem like the right sort of thing to proclaim as a right in itself.

The trouble is that a right to the pursuit of happiness may be counterproductive. For most people, actively pursuing happiness isn't a reliable route to attaining it.

Studies conducted have consistently found that actively seeking happiness can backfire: Those who strongly value and pursue happiness are more likely to feel disappointed about their own feelings, to report loneliness, and to have depressive symptoms. One reason for these negative effects is that in many Western cultures, happiness is conceptualized in individualistic terms — as a personal pursuit that leads to personal achievements. Actively pursuing happiness (so defined) can thus decrease social connection, which is one of the best predictors of a person's wellbeing.

These findings suggest that, promoting a right to pursue happiness could lead to behaviors and outcomes that are quite distinct from those that support happiness itself. Putting more strongly, supporting people in actively pursuing happiness could actually prevent people from achieving happiness. And it is presumably the latter — the actual achievement of happiness — that the UN resolution aims to recognize and support.

In the light of this research, a right to the pursuit of happiness may seem deeply misguided — a right we should simply abandon. Instead of a right to pursue happiness, we should endorse a right to the conditions that successfully foster happiness. Or, to borrow the WHO's formulation regarding health, we should endorse a right to the highest attainable standard of mental health and wellbeing.

But here's another thought: Maybe the problem isn't with the pursuit of happiness, but with how we conceptualize happiness itself. When it comes to defining happiness, perhaps there's another way — a better way. Cross-cultural research suggests that there is.

In a paper published in 2015, psychologist Brett Ford and her colleagues found that the negative association between pursuing happiness and achieving happiness isn't cross-culturally universal. In the U.S., they found the previously reported link between pursuing happiness and failing to achieve it. But in Germany, there was no reliable association between the strength of individuals' motivation to pursue happiness and their actual wellbeing. And in Russia, Japan, and Taiwan, the association was positive: Those who were more motivated to pursue happiness also reported greater wellbeing.

The researchers hypothesized that these cross-cultural differences were driven by differing conceptions of happiness itself. They expected — and found support for — the idea that in more collectivist cultures, happiness is more likely to be defined in terms of social engagement, including pro-social behaviors (such as seeing to other people's wellbeing) and social relationships (such as being surrounded by caring family and friends). For those with a socially-engaged definition of happiness, pursuing happiness presumably supported the kinds of social connections that are known to foster wellbeing, reversing the negative pattern observed in the U.S.

If these ideas are right, then the effects of pursuing happiness crucially depend on one's notion of happiness itself. Promoting a right to the pursuit of happiness could yield positive consequences when happiness is understood in social terms. But with the more individualistic definition prevalent in the U.S., promoting the active pursuit of happiness could lead to less happiness, not to more.

More likely than not, the UN's original advocates for the International Day of Happiness had a broad and community-oriented notion of happiness in mind — not the more narrowly individualistic one that many Americans seem to possess. For instance, the resolution itself doesn't simply call for more personal wellbeing, but for "a more inclusive, equitable and balanced approach to economic growth that promotes sustainable development, poverty eradication, happiness and the well-being of all peoples."

In celebrating the International Day of Happiness, then, we might do well to examine rather than reaffirm our tacit assumptions about happiness and its pursuit. And we might do well to join the UN's resolution in aspiring to the wellbeing of all peoples, not only to our own happiness as individuals.

A "right to happiness" has been proposed as part of third generation human rights. A gross distinction can be made between "internalist" and "externalist" ideas of happiness. Internalist ideas hold that happiness requires free action. Externalist ideas hold that happiness can be achieved independent of the will of the person, simply by obtaining certain objects, circumstances or events. It is argued that a right to happiness makes no sense in light of either of these interpretations, since it is impossible to comply universally with an "externalist" right to happiness. The state can only make someone "happy" at the expense of the happiness of others. Conversely, a right to happiness according to the internalist interpretation is impossible as well, simply because there is nothing a state or a third party can do to replace the free action of a person.

3.4 Right to Happiness in three Traditions

Three wellbeing philosophies of the Global South - Gross National Happiness (Bhutan), Ubuntu (South Africa), BuenVivir/SumakKawsay (Ecuador) – each articulate their own understanding of the right to happiness (wellbeing). These theories add dimensions to concepts of human dignity and fundamental freedoms that go beyond the traditional conception of rights. Gross national happiness understands human freedom and dignity from a Buddhist perspective to extend over several lifetimes, viewing it from the perspective of codependent origination and dignity of all sentient beings. Freedom is reinterpreted as freedom from delusion and desire. Ubuntu stresses human boundedness rather than human freedom as well as interdependence as a grandmother principle of law (my dignity is interwoven with your dignity). The community of people includes those who have come before and those who will come after you, all having equal rights. BuenVivir accords rights to mother earth (thereby to spirits, as Pachamama is a spiritual concept) and nature. It expands human dignity to encompass dignity for nature.

Ubuntu can be defined as the continuous motion of the enfoldment of the universe, but more popularly as 'I am because we are' (a person is a person through other persons). It is a collective ontology which stresses the value of compassion or 'life as mutual aid. It is embodied in national Batho Pele (People First) policies related to government conduct. The interim South African Constitution mentioned Ubuntu, to enable the Truth and Reconciliation Commission, and this legal history inspired activist judges into civil and criminal Ubuntu jurisprudence based on victim participation, forgiveness, reintegration of criminals in society, dialogue, relatedness, meaningful engagement, the value of apologies, mutual respect, extended family and hospitality with concrete results such as abolition of the death penalty and prevention of eviction from housing (less strict property rights).

BuenVivir can be defined as derived from the Quecha Sumak Kawsay, Good Living based on living in harmony with (and not at the cost of) others or nature and in balance between spiritual and material wealth . Ecuador enshrines BuenVivir principles in its Constitution and national and international policies. Rights of nature (Mother Earth) are central to BuenVivir, as a form of restorative justice (between humans and nature) articulated in a modest jurisprudence enabling persons to protect nature without proving personal damage, however, not preventing large scale natural resource exploration. It deconstructs legal concepts centered around individual humans, the utility value of nature (defined as property), nature conservation, and reconstructs them based on the earth as central system (mother), collective rights, the redefinition of economy-society-nature-relationship and the intertwinement of culture and nature as well as plurinationality.

Some countries are experimenting with the right to happiness in their constitutions and policies. Happiness needs to be understood as a broad term defining the right way of living, leading to wellbeing. This is interpreted in different ways in various continents and includes the 'happiness' of nature and of communities.

CHAPTER FOUR

GROSS NATIONAL HAPPINESS (GNH)

4.1 What is Gross National Happiness?

Bhutan, a Himalayan landlocked country of just about 750,000 inhabitants, has since the 1980s adopted a unique, holistic approach to development governance commonly referred to as 'Gross National Happiness' (GNH), which aims at achieving equitable socio-economic progress in harmony with other fundamental 'pillars' such as environmental preservation, good governance, and protection of the local cultural identity.

GNH, as the guiding philosophy of Bhutan's development process, was pronounced by King Jigme Singye Wangchuck (the then King of Bhutan), soon after his enthronement in 1972. He was clear that happiness is the ultimate common goal and everything else was the means or instruments for fulfilling this wish that every human being has.

Despite an average per capita Gross Domestic Product (GDP) of 2,560 USD in 2014 (World Bank, 2015a), a consistent presence in the UN's list for Least Developed Countries (United Nations [UN], 2015) and a ranking as 132nd in the latest Human Development Report (United Nations Development Programme [UNDP], Bhutan - sandwiched between China and India - has often been considered an important benchmark by modern development strategists. This owes certainly to the significant reduction in the levels of income poverty registered in the country, slowly but steadily, in the last two decades – thanks mainly to the performance of the main revenue-earning sector, i.e. export of hydropower, and, to a lesser extent, the tourism industry – but even more so to a peculiar development paradigm emerged from the early 1970s onwards. It was then, in fact, that Jigme Singye Wangchuck, young 4th King of the Wangchuckdynasty, spoke for the first time about the need for his administration to pursue not just mere GDP growth, but the general increase of 'Gross National Happiness' (GNH) instead.

Bhutan remains in the UN list of Least Developed Countries, which does, currently offer benefits in the form of lower tariff-barriers to export into developed countries. Said benefits, though, are yet to be fully tapped into due to limited exports available in the first place, significant non-tariff barriers, and the fact that most of Bhutan current exports end into neighboring countries with which preferential agreements are already in place.

GNH can become the unifying goal of development process for several reasons, including the following:

i. GNH stands for holistic needs of human being - both physical and mental wellbeing. While poverty alleviation and other material development measures are consistent with physical well-being, the misery of mental conditions, that is independent of material living conditions, cannot be addressed by favorable material circumstances alone.
ii. Second, which is a related point to the first, GNH seeks to complement inner skills of happiness with outer circumstances. Both sources have to be harmonized to bring about happiness.
iii. GNH recognizes that happiness can be realized as a societal goal; it cannot be left as an individualized goal; though individual happiness too contributes to GNH. It stresses collective happiness to be addressed directly through public policies in which happiness becomes and programmes.
iv. GNH, as it mirrors individual feeling directly, suggests that public policies based on GNH can be far less arbitrary than those based on standard economic tools.

4.2 Bhutan's Choice of Four Policy Areas of GNH

(i) Sustainable and equitable socio-economic development:

The necessity for materialistic development is obvious from the scale of economic suffering faced by majority of global population. But the need for spiritual development is no less obvious from the scale of spiritual suffering in terms of anxiety, insecurity, stress, and pain also in the affluent North. Economic aspect of development emphasizes economic growth so that employment and livelihood is secured. As it has been said, it is easier to identify and alleviate misery than to maximize happiness. At low levels of income, bordering on poverty, income policies are same as happiness policies, but not otherwise. Economic growth is vitally important to resolve poverty. Yet here too, there are three differences for a GNH driven economic development.

First, in a GNH economy, the means and nature of economic activities chosen are as important as their result in terms of economic growth. A GNH economy must make qualitative distinctions in the mix of economic activities for the same level of growth and size of economy.

Second, the measurement system for a GNH economy must necessarily be different from conventional measurement of GDP, because the measurement system must value social and economic services of households and families, free time and leisure given the roles of these factors in happiness. The measurement system must not be biased towards consumption against conservation of social, environmental, and human capitals. At the same time, happiness cannot be found in ever increasing consumption. Detachment from proliferation of wants can contribute to happiness. It leads logically to the possibility of considering steady state economy as a sign of progress. Current economies are, however, biased towards proliferation of wants and consumption.

Third, a GNH economy must concentrate on redistribution of happiness by income redistribution far more seriously. This is ethical on its own, but also because inequality sets in, as far as collective happiness is concerned, a self-defeating, vicious spiral of catching up process in a world where people derive satisfaction from relative, not absolute consumption, contrary to an axiom of economics. Of course, the distortion of our perception and choices which make us derive satisfaction from relative rather than absolute consumption itself needs enormous re-education in a GNH economy.

(ii) Conservation of Environment:

Moving on to policy priority on environment, it would first seem from happiness researches that environment and biodiversity are not strong correlate of happiness. Partly this is because it seems that no one has measured happiness against environmental variables. Nevertheless, no one would argue against the value of environment in everyday life and hence our happiness, given that our health and aesthetic experiences depend on the quality of physical environment around us. Among farming communities, such as majority of Bhutanese, living not only close to, but in, nature, livelihood depends directly on richness of their immediate natural environment which bestows on them truly free, wholesome, natural, forest foods, fruits and medicines that man need not labour and sweat to cultivate. Even the elevation of their aestheticsenses depend on our regular, if not daily, access to great natural environment. Thus, there is a demonstrable relationship between happiness and natural environment.

From this point of view, there is a pattern of deep relationship between environment and Man. So a relationship of access to quality natural environment on regular, if not daily, basis is crucially important. If a substantial population in a country live without access to quality natural environment, although the nation as a whole has substantial natural environment, a close pattern of relationship between Man and Nature cannot be fostered. Thus, it would be a case of existence of Man apart from natural environment that could result in a narrower basis of happiness.

Given this intuition about environment and happiness, Bhutan launched vigorous greening and biodiversity preservation policies, whose implementation of course have not been without costs in terms of foregone food self-sufficiency. But Bhutan is greener than it has been in living memory, with 26 percent of it turned into protected areas and 72 percent forest coverage. Someone called Bhutan an acupuncture point in the leviathan body of our ailing planet! It is an appropriate metaphor given the unthinkable consequences of environmental disasters in Bhutan and in the Himalayas on its own inhabitants and billions living on either side of the Himalayas.

(iii) Preservation and Promotion of Culture:

The priority area of culture for GNH that culture received has a rare global attention last year through the UNDP's Human Development Report titled "Cultural Diversity in Today's World." Free choice is equated with cultural liberty and as being central to human rights and human development. This report resonates with the message that individuals must be have the right to choose, change, and revise various elements of his multiple cultural identities. While there should be all the space for choice, we should distinguish situations where individuals change their identities voluntarily from situations where powerless individuals are changed by profoundly pervasive forces such as open-sky and free trade regimes which spawn cultural hybridization, creolization, and displacement of vernacular economies, even before one realizes. This is especially true in highly asymmetric situations like Bhutan involving massive outside cultures encountering small scale Bhutanese culture when the border opens wide open, and hence the need to have a vigorous promotion of indigenous cultures as a context of individuals choice. Rich cultural heritage itself provides options and choices for us to select life plans. So, not having a rich and intact culture is a diminishment of choices. A state which does not preserve cultural richness is thus one where the choices and wellbeing of its citizens are constrained.

(iv) Good Governance:

Securing any public good, such as collective happiness, depends on realizing governance oriented to it. Logically, if a government should reflect the ultimate democratic desire or opinion of the people, which is happiness, then the nature of governance should also be attuned to it. But both theoretically and practically, Bhutan is far from grounding GNH in any contemporary system of government and political structures in the world, of which the most well-established is liberal democratic system. So far in Bhutan, the scholars seem to have reflected more on cultivating values of liberating leadership, such as epitomizing His Majesty the

King rather than sharpening external institutions of check and balances. However, in keeping with times, Bhutanese are about to formally take up parliamentary democracy. His Majesty the King, the fountainhead of all positive changes, has recently placed the Draft Constitution of the Kingdom of Bhutan that opts for liberal democratic institutions before the people. The liberal democratic system as an institutional arrangement is possibly as a best path for securing any public good and good governance. But one should forgo seeking any better system by betraying ourselves that liberal democratic system is the climax in a linear and convergent evolution of political institutions, as some scholars have supposed.

4.3 Calculation of GNH Index of Bhutan

During the process of reforms investing Bhutan's political life in the early 2000s, it appeared clear that if GNH was to realistically represent a practical tool shaping day-today policymaking, it had to be measurable. Only standardized, replicable methodologies producing objective numerical results, in fact, could allow meaningful evaluations, and even comparisons of development policy outcomes. Therefore, since 2005 the Bhutanese government, through ad-hoc institutions such as the GNH Commission and the Centre for Bhutan Studies and GNH Research, focused its attention onto the very structuring of a rigorous system to survey its people, assess their levels of satisfaction, and ultimately produce a single-figure 'GNH Index'. Based on Alkire-Foster multidimensional methodology, the GNH Index consists of a weighted average gathered from 33 'cluster' indicators - both subjective and objective in nature, statistically reliable, relevant to and comprehensible by potential local respondents - across nine domains representing significant components of Bhutanese citizens' wellbeing, namely: psychological wellbeing; living standards, good governance; health, education; community vitality; cultural diversity and resilience; ecological diversity and resilience; and time use.

Domains are equally weighted, but the subjective and self-report-based indicators within them, though, carry, in general, lighter weights than the objective ones. 'Happiness' is defined as the achievement of 'sufficiency' in six of the nine domains, or, in other terms, by overall positive achievement in 66 percent of all weighted indicators. Such 'cutoff' delivers relevant quantitative outcomes, while still acknowledging that not all indicators are relevant to everyone in the same way.

The calculation undergoes two distinctive, subsequent procedures of 'identification' and 'aggregation'. The first reveals whether each household has attained sufficiency in each of the nine domains, and it is pursued by applying a sufficiency cutoff to every single indicator. Achievements exceeding the cutoff are replaced by the sufficiency levels themselves, so that they do not further affect the GNH Index score.

In the following 'aggregation' phase, data of the population are merged into a decomposable index that must be able to inspire policies that may increase the level of satisfaction both of 'happy' citizens and of those who aren't happy yet. The GNH Index looks straight at the very shortcomings of GNH implementation so that they are remedied, and the overall GNH improved, by 'subtracting' them from the ideal value of '1'. The GNH Index is thus equal to 1 minus the product of two measures, 'H' and 'A' (GNH = 1-HA), where 'H' is the headcount representing the percentage of people who do not enjoy sufficiency in six or more domains (obtained dividing the number of nonhappy people by the total number of respondents) and 'A' is the average number of dimensions in which people are deprived (obtained dividing the number of insufficient indicators by the number of 'unhappy' people).

It is possible to break down the equation and obtain different values. For instance, the percentage of people who are happy would be given by H_h = 100% - H .; similarly, the percentage of domains in which people who are not yet happy do enjoy sufficiency will be given by A_h = 100% - A. Additional cutoffs are selected to further differentiate among Bhutanese who are 'unhappy' (0-49.9%), 'narrowly happy' (50-65.9%), 'extensively happy' (66-76.9%), or 'deeply happy' (77-100%). Values can also be decomposed and evaluated by district, time frame, single domain, gender, occupation, level of education etc.

The advantages of this methodology are that it delivers a wide array of informative inputs for public policymaking, and it can coherently synthesize many different relevant phenomena in basic mathematical formulas. In addition, domains and indicators are chosen on the basis of their actual relevance to the local context; questionnaires are conceived to be understandable by their target audience; the calculation relies on a 'cutoff approach' which is purposefully focused on the middle tier of achievements that are relevant to the wellbeing of most people; the index can be broken down by groups, and performance patterns can be monitored in detail over time. Above all, this methodology highlights the very sections of the population which do not yet enjoy sufficient quality of life, setting therefore very concrete, people-centered objectives for the country's development governance agenda.

4.4 Decision-Guiding Tool: GNH Policy Screening Tools

The main objective of the GNH screening tool is to systematically assess impacts of any policy and project on GNH. Two kinds of tools were developed: a general GNH policy screening tool for appraising draft policies and sixteen GNH project screening tools for selection of projects. The aim through this endeavor is to select GNH enhancing policies and projects and reject those that adversely affect key determinants of GNH. Currently, only the general GNH policy screening tool is being implemented and tested across ministries. The 26 criteria of GNH policy screening are

1. Equity
2. Economic Security
3. Material well-being
4. Engagement in productive activities
5. Decision-making opportunity
6. Corruption
7. Judiciary efficiency
8. Judiciary access
9. Rights
10. Gender Equality
11. Information
12. Learning
13. Health
14. Water Pollution
15. Air pollution
16. Land degradation
17. Conservation of plant

18. Conservation of animals
19. Social support
20. Family
21. Nature
22. Recreation
23. Culture
24. Values
25. Spiritual pursuits
26. Stress.

Each of the screening 26 criteria is to be weighed on a 4-point scale ranging from 1 to 4. This 4-point scale is ranked from the most negative to the most positive score. One denotes a negative score, two uncertain (lack of knowledge of the effect of the policy), three is a neutral score and 4 denotes a positive score. The final outcome depends of the accumulation of positive scores.

It can also serve as a tool for policymaking when confronted with conflicting interests. Typically, political decisions are made on the basis of trade-offs. For example, when faced with the choice between providing employment versus the preservation of environment, most governments would choose the former. The GNH model shows that these tradeoffs should be made in the context of a certain hierarchy of values. Otherwise policymakers will continue to sacrifice higher values for lower values, longer term interests for shorter term interests, and causing investments in sustainable development to be put off. If GNH can be developed into a comprehensive tool incorporating all relevant values for a happy life, it will free governments from defaulting to economic decisions on the narrow paradigm of materialism. The holistic nature of GNH will also allow for market forces to remain active. In fact, as long as we treasure the freedom and opportunities that the market economy provides, GNH will have to include principles of competition and market forces – but only as a supportive force for higher valued well-being. Competition is so much valued in our capitalist economies because it has proven to be an effective incentive for bringing out the best of our selves. That is why capitalism has “defeated” communism. But competition without a higher moral dimension is like an elephant gone wild – it will destroy the very earth it depends on.

In summary, GNH is congruent with what is known as a “mixed economy”, the idea that market forces could do many things well – but not everything. This will require government and all actors in the economy to reclaim responsibility for their lives and start defining economic objectives in more human terms. The neoclassical principle of “laisser faire” has wrongly created a mentality of taking things for granted and we have become enslaved by the market and its monetary values. The alternative is not a return to rigid central planning and closing one’s border, but rather the development of an alternative economic model tailor-made to suit the condition of our own society and life itself.

4.5 Happiest Countries in the World 2021

Since 2002, the World Happiness Report has used statistical analysis to determine the world’s happiest countries. In its 2021 update, the report concluded that Finland is the happiest country in the world.

To determine the world’s happiest country, researchers analyzed comprehensive Gallup polling data from 149 countries for the past three years, specifically monitoring performance in six particular categories:

- Gross domestic product per capita;
- Social support;
- Healthy life expectancy;
- Freedom to make your own life choices;
- Generosity of the general population; and
- Perceptions of internal and external corruption levels.

In order to properly compare each country’s data, the researchers created a fictional country—christened Dystopia—filled with "the world’s least-happy people." They then set Dystopia as the rock bottom value in each of the six categories and measured the scores of the real-world countries against this value. All six variables were then blended to create a single combined score for each country.

Interestingly enough, the top seven happiest countries in the world for 2021 were all Northern European countries. Finland took top honors—for the fourth year in a row—with an overall score of 7.842, followed (in order) by Denmark (7.620), Switzerland (7.571), Iceland (7.554), the Netherlands (7.464), Norway (7.392), and Sweden (7.363).

The least happy country in the world for 2021 was Afghanistan, whose 149th-place ranking of 2.523 can be attributed in part to a low life expectancy rate and low gross domestic product rates per capita. It's worthwhile to note that the report was released before the recent Taliban takeover of Afghanistan, which will undoubtedly impact future scores in one way or another.

Rounding out the bottom five are Zimbabwe (3.145), Rwanda (3.415), Botswana (3.467), and Lesotho (3.512).

A happiness profile would be the profile of the kind of person who is most likely to be happy, as we can also see in the following classic description:

"Happy persons are more likely to be found in the economically prosperous countries, whose freedom and democracy are held in respect and the political scene is stable. The happy are more likely to be found in majority groups than among minorities and more often at the top of the ladder than at the bottom. They are typically married and get on well with families and friends. In respect of their personal characteristics, the happy persons appear relatively healthy, both physically and mentally. They are active and openminded. They feel that they are in control of their lives. Their aspirations concern social and moral matters rather than money making. In matters of politics, the happy tend to the conservative side of middle."

The Top 7 Happiest Countries in the World (plus an inspiring honorable mention) for 2021:

(i) Finland

Finland ranks as the world's happiest country based on the 2021 report, with a score of 7.842 out of a total possible score of 10. The report writers credited the citizens of Finland's strong feelings of communal support and mutual trust with not only helping secure the #1 ranking, but (more importantly) helping the country as a whole navigate the COVID-19 pandemic. Additionally, Finlanders felt strongly that they were free to make their own choices, and showed minimal suspicion of government corruption. Both of these factors are strong contributors to overall happiness.

(ii) Denmark

The second-happiest country in the world is Denmark, which scores 7.620. Denmark's values for each of the six variables are quite comparable to those of Finland. In fact, Denmark even outscored the leader in multiple categories, including GDP per capita, generosity, and perceived lack of corruption, demonstrating that it may claim the top spot sometime in the near future.

(iii) Switzerland

As the third-happiest country in the world, Switzerland scored a total of 7.571 out of 10. In general, the Swiss are very healthy, with one of the world's lowest obesity rates and a long-life expectancy. The Swiss also have a very high median salary, about 75% higher than that of the United States, and the highest GDP per capita in the top seven. Additionally, there is a strong sense of community in Switzerland and a firm belief that it is a safe and clean country—which is statistically true. Along with Iceland and Denmark, Switzerland is one of the world's safest countries.

(iv) Iceland

Iceland ranks as 2021's fourth-happiest country in the entire world, with a total score of 7.554. Of the top seven happiest countries around the globe, Iceland has the highest feeling of social support (higher even than Finland, Norway, and Denmark, which all tied for second place). Iceland also had the second-highest generosity score in the top seven, though it's worth noting that it ranked only 11th worldwide.

(v) Netherlands

Edging out Norway for the honor of fifth-happiest country in the world is the Netherlands (also known as Holland to many tulip lovers), with a score of 7.464. The Netherlands scored higher in the generosity category than any other top-seven country and also displayed an impressive lack of perceived corruption

(vi) Norway

The citizens of sixth-place Norway (7.392) feel they are being well cared for by their government thanks to universal healthcare and free college tuition. Norwegians also enjoy a healthy work-life balance, working an average of 38 hours per week vs. 41.5. hours per week in the United States. Additionally, Norway has a low crime rate and a strong sense of community among its citizens—a quality it shares with many of the top seven.

(vii) Sweden

Seventh-place Sweden (7.363) ranks high, if not quite highest, in virtually every category measured. For example: Sweden has a higher lack of corruption score than all but four countries worldwide (two of which are Finland and Denmark), the fourteenth-highest GDP per capita of all 149 countries measured, and the fourth-highest life expectancy in the top seven.

Honorable Mention: Bhutan

Bhutan was excluded from the 2021 report due to a technicality: Each country's scores are based upon detailed Gallup polls, but Gallup did not conduct polling in Bhutan during the required timeframe. However, the report's writers made a special effort to pay tribute to Bhutan, saying it "once again provided an inspiring example for the world about how to combine health and happiness. They made explicit use of the principles of Gross National Happiness in mobilizing the whole population in collaborative efforts to avoid even a single COVID-19 death in 2020, despite having strong international travel links." Impressive indeed. If Gallup begins polling in Bhutan, Northern Europe's hold on happiness may soon have competition.

4.6 Why are Nordic Countries Happier in the World?

From 2013 until today, every time the World Happiness Report (WHR) has published its annual ranking of countries, the five Nordic countries – Finland, Denmark, Norway, Sweden, and Iceland – have all been in the top ten, with Nordic countries occupying the top three spots in 2017, 2018, and 2019. Clearly, when it comes to the level of average life evaluations, the Nordic states are doing something right, but Nordic exceptionalism isn't confined to citizen's happiness. No matter whether we look at the state of democracy and political rights, lack of corruption, trust between citizens, felt safety, social cohesion, gender equality, equal distribution of incomes, Human Development Index, or many other global comparisons, one tends to find the Nordic countries in the global top spots.

What exactly makes Nordic citizens so exceptionally satisfied with their lives? This is the question that this article aims to answer.

Through reviewing the existing studies, theories, and data behind the World Happiness Report, we find that the most prominent explanations include factors related to the quality of institutions, such as reliable and extensive welfare benefits, low corruption, well- functioning democracy and state institutions. Furthermore, Nordic citizens experience a high sense of autonomy and freedom, as well as high levels of social trust towards each other, which play an important role in determining life satisfaction. On the other hand, we show that a few popular explanations for Nordic happiness such as the small population and homogeneity of the Nordic countries, and a few counterarguments against Nordic happiness such as the cold weather and the suicide rates, actually don't seem to have much to do with Nordic happiness.

Most of the potential explanatory factors for Nordic happiness are highly correlated with each other and often also mutually reinforcing, making it hard to disentangle cause from effect. Therefore, focusing on just a single explanation may result in distorted interpretations. For example, does trust in institutions and other citizens create a fertile ground for building a welfare state model with extensive social benefits? Or does the welfare state model contribute to low crime and corruption, which leads citizens to trust each other more? Most likely, both directions of influence play a role, leading to a self-reinforcing feedback loop that produces high levels of trust in the Nordic region, and a high-functioning state and society model.

We seek insight on this by taking a brief look at the history of the Nordic countries, which helps us to identify some practical takeaways about what other countries could learn from the Nordic region to ignite a positive feedback loop and enhance the happiness of their citizens. The care of human life and happiness and not their destruction is the first and only legitimate object of good government.

4.6.1 Review of existing explanations

Many theories have been put forth to explain the high level of Nordic happiness, from successful modernization and the ability to support better the less well off, to high levels of social capital. Here the most prominent theories are reviewed to see the strength of their explanatory power as regards Nordic happiness. After having reviewed each explanation individually in this section, we turn to the more difficult question of how these factors are linked together, as there are crucial interlinks and feedback mechanisms between them.

1. Weather, smallness, homogeneity, and suicides –Dispelling four myths contradicting the idea of Nordic happiness

Before turning to what we see as the most probable explanations for Nordic happiness, we will dispel some myths that challenge Nordic happiness by discussing a few factors sometimes raised in popular press that in fact don't have much to do with Nordic happiness.

First, it is true that the Nordic countries do not have the pleasant tropical weather that popular images often associate with happiness; rather, the Nordic winter tends to be long, dark, and cold. It is true that people account for changes in weather in their evaluations of life satisfaction, with too hot, too cold, and too rainy weather decreasing life satisfaction. However, effect sizes for changes in weather tend to be small, and are complicated by people's expectations and seasonal patterns. For example, people in the tropics are found to be happier during winter but less happy less happy during spring, as compared to people in more temperate zones. Average weather is something people adapt to and thus typically doesn't much affect the life satisfaction of those used to a given weather. Accordingly, although the warming of the weather due to climate change could slightly increase the life satisfaction of people living in cold countries such as the Nordic countries, based on current evidence, weather probably doesn't play a major role in increasing or decreasing Nordic happiness.

Second, there is a myth that in addition to high happiness metrics, the Nordic countries have high suicide rates, a seeming paradox. However, even though the Nordic countries, especially Finland, used to have relatively high suicide rates in the 1970s and 1980s, these rates have declined sharply since those days, and nowadays the reported suicide rates in the Nordic countries are close to the European average, and are also similar to rates in France, Germany, and the United States, for example. Although wealthy countries, such as the Nordics, tend to have higher suicide rates than poorer countries, in general, the same factors that predict higher life satisfaction tend to predict lower suicide rates. For example, higher national levels of social capital and quality of government predict both higher subjective well-being and lower suicide rates, while higher divorce rates predict more suicides and lower life satisfaction – although quality of government seems to have bigger effects on life satisfaction and divorces on suicide. Thus, this seeming paradox seems to be based on outdated information, as Nordic suicide rates are not especially high and are well predicted by the theoretical models where the same factors contribute to both higher life satisfaction in the Nordics and to lower suicide rates.

Third, it is often suggested that it is easier to build welfare societies in small and homogenous countries such as the Nordics, compared to larger and more diverse countries. However, research has not found a relationship, either negative or positive, between the size of a country's population and life satisfaction. In addition, smaller countries on average are not more homogenous than larger countries. In fact, today the Nordic countries are actually quite heterogenous, with some 19 % of the population of Sweden being born outside the country. Some empirical studies have found that increased ethnic diversity is associated with reduced trust. This is attributed to ethnically diverse societies having more difficulty generating and sharing public goods, but that it is not ethnic diversity per se, but rather ethnic residential segregation that undermines trust. Corroborating to this, other research has demonstrated that the economic inequality between ethnic groups, rather than cultural or linguistic barriers, seems to explain this effect of ethnic diversification leading to less public goods. Thus, the historical fact that the Nordic countries have not had an underclass of slaves or cheap labor imported from colonies could play some role in explaining the Nordic path to welfare societies. Furthermore, Charron & Rothstein show that the effect of ethnic diversity on social trust becomes negligible when controlling for quality of government, indicating that in countries of high-quality institutions such as the Nordic countries, ethnic diversity might not have any effect on social trust. Furthermore, according to the analysis in World Happiness Report 2018, the ratio of immigrants within a country has no effect on the average level of happiness of those locally born, with the ten happiest countries having foreign-born population shares averaging 17.2 %, about twice as much as the world average. Other studies have tended to find a small positive rather than negative effect of immigration on the well-being of locally born populations. Ethnic homogeneity thus provides no explanation of Nordic happiness. Also, immigrants within a country tend to be about as happy as people born locally. The quality of governmental institutions play a big part of Nordic happiness and these institutions serve all people living within the country, including immigrants. This is a probable explanation for the high ranking of the Nordics in the comparison of happiness of foreign-born people in various countries, in which Finland, Denmark, Norway, and Iceland occupy the top four spots, with Sweden seventh globally. The well-being advantage of the Nordic countries thus extends also to those immigrating to these countries.

4.7 Formula for Happiness

4.7.1 Dr Kashdan's Formula:

According to Dr Kashdan, author of 'Curious', there are six factors which, when put together in the right combination, make a happy soul.

The factors are: (i) Live in the moment (M), (ii) be curious (C), (iii) do something you love (L), (iv) think of others (T), (v) nurture relationships (N), and (vi) taking care of your body (B).

The equation sets out the perfect formula which incorporates the 'happiness six'. They include: Living in the moment, curiosity, spending time with family, doing something you love, thinking of others first and taking care of your body

The winning formula for Feeling Good = (Mx16 + Cx1 + Lx2) + (Tx5 + Nx2 + Bx33).

Following is the clearer explanation of these six terms:

i. **M: Live in the moment** - Appreciate the sounds, smells and sights that you take for granted every day. Pay attention to your breathing. Remind yourself every waking hour to do this.
ii. **C:Be curious** - Explore the unfamiliar, mysterious, complex, and uncertain aspects of our world once a day.
iii. **L:Do something you love** - If there is anything that provides the framework for a well-lived life it is the presence of activities that are important to us and excite us. Do this once at work and once at play.
iv. **T: Think of others first** - Offer compliments, do a good deed and listen. This is not intuitive because many believe you need to love yourself before you can love others. Science has found this to be false. Do this five times a day and you'll soon see it feels good to make someone feel good.
v. **N: Nurture relationships** - Dedicate time to a partner, friend or family member twice a day. Scientists have discovered that when you observe the happiest people on the planet, every single one has a close, significant relationship with another person.
vi. **B: Take care of your body** - No, you do not need three per cent body fat, nor do you need to be able to pound through three sets of 15 unassisted handstand push-ups. Taking care of your body is about healthy eating at least three times a day and committing 30 minutes per day to exercise.

Scientists reviewed the results of nationwide research carried out into how Brits truly feel, inside and out.

4.7.2 Einstein's Formula:

A few days before Einstein fell into the Reaper's grim arms, his assistant — Dukas — found him in the hospital bed, "in agony, unable to lift his head."

Yet on the very next day, a mere 24 hours or so away from his death-day, Einstein "asked Dukas to get him his glasses, papers, and pencil, and he proceeded to jot down a few calculations."

"He worked as long as he could," noted biographer Walter Issacson, "and when the pain got too great he went to sleep," for the final time. Indeed, Einstein died doing the one thing he loved most — working.

"Genius is one percent inspiration," said Einstein, "and 99 percent perspiration." Indeed, it's not by accident that no one has ever become great by accident. After all, as Einstein once noted: "Only a monomaniac gets what we commonly refer to as results."

For the above reason, when Einstein was asked for the secret to a happy life, though the questioner expected an answer long and sour, Einstein kept it short and sweet:

> *"If you want to live a happy life, tie it to a goal, not to people or things."*

Here lies Einstein's formula for a happy life.

Given that great minds think alike for the same reason, passengers boarded the same train of thought inevitably end up at the same destination, we should hardly be surprised that **Newton** and Einstein — arguably the two greatest scientists in history — when confronted with life's storms both used the same formula for a happy life.

In 1665, the bubonic plague struck London. Never before nor since has the world seen anything like the deadly pandemic. And just as a pandemic shut down today's stores and universities, the same held true back then. History repeats itself indeed.

While the world's stage was seemingly crumbling underneath his feet, Isaac Newton applied the formula for a happy life. How? He merely tied his life to an abstract goal, not to physical people or concrete things. Over the span of roughly eighteen months, Newton would revolutionize science.

Newton was later asked how he discovered the law of gravity. He replied: "By thinking about it all the time."

In short, because Newton had hitched his star to an abstract goal, which remains forever fixed, and not to life — which is forever unpredictable — he in effect found shelter from life's storms.

When Einstein's wife Elsa died, needless to say — he was crushed. After all, Elsa served as a somewhat maternal figure to Einstein.

"She told him when to eat and where to go," "She packed his suitcases and doled out his pocket money. In public, she was protective of the man she called 'the Professor.' "

Fortunately for Einstein, his formula for a happy life served as shelter from the storm. "As long as I am able to work, I must not and will not complain, because work is the only thing that gives substance to life."

In Closing: Dream With Mind + Chase with Body = the Formula for a Happy Life.

What Einstein fully grasped — regarding his concise formula for a happy life — appears to boil down to this:

Indeed, the best things in life are not only free but they're not even "things." After all, never has a hand touched love. Never has an eye spotted peace. Never has a nose sniffed dreams. Here lies the DNA of Einstein's formula for a happy life.

CHAPTER FIVE

HAPPINESS IN HINDUISM

Pursuit of happiness is the goal of all religions and almost all spiritual writings describe the ways how to achieve it.

5.1 Concept of Happiness in Hinduism

To secure happiness here in mortal life, Hinduism prescribes a holistic method, which takes into consideration both the material and spiritual needs of human beings. It recognizes four chief aims of human life, called purusharthas, by pursuing which human beings can experience physical, mental, and spiritual happiness. They are also called the four chief purposes (purusharthas) of existence, because they are also chosen by God (Purusha) Himself for his own enjoyment. Broadly speaking, in a secular sense, they refer to the pursuit of morality, prosperity, enjoyment, and spirituality. Specifically, in a religious sense, they refer to religious and moral duty (dharma), wealth (artha), conjugal bliss (kama) and liberation (moksha).

Let us examine how they contribute to our happiness. By pursuing dharma, you enjoy name and fame, social status, and respect in society. By pursuing wealth, you enjoy the comforts of life, status in society, and the satisfaction of fulfilling your obligations to family and society. By pursuing kama (sex) you enjoy conjugal bliss, companionship with your spouse, family life, and the happiness of having children, relations, and continuation of family lineage. Finally, pursuing liberation, you can secure the ultimate happiness of being absolutely and eternally free from all obligations. For a human being, the four aims are the best means to secure happiness upon earth and lay a firm foundation for future happiness in the world of Brahman, the highest Self.

Hindu scriptures further suggest that a person has better chances of securing happiness and enjoying life if he pursues these four aims according to the four phases of human life, called ashramas, during which he has to fulfil the duties and obligations that are specific to each of them. The **four phases of human life are, brahmacharya, grihastha, vanaprastha, and Sanyasa.** (i) In Brahmacharya, which corresponds to childhood and young age, a person has to study the Vedas and other scriptures and learn about his duties and responsibilities (dharma), apart from the knowledge of the Self and the Supreme Self. (ii) In Grihastha, which corresponds to the adult life, he has to perform his obligatory duties (dharma) and earn wealth (artha) to ensure the welfare, order and regularity of his family and society. (iii) In Vanaprastha, which corresponds to the old age, he has to retire into seclusion and contemplate upon his experiential wisdom (dharma) and the ultimate purpose of human life (liberation). (iv) In Sanyasa, which corresponds to the last phase of human life, he has to renounce everything, including his knowledge of the scriptures (dharma), and work for his liberation (moksha). In each of these stages it is possible to experience peace and happiness by following the injunctions specified in the scriptures. If he follows them strictly, at the end of the journey he is bound to become liberated and enter the world of bliss.

Chasing happiness upon earth by worldly means is like chasing a mirage. To escape from this predicament, one should subordinate earthly happiness to spiritual happiness and, earthly goals to spiritual goals, and aim for permanent happiness, which can be secured only when a being is completely free from all attachments, and the limitations of mortal life. True happiness of the divine kind arises not from having things or fulfilling our desires, but by restraining our minds and bodies, and becoming free from our dependence upon them. When we are free from all attachments, from the impurity of maya and desires, we return to our soul's essential nature, which is permanent bliss. Reaching this state is called liberation, which one can achieve even when one is alive upon earth.

5.2 Three types of Happiness

Just as everything in creation is coloured by the gunas, our happiness upon earth is also influenced by our predominant nature. According to the predominance of the gunas, we can identify three types of happiness.

i. **Sattvic happiness**, which arises from moral and mental purity, and from being good and doing good. This also corresponds to spiritual happiness.

ii. **Rajasic happiness,** which arises from fulfilling your desires, and securing power, position, name and fame, etc. This corresponded to mental happiness.

iii. **Tamasic happiness,** which arises from bodily pleasures and base desires. This corresponds to physical happiness.

While sattvic happiness is the best of the three, it does not by itself guarantee liberation or true enjoyment. All types of happiness that arise from fulfilling desires and likes and dislikes are binding and have consequences. True happiness is freedom from the compulsion to be happy, dualities, and conditionality. It should arise in one as a reflection of the soul in the pure consciousness.

Bhagavad Gita reaffirms in the following shlokas:

Sri Krishna enlightens us about this elusive concept through his conversation with Arjun in Bhagavad Gita.

In Chapter II, Verse 70 of the Bhagavad Gita, Sri Krishna says,

"aapurya-manam achala-prathistham
samudram apah pravishanti yadvat
tadvat-kama yam pravishanti sarve
sa shantim-apnoti na kama-kaami"

Meaning: As the waters (of different rivers) enters the Great Ocean, which though full on all sides remains undisturbed, likewise a person who is not disturbed by the incessant flow of desires, can alone achieve peace, and not the man who runs after these desires & strives to satisfy such desires.

Sri Krishna says to Arjun,

sukhaṁ tu idaniṁ tri-vidhaṁ shrinu me bharatarshabha
abhyasad ramate yatra duhkhantam cha nigachchhati.

Meaning: And now hear from me, O Arjun, of the three kinds of happiness in which the embodied soul rejoices, and can even reach the end of all suffering

-Bhagavad Gita, Chapter 18, Verse 36

yat tad agre viham iva pariname mitopamam
tat sukham sattvikam proktam atma-buddhi-prasada-jam.

Meaning: That which seems like poison at first, but tastes like nectar in the end, is said to be happiness in the mode of goodness. It is generated by the pure intellect that is situated in self-knowledge.

-Bhagavad Gita, Chapter 18, Verse 37

It is the happiness that arises from the elevation of the soul. However, attaining this is not easy. One pursuing satvik or pure happiness one has to practice a lot of discipline. That is why, it feels like poison in the beginning but nectar in the end.

vishayendriya-sanyogad yat tad agre mritopamam
pariname visham iva tat sukham rajasam smritam.

Meaning: Happiness is said to be in the mode of passion when it is derived from the contact of the senses with their objects. Such happiness is like nectar at first but poison at the end.

-Bhagavad Gita, Chapter 18, Verse 38

This is the materialistic pleasure that is derived when the senses come in contact with external objects that create a feeling of gratification. However, this kind of happiness is temporary.

yad agre chanubandhe cha sukham mohanam atmanah
nidralasya-pramadottha tat tamasam udahritam.

Meaning: That happiness which covers the nature of the self from beginning to end, and which is derived from sleep, indolence, and negligence, is said to be in the mode of ignorance.

-Bhagavad Gita, Chapter 18, Verse 39.

This is the lowest form of happiness and is derived from sleeping or being lazy. The soul is never nurtured through these practices yet since there is a tiny sense of pleasure associated with it, people wrongfully consider it to be a state of happiness.

5.3 Some More Bhagavad Gita Quotes on Happiness

yah shaastravidhimutsrijya vartate kaamakaaratah
na sa siddhimavaapnoti na sukham na paraam gatim // 16.23 //

Meaning: He, who has cast aside the ordinances of the scriptures, acts under the impulse of desire, attains neither perfection nor happiness nor the Supreme goal.

Scriptures need not mean the ritualistic ones but they mean the texts discussing the theory of Truth - Brahma Vidya. A seeker should renounce desire, anger and greed. Anger is the result when fulfilment of desire is obstructed and greed is the consequence of satisfaction of one desire.

Sri Krishna warns that if one were not to obey the life advocated in the scriptures he will live a life of restless agitations and passions. Such a man cannot feel any happiness or attain any cultural development.

tatra Sattvam nirmalatwaat prakaashakam anaamayam
sukhasangena badhnaati jnaanasangena chaanagha // 14.6 //

Meaning: Of these, Sattva, the luminous, free from evil and because of its unblemishness, binds, O Sinless One, by attachment to happiness and by attachment to knowledge. Gunas cannot be defined directly without explaining their symptoms and processes.

tamastwajnaanajam viddhi mohanam sarvadehinaam
pramaadaalasyanidraabhis tannibadhnaati bhaarata // 14.8 //

Meaning: And know Tamas to be born of ignorance, deluding all embodied beings, it binds fast, O Bharata, by mis-comprehension, indolence and sleep.

Sattvam sukhe sanjayati rajah karmani bhaarata
jnaanamaavritya tu tamah pramaade sanjayatyuta // 14.9 //

Meaning: Sattva attaches to happiness and Rajas to action, O Bharata, while Tamas, verily,
shrouding knowledge attaches to mis-comprehension.

rajastamashchaabhibhooya Sattvam bhavati bhaarata
rajah Sattvam tamaishchaiva tamah Sattvam rajastathaa // 14.10 //

Meaning: O Bharata, Sattva arises predominating over Rajas and Tamas ; likewise Rajas (prevails) overpowering Sattva and Tamas ; so Tamas (prevails) over Sattva and Rajas. The question whether these three Gunas act on the mind all at a time or each separately at different points of time is answered here. The Lord says that these Gunas act at different times - each one of them becoming powerful at any one point of time. At a given time human personality works under the influence of one predominant Guna when the other two Gunas get subdued but not totally absent.

Thus when Sattva predominates over Rajas and Tamas it produces on the mind its own nature of happiness and knowledge ; when Rajas predominates over the other two it produces passions, desires, attachments and actions. When Tamas is prominent over Sattva and Rajas it shrouds discrimination and makes the mind unaware of its nobler duties.

The Gita points out that our happiness is inward. It invites our attention to the manner of our life, the state of human consciousness, which does not depend upon the outward machinery of life. The body may die and the world pass away but the life in spirit endures. Our treasures are not the things of the world that perish but the knowledge and love of God that endure. We must get out of the slavery to things to gain the glad freedom of spirit.

baahyasparsheshwasaktaatmaa vindatyaatmani yatsukham
sa brahma yoga yuktaatmaa sukham akshayamashnute // 5.21 //

Meaning: With the heart unattached to external contacts he discovers happiness in the Self; with the heart engaged in the meditation of Brahman he attains endless bliss.

The happiness from the enjoyment of outer objects is transitory while the Bliss of Brahman is eternal. When the mind is not attached to the external objects of the senses, when one is deeply and constantly engaged in the contemplation of the Self, one finds eternal peace within. If one wishes to enjoy the imperishable happiness of the Self within, one has to withdraw the senses from their respective objects and enter in deep meditation on the Self within. It is to be noted that through self-control a void is created in the mind and heart which will have to be filled in with bliss through contemplation of Brahman.

ye hi samsparshajaa bhogaa duhkhayonaya eva te
aadyantavantah kaunteya na teshu ramate budhah // 5.22 //

Meaning: The enjoyments that are born of contacts with objects are generators of pain only, for they have a beginning and an end, O Son of Kunti, and the wise do not find delight in them.

Man goes in search of happiness among the external and perishable objects. He finds no permanent joy in them but receives a load of sorrows instead. One should, therefore, withdraw the senses from the sense objects which are not at all a source of permanent joy. One should fix the mind on the immortal, blissful Self within. The sense objects have a beginning and an end. The pleasure out of them is therefore momentary and fleeting during the interval between the contact of the senses with the objects and their separation. One who has discrimination or knowledge of the Self will never rejoice in the objects of the senses.

naasti buddhir ayuktasya na chaayuktasya bhaavanaa
na chaabhaavayatah shaantir ashaantasya kutah sukham // 2.66 //

Meaning: The man whose mind is not under his control has no Self-Knowledge and to the unsteady no meditation is possible and to the unmeditative there can be no peace and to the man who has no peace how can there be any happiness?

ajnashchaashraddhaadhaanashcha samshayaatmaa vinashyati
naayam loko'sti na paro na sukham samshayaatmanah // 4.40 //

Meaning; The ignorant, the faithless, the doubting self goes to destruction; there is neither this world nor the other nor happiness for the doubting soul.

5.4 Eternal Happiness through Complete Freedom

True enjoyment and happiness in life are not possible, unless it is secured on a lasting basis. Like Buddhism, Hinduism also clearly and emphatically recognizes the suffering that is inherent to earthly life and traces its root cause to desire only. Human beings are unhappy because they are bound to impermanent things and cannot easily escape from their attraction and aversion to them. Because they are driven by their desire for impermanent things, and pairs of opposites, their happiness upon earth remains temporary and elusive. No one is free from suffering because of impermanence, which manifests in our lives as loss, union, aging, sickness, decay, death, and destruction.

Duality is another important cause. We experience unhappiness, because of union and separation, or attraction and aversion to the objects and conditions that we like or dislike. We are happy when we are with those that we like, or unhappy when we are with those that we dislike. One may experience temporary happiness when we pursue sense objects. However, it is a trap, since the pursuit of objects results in attachment. From attachment arise karma, delusion, and bondage, which aggravate our suffering and make our chances of enjoying life increasingly difficult.

5.5 Happiness in Ancient Hindu Scriptures

Patanjali Yoga Sutra 1.12 says:

abhyasavairagyabhyam tan nirodhaha

Meaning: The restless mind, accustomed to act on impulse, can be controlled only by nonattachment and practice. Of these two methods, the attempt to make the mind steady is called practice. (Sutra 1.13)

Yoga Sutra 1.33 (of Patanjali) says:

maitrī karuṇā mudito-pekṣāṇāṁ-sukha-duḥkha puṇya-apuṇya-viṣayāṇāṁ bhāvanātaḥ citta-prasādanam

Meaning: The mind becomes purified by practicing friendship over wellness, kindness over suffering, pleasure over virtuosity and indifference over immorality.

Brihadaaranyaka Upanishad (1.4.14), an ancient Hindu scripture, says:

Sarve Bhavantu Sukhinah, Sarve Santu Niraamayah,
Sarve Bhadraani Pashyantu, Maa Kaschid Dukha Mapnuyat.

Meaning: May all be happy; May all be without disease; May all look for well-being of others; May none have misery of any sort.

- Brihadaaranyaka Upanishad 1.4.14

According to Sri Aurobindo, happiness is the natural state of humanity, as he mentions in his book 'The Life Divine', he informs about it as the delight of existence. Srimad Bhagavad Gita interprets happiness as derived via good thoughts and good deeds that depend on the state and on the control of the mind. Through evenness of temper and mind, the state of supreme bliss is reached in all aspects of one's life. According to the Vishishtadvaita Vedanta school, which was proposed by Ramanujacharya, true happiness can only be through divine grace, which can be achieved by surrender of one's ego to the Divine. According to Ramana Maharshi, happiness is within us and can be known only through discovering our true self. The happiness can be attained by inner enquiry, using the thought "Who am I?

According to Hinduism, an embodied being's ultimate purpose is enjoyment of supreme bliss as a free soul (mukta) in the highest heaven. This aspect will be described in a subsequent chapter in this book. Enjoyment is also the basis of happiness upon earth. However, in mortal life happiness should not be pursued for happiness sake alone, because mere pursuit of happiness in a bound state (baddha) leads to attachment (Yogasutras 2.7), and bondage. It should be pursued as part of a way of life in which liberation or union with the Self should be the highest goal. Human beings can temporarily secure happiness upon earth by doing their duties, or permanently in the highest heaven by achieving liberation.

An intermediary approach is to prolong happiness by doing good karmas and going to the ancestral heaven where souls can stay for longer periods than upon earth. However, such happiness would not last forever, because when their good karma is exhausted souls have to return to the earth and take another birth to continue their existence. The best strategy therefore is to secure happiness here, and liberation hereafter. In the following discussion we will examine how Hinduism expects each practitioner to achieve this rather difficult goal. The impediments to peace and happiness are egoism (aham), ignorance (avidya), impurities (malas), delusion (maya), past actions (karma), desires (kama) and attachments (pasas).

5.6 Happiness in Upanishads

The Upanishads advance a unique and powerful notion that the qualitative distinction between pleasure and happiness resides within a temporal context. To elaborate, the pleasure is short-lived: meaning that it is temporally local; on the other hand, happiness is long lasting: meaning that it is temporally nonlocal.

Isa-Vasya-Upanishad gives knowledge of the All-pervading Deity. The dominant thought running through it is that we cannot enjoy life or realize true happiness unless we consciously "cover" all with the Omnipresent Lord. If we are not fully conscious of that which sustains our life, how can we live wisely and perform our duties? Whatever we see, movable or immovable, good or bad, it is all "That." We must not divide our conception of the universe; for in dividing it, we have only fragmentary knowledge and we thus limit ourselves.

Katha Upanishad beautifully distinguishes between the 'happiness' and the 'pleasure' in the following two shlokas:

anyacchreyo'nyadutaiva preya-
ste ubhe nānārthe puruṣa~ sinītaḥ ।
tayoḥ śreya ādadānasya sadhu
bhavati hīyate'rthādya u preyo vṛṇīte (1.2.1)

śreyaśca preyaśca manuṣyametaḥ
tau samparītya vivinakti dhīraḥ ।
śreyo hi dhīro'bhi preyaso vṛṇīte
preyo mando yogakṣemādvṛṇīte (1.2.2)

Meaning: There is the path of happiness, and there is the path of pleasure.

Both attract the soul. Who follows the first (means the happiness) comes to good; who follows the path of pleasure fails to reach the end goal. The two paths lie in front of man. Discriminating between them the wise one chooses the path of happiness; the simple-minded choose the path of pleasure.

-(Katha Upanishad I.2, 1-2).

In this context, some shlokas from the **Chandogya Upanishad** are quoted here below:

yadā vai sukhaṃ labhate'tha karoti nāsukhaṃ labdhvā karoti sukhameva labdhvā karoti sukhaṃ tveva vijijñāsitavyamiti sukhaṃ bhagavo vijijñāsa iti (7.22.1)

Meaning: A person works when he gets happiness. He does not care to work if he does not get happiness. By getting happiness one does one's duty. But one must try to understand the true nature of this happiness. Nārada replied, 'Sir, I want to know well the true nature of happiness'.

yo vai bhūmā tatsukhaṃ nālpe sukhamasti bhūmaiva sukhaṃ bhūmā tveva vijijñāsitavya iti bhūmānaṃ
bhagavo vijijñāsa iti || 7.23.1 ||

Meaning: That which is infinite is the source of happiness. There is no happiness in the finite. Happiness is only in the infinite. But one must try to understand what the infinite is.' Nārada replied, 'Sir, I want to clearly understand the infinite'.

yatra nānyatpaśyati nānyacchṛṇoti nānyadvijānāti sa bhūmātha yatrānyatpaśyatyanyacchṛṇotyanyadvijānāti tadalpaṃ yo vai bhūmā tadamṛtamatha yadalpaṃ tanmartyṃ sa bhagavaḥ kasminpratiṣṭhita iti sve mahimni yadi vā na mahimnīti (7.24.1)

Meaning: Bhūmā [the infinite] is that in which one sees nothing else, hears nothing else, and knows [i.e., finds] nothing else. But alpa [the finite] is that in which one sees something else, hears something else, and knows something else. That which is infinite is immortal, and that which is finite is mortal.' Nārada asked, 'Sir, what does bhūmā rest on?' Sanatkumāra replied, 'It rests on its own power—or not even on that power [i.e., it depends on nothing else]'.

sa evādhastātsa upariṣṭātsa paścātsa purastātsa dakṣiṇataḥ sa uttarataḥ sa evedaṃ
sarvamityathāto'haṃkārādeśa evāhamevādhastādahamupariṣṭādaham paścādaham purastādaham
dakṣiṇato'hamuttarato'hamevedaṃ sarvamiti || 7.25.1 ||

Meaning: That bhūmā is below; it is above; it is behind; it is in front; it is to the right; it is to the left. All this is bhūmā. Now, as regards one's own identity: I am below; I am above; I am behind; I am in front; I am to the right; I am to the left. I am all this.

VII-xxii-1: 'When one obtains happiness', then alone does one act. Without obtaining happiness one does not act. Only on obtaining happiness does one act. But one must desire to understand happiness'. 'Revered sir, I desire to understand happiness'.

The **Isha Upanishad**, in hymns 2–6, acknowledges the contrasting tension within Hinduism, between the empirical life of householder and action (karma) and the spiritual life of renunciation and knowledge (jnana).

Should one wish to live a hundred years on this earth, he should live doing Karma. While thus, as man, you live, there is no way other than this by which Karma will not cling to you. Those who partake the nature of the Asuras [evil], are enveloped in blind darkness, and that is where they reside who ignore their Atman [Self]. For liberation, know your Atman, which is motionless yet faster than mind, it is distant, it is near, it is within all, it is without all this. It is all pervading. And he who beholds all beings in the Self, and the Self in all beings, he never turns away from it [the Self].— Isha Upanishad, Hymns 2-6

It is generally felt that this verse–and other passages from scriptures and books on spiritual life–indicates that one hundred years is the normal lifespan for a human being. On the other hand, the figure of one hundred years may also symbolize the complete lifespan of a person, however brief or long, the idea here being that not one moment of our life need be a burden nor should we ever wish to shorten our life by a single breath–that life should be lived in fulfillment with peace and happiness all the way through. That this is possible has been shown well by the saints and Masters of all religions and ages. We need only know how to do it; and these words give the way.

Katha Upanishad (2-II-12):

Eternal happiness belongs to the intelligent – not to others – who realize in their hearts Him who is one, the controller and the in-dwelling Self of all beings, and who makes the one form manifold.

Mandukya Karika of Gaudapada. III. ADVAITA PRAKARANA:

III-5. Just as when the ether confined within a particular jar contains dust and smoke, that is not the case with all jars, in the same way, all the individual souls are not associated with happiness etc.

III-45. In that state one should not enjoy the happiness, but should, by means of discrimination, become unattached. When the mind that has become still tends towards wandering, it should be unified (with the self) with efforts.

Alatasanti Prakarana

IV-2. I bow down to that Yoga which is devoid of touch with anything (that implies relationship), which conduces to the happiness of all beings and is beneficial, and which is free from dispute and contradiction and is taught by the scriptures.

Taittiriya Upanishad 1:4:2

Thou art the source of all happiness and of all prosperity. Do thou come to me as the goddess of prosperity and shower thy blessings upon me. May the seekers after truth gather round me, may they come from everywhere, that I may teach them thy word.

Yoga Tattva Upanishad

11. Know that to be Jiva which is associated with happiness and misery and hence is the term Jiva applied to Paramatman which is pure.

Rama Uttara Tapaniya Upanishad

Om! He who is Ramachandra is verily the God. He is the 'non-dual soul of great happiness'. I salute him again and again in earth, bhuvar loka and Suvar loka. 3.1

5.7 Some more Sanskrit Shlokas On Happiness

Lokah Samastah Sukhino Bhavantu

Meaning:Let the entire world be happy.

svastiprajābhyaḥ paripālayantāṃ nyāyena mārgeṇa mahīṃ mahīśāḥ।
gobrāhmaṇebhyaḥ śubhamastu nityaṃ lokāḥ samastāḥ sukhino bhavantu॥

Meaning:May the well-being of all people be protected by the powerful and mighty leaders be with law and justice. May the success be with all divinity and scholars, May all the worlds become happy.

Chitte prasanne bhuvana chitte vishanne bhuvanam .
Atoabhilasho yadi te sukhe syat chittaprasade prathamam yatasva.

Meaning:If the mind is happy, the entire world (seems) happy. If the mind is despondent, the entire world (seems) despondent. Hence, if you desire happiness, strive towards the happiness of the mind first.

CHAPTER SIX

HAPPINESS IN BUDDHISM

If you want others to be happy, practice compassion.
If you want to be happy, practice compassion.- Dalai Lama

6.1 Concept of Happiness in Buddhism

Happiness forms a central theme of Buddhist teachings. For ultimate freedom from suffering, the Noble Eightfold Path leads its practitioner to Nirvana, a state of everlasting peace. Ultimate happiness is only achieved by overcoming craving in all forms. More mundane forms of happiness, such as acquiring wealth and maintaining good friendships, are also recognized as worthy goals for lay people. Buddhism also encourages the generation of loving kindness and compassion, the desire for the happiness and welfare of all beings.

Among the early scriptures, 'Sukha' (happiness, pleasure, ease, joy or bliss, in Sanskrit and Pali) is set up as a contrast to 'preya' meaning a transient pleasure, whereas the pleasure of 'Sukha' has an authentic state happiness within a being that is lasting. In the Pail Canon, the term is used in the context of describing laic pursuits, meditative absorptions, and intra-psychic phenomena.

The term 'sukha' is used in a general sense to refer to "well-being and happiness" (hita Sukha) in either this present life or future lives. In addition, it is a technical term associated with describing a factor of meditative absorption (jhāna) and a sensory-derived feeling (vedanā).

The Buddha discusses with different lay persons "well-being and happiness", "visible in this present life" (diṭṭha-dhamma) and "pertaining to the future life" (samparāyika).

In the Anaṇa Sutta (AN 4.62), the Buddha describes the following types of happiness for a "householder partaking of sensuality" (gihinā kāma-bhoginā):

The happiness of earning (atthi-sukha) wealth by just and righteous means the happiness of using (bhoga-sukha) wealth liberally on family, friends, & on meritorious deeds

The happiness of debt-lessness (anaṇa-sukha) be free from debts;

The happiness of blame-lessness (anavajja-sukha), to live a faultless and pure life without committing evil in thought, word, and deed.

In the Dighajānu Sutta (AN 8.54), Dighajānu approaches the Buddha and states:

"We are lay people enjoying sensuality; living crowded with spouses & children; using Kasi fabrics & sandalwood; wearing garlands, scents, & creams; handling gold & silver. May the Blessed One teach the Dhamma for those like us, for our happiness & well-being in this life, for our happiness & well-being in lives to come."

The Buddha identifies four sources that lead to well-being and happiness in the current life:

productive efforts (uṭṭhāna-sampadā) in one's livelihood, protective efforts (ārakkha-sampadā) regarding ones wealth in terms of possible theft or disaster, virtuous friendship (kalyāṇa-mittatā), and even-headed living (sama-jīvikatā), abstaining from womanizing, drunkenness, gambling and evil friendships.

In terms of well-being and happiness in the next life, the Buddha identifies the following sources:

faith (saddhā) in the fully enlightened Buddha; virtue (sīla), as exemplified by the Five Precepts; generosity (cāga), giving charity and alms; and, wisdom (paññā), having insight into the arising and passing of things.

6.2 Classifications or Levels of Happiness in Buddhism

In Buddhism, there are different kinds of classifications or levels of "sukha". No matter how many levels it is classified, its range starts from the lowest level – kāmasukha – which is happiness from acquisition or meeting sensual pleasures, to the highest level – nirodha samāpattisukha – with total extinction of suffering. Kāmasukha is a kind of happiness, but it can also cause and increase dukkha or suffering. Therefore, it is not considered as real happiness. Different ranks or levels of happiness also reflect degrees of real happiness.

However, this lowest rank of happiness at physical or material level is required for basic needs to relieve person's physical sufferings. After the basic needs are fulfilled, that person should develop further to gain higher level of happiness. Excessive material accumulation driven by greed may not lead to the increase of happiness and never keep happiness sustainable. Instead, it may increase problems, resulting in suffering and reducing happiness. This type of happiness depends on external pleasures to serve one's needs and may cause conflicts with others who also need them. People can get stress and tensions for that object dependent and their happiness can be faded down with higher desire and pressure. Thus, this type of happiness needs to be watched out or monitored by one's own mind and managed with wisdom that understands the natural truth of changes and true happiness.

Buddhism encourages human beings to have happiness with less dependent from materials outside oneself. Happiness can be obtained from non-acquisition which is mind- and wisdom- based. This is the higher level of happiness or inner happiness which can be generated inside human beings and independent to external factors. This level of happiness is considered as a neater type of happiness that human beings should be trained for and it should be the goal for complete human development. The advancement in developing oneself to gain happiness at higher level is the progress from practicing Dhamma, which can be achieved by continued practicing rightly. When people reach the true happiness with full wisdom, they are free from any attachment and will not move back to enjoy the lower level of happiness. In other words, true happiness means realizing Dhamma, and reaching true happiness means reaching Dhamma. Buddhism teaches how to achieve a good and happy life by reaching the essence of Dhamma. Human beings have to understand what is a good life and genuine happiness. However, there are many steps to reach true happiness and many detailed classifications of happiness in various Dhamma books.

6.2.1 Sensual Pleasures

As described before, happiness from sensual pleasures is the lowest level of Buddhist happiness, obtained from 5 senses: eye, ear, nose, tongue, and body; such as nice forms, pleasant noises, good smell, sweet taste, and comfortable touches. These are the pleasures one enjoys these things at physical level. These sensual pleasures or kāmasukha are not real happiness because it may involve dissatisfaction and suffering (dhukha). Happiness at this level can be further divided into two categories: undeveloped and developed ones.

(a) First, the undeveloped one from untrained mind, driven by kilesa (defilements) which is a troublesome desire: This type of desire is driven with the ignorance of the three signs of truth (impermanent, suffering, and non-existing) and can push people into trouble with dissatisfaction and unlimited wants. This type of desire may be called as "taṇhā" (craving and attachment). When the desire is not met, it can cause frustration due to attachment from being anticipated.

(b) It is acceptable that people can be happy with sensual pleasures, if they have wisdom and practices for living appropriately in the society. People can have materials and wealth, but they know how to develop their lives as well as others' towards higher goals. In other words, material accumulations can be used to improve human development to benefit the society as a whole. Also, human sensual desires should limit and people must know what level is appropriate for themselves and well behave towards others. In the process of acquisition, of material wealth, one should not burden oneself as well as the others.

If people in the society have sīla (morality), dāna (generiousity, sharing), and paññā (wisdom), the society can gain positively from material development. Therefore, Buddhism does not reject materials or physical development, if it is supervised by Dhamma.

6.2.2 Mind-Based Happiness

This is the happiness that can be generated as mind-based, not from getting more materials or dependence with external factors. Happiness can be developed inside one's own mind. Therefore, this level of happiness is higher than the level of physical well-being which has to depend on other things outside oneself.

As indicated in Buddha Dhmama, development on the mind-level will allow the individual to have a mind that contains virtues like loving-kindness (mettā), compassion (karuṇa), faith (saddhā), gratitude (kataññūkataveditā) and so on. It is a mind with efficiency, strength, stability, diligence and patience, a mind that has mindfulness (sati) and knows its responsibilities, and so, it is in good health because it is peaceful, relaxed, clear, fresh, joyful, and happy.

With loving-kindness (mettā) and compassion (karuṇā) in mind, we want other people to be happy. Therefore, we are happy to give, share, or help others, instead of taking advantage from them. People can be generous (dāna) towards others rather than selfishness, and that can generate happiness to the givers. Instead of being happy from acquisitions, individuals can be happy from giving away and less acquisition. In that case, individual happiness from mind.

6.2.3 Happiness at the Level of Liberation

Happiness at this level is characterized by wisdom or insight (paññā), with full understanding of natural changes from the three signs of truth: the impermanance, the state of suffering, and the non-existing (or selflessness). Realizing that it is not worth to attach with, human beings then have purified minds and free from any attachment. Therefore, they are completely free from suffering as they have insight to understand all the natural laws, that is, changes as well as causes and effects. This is the highest level of happiness and the individual who has progressed to reach this level is completely awakened or enlightened with natural freshness and joyfulness. Nothing can cause suffering to that person whose wisdom is able to solve all problems wisely with the mind of emptiness and unattached. They will neutrally understand everything under the natural truth without suffering. Although the person can have happiness at sensual pleasures (level 1) and mind-based (level 2), there would be no danger as that are supervised by wisdom and can positively be utilized for the benefits of others and the society.

This level is the ultimate goal of dhamma practice or happiness development to be called as lokuttara (beyond the world) level or paramattha (the highest level). Those who can achieve this level are noble individuals or called "Ariya". That individual who has achieved the highest happiness does not want anything for oneself anymore; therefore, that one can fully work for others for the benefit of the society. Whatever the individual does is driven from "chanda" to do good things with selflessness, as well as pure and perfect compassion. Consequently, the society has received benefit fully from this type of highly developed person.

6.3 Training Mind for Happiness

For Buddha, the path to happiness starts from an understanding of the root causes of suffering. Those who consider Buddha a pessimist because of his concern with suffering have missed the point. In fact, he is a skilful doctor — he may break the bad news of our suffering, but he also prescribes a proactive course of treatment. In this metaphor, the medicine is the Buddha's teachings of wisdom and compassion known as Dharma, and the nurses that encourage us and show us how to take the medicine are the Buddhist community or Sangha. The illness however, can only be cured if the patient follows the doctor's advice and follows the course of treatment: the Eightfold Path, the core of which involves control of the mind.

In Buddhism, this treatment is not a simple medicine to be swallowed, but a daily practice of mindful thought and action that we ourselves can test scientifically through our own experience. Meditation is, of course, the most well-known tool of this practice, but contrary to popular belief, it is not about detaching from the world. Rather it is a tool to train the mind not to dwell in the past or the future, but to live in the here and now, the realm in which we can experience peace most readily.

All that we are is the result of what we have thought. It is founded on our thoughts. It is made up of our thoughts. If one speaks or acts with an evil thought, pain follows one, as the wheel follows the foot of the ox that draws the wagon.

- (Dhammapada-1)

All that we are is the result of what we have thought. It is founded on our thoughts. It is made up of our thoughts. If one speaks or acts with a pure thought, happiness follows one, like a shadow that never leaves

- (Dhammapada-2)

The first and second verses (above) of the Dhammapada, the earliest known collection of Buddha's sayings, talk about suffering and happiness. So, it's not surprising to discover that Buddhism has a lot to offer on the topic of happiness. Buddha's contemporaries described him as "ever-smiling" and portrayals of Buddha almost always depict him with a smile on his face (***Laughing Buddha***). But rather than the smile of a self-satisfied, materially-rich or celebrated man, Buddha's smile comes from a deep equanimity from within.

6.3.1 The Problem & The Solution: The Four Noble Truths & The Eightfold Path to Happiness

6.3.1.1 Four Noble Truths – Dukkha and its Ending in Buddhism

The Four Noble Truths are the very foundation of the Buddhist teaching, and that is why they are so important. In fact, if you don't understand the Four Noble Truths, and if you have not experienced the truth of this teaching personally, it is impossible to practice Buddha Dharma. In Buddhism, the Four Noble Truths ("The four Arya Satyas") are "the truths of the Noble Ones", the truths or realities for the "spiritually worthy ones".

The truths are:

(i) Dukkha (suffering, incapable of satisfying, painful) is an innate characteristic of existence in the realm of samsara;

(ii) Samudaya (origin, arising) of this dukkha, which arises or "comes together" with taṇhā ("craving, desire or attachment");

(iii) Nirodha (cessation, ending) of this dukkha can be attained by the renouncement or letting go of this taṇhā;

(iv) Marga (path, Noble Eightfold Path) is the path leading to renouncement of tanha and cessation of dukkha.

6.3.1.3 The Eightfold Path

1. Right View/ understanding (wisdom), 2. Right Intention/ thought (wisdom), 3. Right Speech (Ethical conduct), 4. Right Action (Ethical conduct), 5. Right Livelihood (Ethical conduct), 6. Right Effort (Mental cultivation), 7. Right Mindfulness (Mental cultivation), and 8. Right Concentration (Mental cultivation).

The Eightfold Path is a practical and systematic way out of ignorance, eliminating dukkha from our minds and our lifestyle through mindful thoughts and actions. It is presented as a whole system, but the three paths associated with the area of mental cultivation are particularly relevant to the happiness that we can find in equanimity, or peace of mind.

By following the Noble **Eightfold Path**, to moksha, liberation, restraining oneself, cultivating discipline, and practicing mindfulness and meditation, one starts to disengage from craving and clinging to impermanent states and things, and rebirth and dissatisfaction will be ended. The term "path" is usually taken to mean the Noble Eightfold Path, but other versions of "the path" can also be found in the Nikayas. The Theravada tradition regards insight into the four truths as liberating in itself.

The well-known eightfold path consists of the understanding that this world is fleeting and unsatisfying, and how craving keeps us tied to this fleeting world; a friendly and compassionate attitude to others; a correct way of behaving; mind-control, which means not feeding on negative thoughts, and nurturing positive thoughts; constant awareness of the feelings and responses which arise; and the practice of dhyana, meditation. The tenfold path adds the right (liberating) insight, and liberation from rebirth.

The four truths are to be internalized, and understood or "experienced" personally, to turn them into a lived reality.

The four truths describe dukkha and its ending as a means to reach peace of mind in this life, but also as a **means to end rebirth**.

The Four Noble Truths describe the knowledge needed to set out on the path to liberation from rebirth. By understanding the four truths, one can stop this clinging and craving, attain a pacified mind, and be freed from this cycle of rebirth and re-death. The moksha is a central concept in Indian religions, and "literally means freedom from samsara. The desire is the cause of suffering because desire is the cause of rebirth. When desire ceases, rebirth and its accompanying suffering ceases.

Once birth has arisen, "ageing and death", and various other dukkha states follow. While saying that birth is the cause of death may sound rather simplistic, in Buddhism it is a very significant statement; for there is an alternative to being born. This is to attain Nirvāna, so bringing an end to the process of rebirth and re-death. Nirvāna is not subject to time and change, and so is known as the 'unborn'; as it is not born it cannot die, and so it is also known as the "deathless". To attain this state, all phenomena subject to birth – the khandhas and nidānas – must be transcended by means of non-attachment.

The last sermon, the Maha-parinibbana Sutta (Last Days of the Buddha,

Digha Nikaya 16), states it as follows:

[...] it is through not realizing, though not penetrating the Four Noble Truths that this long course of birth and death has been passed through and undergone by me as well as by you [...] But now, bhikkhus, that these have been realized and penetrated, cut off is the craving for existence, destroyed is that which leads to renewed becoming [rebirth], and there is no fresh becoming.

6.4 Kindness and Compassion are the Pre-requisites for Happiness

There is an inextricable link between one's personal happiness and kindness, compassion, and caring for others. And this is a two-way street: increased happiness leads to greater compassion, and increased compassion leads to greater happiness.

In other words, studies have found not only that happier people tend to be more caring and more willing to reach out and help others, but that by deliberately cultivating greater kindness and compassion, a person will experience increased happiness. It is easy to see how such principles could have a profound impact on any society if people adopted them on a widespread scale. However, since it is unlikely that most people will "convert" to Buddhism as their primary spiritual path, they need to be presented in a secular context, which generally means investigating them from a scientific perspective.

6.5 Sources of Happiness

Talking at a superficial lever, a pay raise, a new car, or recognition from our peers may lift our mood for a while, but we soon return to our customary level of happiness. In the same way, an argument with a friend, a car in the repair shop, or a minor injury may put us in a foul mood, but within a matter of days our spirits rebound. This tendency isn't limited to trivial, everyday events but persists even under more extreme conditions of triumph or disaster. Researchers surveying Illinois state lottery winners and British pool winners, for instance, found that the initial high eventually wore off and the winners returned to their usual range of moment-to-moment happiness. And other studies have demonstrated that even those who are struck by catastrophic events such as cancer, blindness, or paralysis typically recover their normal or near-normal level of day-to-day happiness after an appropriate adjustment period.

So, if we tend to return to our characteristic baseline level of happiness no matter what our external conditions are, what determines this baseline? And, more important, can it be modified, set at a higher level? Some researchers have recently argued that an individual's characteristic level of happiness or well-being is genetically determined, at least to some degree. Studies such as one that found that identical twins (sharing the same genetic constitution) tend to have very similar levels of well-being—regardless of whether they were raised together or apart have led these investigators to postulate a biological set point for happiness, wired into the brain at birth.

But even if genetic makeup plays a role in happiness—and the verdict is still out on how large that role is—there is general agreement among psychologists that no matter what level of happiness we are endowed with by nature, there are steps we can take to work with the "mind factor," to enhance our feelings of happiness. This is because our moment-to-moment happiness is largely determined by our outlook. In fact, whether we are feeling happy or unhappy at any given moment often has very little to do with our absolute conditions but, rather it is a function of how we perceive our situation, how satisfied we are with what we have.

6.6 Some Buddha Quotes on Happiness

Buddha was not as chubby as many depictions of him make it seem – he was portrayed this way because, in the east, it was symbolic of happiness. Buddha practiced moderation, fasted regularly, and spent a lot of his time traveling by foot hundreds of miles, spreading his philosophy of enlightenment.

Following are some of the Buddha Quotes on Happiness:

- If you are quiet enough, you will hear the flow of the universe. You will feel its rhythm. Go with this flow. Happiness lies ahead. Meditation is key.

- Thousands of candles can be lit from a single candle, and the life of the candle will not be shortened. Happiness never decreases by being shared.

- There is no path to happiness. Happiness is the path.

- It is ridiculous to think that somebody else can make you happy or unhappy.

- Happiness does not depend on what you have or who you are. It solely relies on what you think.

- A disciplined mind brings happiness.

- Happiness is not having a lot. Happiness is giving a lot.

- Happiness never decreases by being shared.

- If you knew what about the power of giving you would not let a single meal pass without sharing it in some way.

- You only lose what you cling to.

- The past is already gone; the future is not yet here. There's only one moment for you to live.

- Your work is to discover your work and then with all your heart to give yourself to it.

- Teach this triple truth to all: A generous heart, kind speech, and a life of service and compassion are the things which renew humanity.

- Every human being is the author of his own health and happiness.

- One should strive to understand what underlies sufferings and diseases – and aim for health and well-being while gaining in the path.

CHAPTER SEVEN

HAPPINESS IN JAINISM

7.1 Concept of Happiness in Jainism

Life is dear to all even though it may contain misery. Man's desire for an explanation of the existence of a misery, for relief from and extinction of misery and for a consequent increase of **happiness** of life, is the function of religion. True religion is a way of life. It should lead to the mental and moral upliftment of an aspirant and must provide peace and happiness for his soul.

We have to find a thing, where it is. How can we find it where it is not possible to have it at all. For example, consciousness is an attribute of the soul, and can be found in the sentient soul only, not in inanimate entities. Likewise happiness is also an attribute of the soul, not of inanimate beings. Happiness can, therefore, be had in the soul only, not in inanimate objects like human bodies. This soul does not know itself and is, therefore, wandering with wrong faith; in the same manner this being attempts to find happiness in non-self-objects and that is the root cause of his unhappiness. The direction of the search for happiness itself is wrong. When the direction is wrong, the present state will also be full of unhappiness. For getting real happiness, we have to see within, to know our own being, for our happiness lies in ourselves. The soul is a depository of eternal bliss, full of everlasting joy. Therefore, those, in pursuit of happiness should turn their efforts towards their inner beings. Those looking for happiness elsewhere, will never get it.

Real happiness is a matter of experience, not of speech, not of demonstration. It can be had only by being introvert, cutting ourselves from all the non-self-entities and being one with our soul itself. Since the soul is full of happiness, experience of the soul is the experience of happiness. Just as one cannot achieve the soul without experience, in the same manner one cannot get real happiness without the experience of the soul.

If we ponder deeply over the question, we realise that happiness is not to be had from somewhere else, for the soul is itself made of this happiness, is nothing but happiness alone. That which is happiness incarnate has not to find happiness anywhere else. Happiness is not to be possessed, it is to be enjoyed, to be experienced. It is not necessary to torment ourselves for getting happiness. There is no trouble whatsoever in happiness; restlessness has no happiness. Restlessness is itself unhappiness and its absence is happiness. As such there should be no desire for happiness, for desires themselves make us unhappy. Absence of desires is real happiness.

To all questions like, 'what is happiness?'. Where does it lie?' 'How shall we get it?' there is only one answer, only one solution and that is the experience of the soul itself. The first and the foremost means to achieving it is the pondering over the fundamentals of life. However, we should remember that the real experience of the soul is born of the absence of this pondering over the fundamentals of life. Separate treatment is desirable for questions like 'Who am I?' 'What is soul?' and 'How is self-experience achieved?'

7.2 Happiness in Jainism

The name Jainism derives from the Sanskrit verb ji, "to conquer." It refers to the ascetic battle that, it is believed, Jain renunciants (monks and nuns) must fight against the passions and bodily senses to gain enlightenment, or omniscience and purity of soul. The most illustrious of those few individuals who have achieved enlightenment are called Jina (literally, "Conqueror"), and the tradition's monastic and lay adherents are called Jain ("Follower of the Conquerors"), or Jaina. This term came to replace a more ancient designation, Nirgrantha ("Bondless"), originally applied to renunciants only.

Jaina religion (Jainism) is an ancient one. Lord Mahavira, the 24th Tirthankara, rejuvenated it around 2500 years ago. However, it was propagated for thousands of years before Mahavira by the 23 Tirthankaras who preceded him. Even they were not the founders of Jainism, which had existed from time immemorial, they had brought the fundamental principles of Jainism to light by their extraordinary perception and knowledge. They preached, propounded and popularised its principles. Lord Mahavira, however, is credited with having formalised and rejuvenated the religion called Jainism.

The three main pillars of Jainism are ahiṃsā (non-violence), anekāntavāda (non-absolutism), and aparigraha (non-attachment). Jains take five main vows: (i) ahiṃsā (non-violence), (ii) satya (truth), (iii) asteya (not stealing), (iv) brahmacharya (sexual continence), and (v) aparigraha (non-possessiveness). These principles have affected Jain culture in many ways, such as leading to a predominantly vegetarian lifestyle. Parasparopagraho jīvānām (the function of souls is to help one another) is the faith's motto and the Ṇamōkāra mantra is its most common and basic prayer.

According to Jainism, time is without beginning and eternal. The kālacakra, the cosmic wheel of time, rotates ceaselessly. Time is eternal and formless. It is understood as a wheel with 12 spokes (ara), the equivalent of ages, six of which form an ascending arc and six a descending one. In the ascending arc (utsarpini) humans progress in knowledge, age, stature, and **happiness**, while in the descending arc (avasarpini) they deteriorate. The two cycles joined together make one rotation of the wheel of time, which is called a kalpa. These kalpas repeat themselves without beginning or end. Each half cycle is further sub-divided into six epochs. As the universe moves through these epochs, worlds go through changes in **happiness**, life span, and general moral conduct. No divine or supernatural beings are responsible for these changes, rather they happen due to the force of karma. Jains believe that the time cycle is currently in the descending phase.

The **doctrine of karma** is the single most important subject of Jain philosophy. It provides a rational explanation to the apparently inexplicable phenomena of cycles of birth and death, **happiness** and misery, inequalities in mental and physical attainments and the existence of different species of living beings. Jainism believes that from eternity, every soul is ignorant and delusional of its true nature, but nonetheless is bound by karma. The ignorant and deluded soul, while remaining in bondage, continues to attract and bind new karma. It is due to karma that the soul migrates from one life cycle to another, and passes through many pleasures and painful situations. The karma that bind our soul are due not only to the actions of our body, mind, and speech but more importantly, to the intentions behind our actions. Jainism strives for the realization of the highest perfection of the soul, which in its original purity is free from all pain, suffering, desire, and bondage of the cycle of birth and death. This way it provides the basis for the path of liberation.

In Jainism, as in other Indian religions, it is karma which is responsible for the different forms of life that souls will take. Karma is envisioned as a material substance (or subtle matter) that can bind to the soul, travel with the soul in bound form between rebirths, and affect the suffering and **happiness** experienced by the jiva in the Lokas.

The way to salvation demands a deliberate attempt of the soul to purify itself from the Karmic dirt by stopping the fresh accumulation and destroying the old. Darasna Mohaniya Karma makes a man extravagant, seeking **happiness** in external objects and identifying himself with the body and other material things.

According to Jainism, the universe is composed of two main kinds of substances, the jīva (living) and the ajīva (non-living). These are uncreated existents which are always interacting with each other. These substances behave according to natural laws and the intrinsic nature (sahāvō) of a substance. Understanding this intrinsic nature is the true nature of the Jain dharma.

Jīvas are categorized into two types—liberated and non-liberated. A jīva has various essential qualities: knowledge, consciousness (caitanya), bliss (sukha) and vibrational energy (virya). These qualities are fully enjoyed unhindered by liberated souls, but obscured by karma in the case of non-liberated souls resulting in karmic bondage. This bondage further results in a continuous co-habitation of the soul with the body. Thus, an embodied non-liberated soul is found in four realms of existence—heavens, hells, humans and animal world – in a continuous cycle of births and deaths also known as samsāra. According to Jain thinkers, all living beings (even gods) experience extensive suffering and unquenchable desire (while worldly **happiness** is fleeting and small in comparison, like a mustard seed next to a mountain). With the exception of the enlightened ones, all living beings are all subject to death and rebirth.

7.3 Four Infinities

The soul according to Jainism, consists of four infinities, that is, Infinite Knowledge (Ananta Gnana), Infinite Intuition (Anata Darsana), Infinite **Happiness** (Ananta Sukha) and Infinite Potency (Ananta Virya). These are the natural characteristics of the soul and come to full manifestation in the state of salvation. These powers of the soul are neutralized by Karmic influences in the state of spiritual bondage - the state of being engrossed in worldly affairs. The way to salvation consists of the efforts of the soul to remove the karmic obstruction and regain its natural state of four infinities lying dormant since the time immemorial.

Darasna Mohaniya Karma makes a man extravagant, seeking **happiness** in external objects and identifying himself with the body and other material entities. Charitra Mohaniya Karma has also the effects of the emotions of Anger (Krodha), Conceit (Mana), Crookedness (Maya) and Greed (Lobha). The aspirant has to ascend gradually by subduing these passions by degrees. This is minutely and well-described in the Jaina theory of 14 Gunasthanas.

Jainism is useful not only for salvation but also for a man who wishes to live a happy life by rising above his inner conflicts and complexes. It is regrettable that the supreme science of leading a happy life has been wrongly confined to transcendental purposes, on the assumption that benefits are not connected with the present life. That is a wrong notion. A man however materially rich he may be, will sooner or later have to learn this science if he seeks real **happiness** and wants to save himself from destruction.

7.4 What is Real Happiness?

Real happiness is a matter of experience, not of speech, not of demonstration. It can be had only by being introvert, cutting ourselves from all the non-self-entities and being one with our soul itself. Since the soul is full of happiness, experience of the soul is the experience of happiness. Just as one cannot achieve the soul without experience, in the same manner one cannot get real happiness without the experience of the soul.

If we ponder deeply over the question, we realise that happiness is not to be had from somewhere else, for the soul is itself made of this happiness, is nothing but happiness alone. That which is happiness incarnate has not to find happiness anywhere else. Happiness is not to be possessed, it is to be enjoyed, to be experienced. It is not necessary to torment ourselves for getting happiness. There is no trouble whatsoever in happiness; restlessness has no happiness. Restlessness is itself unhappiness and its absence is happiness. As such there should be no desire for happiness, for desires themselves make us unhappy. Absence of desires is real happiness.

To all questions like, 'what is happiness?'. Where does it lie?' 'How shall we get it?' there is only one answer, only one solution and that is the experience of the soul itself. The first and the foremost means to achieving it is the pondering over the fundamentals of life. However, we should remember that the real experience of the soul is born of the absence of this pondering over the fundamentals of life.

7.5 Stoicism in Jainism

Stoicism means the endurance of pain or hardship without the display of feelings and without complaint. Stoicism is a school of Hellenistic philosophy that flourished throughout the Roman and Greek world until the 3rd century AD.

According to the teachings of Stoicism, as social beings, the path to happiness for humans is found in accepting that which we have been given in life, by not allowing ourselves to be controlled by our desire for pleasure or our fear of pain, by using our minds to understand the world around us and to do our part in nature's plan, and by working together and treating others in a fair and just manner.

True happiness is to enjoy the present, without anxious dependence upon the future, not to amuse ourselves with either hopes or fears but to rest satisfied with what we have, which is sufficient, for he that is so wants nothing.

The following Stoic quotes will make you understand Stoicism in a better way and how its applicability can change our lives

- What we desire makes us vulnerable.
- We suffer more of imagination than in reality.
- The best revenge is not to be like your enemy.
- You shouldn't give circumstances the power to rouse anger, for they don't care at all.
- The man who has anticipated the coming of troubles takes away their power when they arrive.

This is the teachings of all major religion also. When we distance philosophy from the religion, we have greater acceptability to the idea and concepts. Philosophy can unite, religion divides.

Eastern philosophies of Jainism, Buddhism, Hinduism, and even the Taoism of Lao Tzu resemble some way or the other with the Happiness thoughts and concepts of Stoicism.

Jainism Philosophy and Happiness:

Our Souls' ignorance of knowing self as a Body is the cause of all unhappiness. Knowing the self as a Soul different from the body is the beginning of the journey of eternal happiness. Soul attracts Karmas by attachment or hatred towards others, things or situations, and can get liberated from Karmas by two means: (i) Knowing the self as a Soul (first and necessary condition), and (ii) The desire-less equanimity in all the situations.

It is the Soul in the body who is suffering, unhappy or happy. Unless the subject of happiness is thought through with this basic premise, search for real happiness will be futile and invariably fail. Physical and Mental happiness are temporary (we all know and experience this), it is the spiritual happiness which is enduring. The only reason is we all are Spiritually different from physique and mind.

Some of the quotes on Jainism Philosophy

- Have compassion towards all living beings. Hatred leads to destruction.
- The greatest mistake of a soul is non-recognition of its real self and can only be corrected by recognizing it.
- All Souls are alike and potentially divine. None is Superior or Inferior.
- One who, even after knowing the whole universe, can remain unaffected and unattached is God.
- Every soul is independent. None depends on another.

CHAPTER EIGHT

HAPPINESS IN SUFISM

8.1 Concept of Happiness in Islam (Sufism)

From Islamic perspective, happiness is expressed by the term *sa'ādah*. The term contrary to *sa'ādah* is *shaqāwah*, which generally conveys the meaning of great misfortune and misery. The term *sa'ādah* isrelated to two dimensions of existence: the hereafter *(ukhrawiyah)* and the present world *(dunyawiyah)*. The term *sa'ādah* has a close relation to both the hereafter and the present world. In the case of thehereafter, *sa'ādah* indicates a meaning of an ultimate form of happiness, which is everlasting contentmentand bliss, the highest vision of God, promised to those, who in the worldly life, have submitted themselvessincerely to serve God by obeying His commands, and avoiding His prohibitions. In other words, theyobserve the tenets of Islamic teachings.

The present world, on the other hand, is related to three things: (i) to the self *(nafsiyyah)*, such as conduct pertaining to knowledge and good character, (ii) to the body *(badaniyyah)*, such as good health and security, and (iii) to things external to the self and the body *(khārijiyyah)*, such as wealth and other attributes. Happiness affects not only our secular and regular life; in fact, it cannot be separated from the spiritual aspects of our existence as interpreted and guided by religion.

There are four group of means *(wasā'il) to happiness*, which man can utilise to achieve happiness in his life. Each of these four means has four forms of virtuousness. Thus, in actual fact, the total number of means amounts to sixteen. Nevertheless, not all of these means are equally relevant to happiness. In other words, they have their own functions, some are useful and some are necessary to attain happiness. The four groups of means are (i) the 'goods' of the *soul (al-faḍā'il an-nafsiyya)*, (ii) the bodily 'goods' *(al-faḍā'il al-jismiyya)*, (iii) the external 'goods' *(al-faḍā'il al-khārijiyya)*, and (iv) the 'goods' of divine grace *(al-faḍā'il at-tawfiqiyya)*.

Al-Ghazzali was a practical mystic. His aim was to make men better by leading them from a merely notional acquiescence in the stereotyped creed of Islam to a real knowledge of God. His magnum opus entitled Iḥyā' 'ulūm ad-dīn ("The Revival of the Religious Sciences") was written in Arabic and Ghazzali himself wrote an abridgment of it in Persian for popular use which he titled Kimiya'e Saadat ("The Alchemy of Happiness"). The real self-knowledge consists in knowing the following things: What art thou in thyself, and from whence hast thou come? Whither art thou going, and for what purpose hast thou come to tarry here awhile, and in what does thy real happiness and misery consist? Some of thy attributes are those of animals, some of devils, and some of angels, and thou hast to find out to which of these attributes are accidental and which essential. Till thou knowest this, thou canst not find out where thy real happiness lies.

Anyone who will look into the matter will see that happiness is necessarily linked with the knowledge of God. Love is the seed of happiness, and love to God is fostered and developed by worship. All Muslims profess to believe that the Vision of God is the summit of human felicity, because it is so stated in the Law; but with many, this is a mere lip-profession which arouses no emotion in their hearts. This is quite natural, for how can a man long for a thing of which he has no knowledge? We must realise why the Vision of God is the greatest happiness to which a man can attain. For perfect happiness mere knowledge is not enough, unaccompanied by love, and the love of God cannot take possession of a man's heart till it be purified from love of the world, which purification can only be affected by abstinence and austerity. In brief, our future happiness will be in strict proportion to the degree in which we have loved God here and now.

8.2 How to Achieve Infinite Happiness according to Sufism?

Man is composed of three bodies. This creature that we call "man" is the most beloved creature of Allah. Allah wills this creature that He has created to be happy, to live in happiness. For this reason, He has created him differently from His other creatures, because we see that he has been created out of three different bodies. Another creature composed of three bodies has not been created in the universe and its being created is out of the question."Tasavvuf" (Sufism) is to act with the whole of the Noble Qur'an. It is to act not only with the verses concerning our physical body but also with the verses laying tasks on our soul and spirit, too. Tasavvuf is to live that which our Master the Prophet and his Companions (sahabe) had lived. The life that all the prophets and their dependents had lived was also "Tasavvuf" (Sufism). Tasavvuf is to surrender to Allâh our trusts (the spirit, the physical body, the soul and the free will) that He has confided to us. It is to reach "irshad", which is to be Islâm.

The first content of the word of Islâm is to believe in One Allah, its second content is the surrender (teslim, submission), its third content is peace and quietness (tranquility, serenity). Whoever has attained to the honour of becoming Islâm has reached the infinite happiness in three respects.

(i) As all the good qualities of the spirit are transferred to the soul in the inner world, man has reached peace and tranquility, because there is not any more state of conflict between the spirit and the soul.

(ii) Man has reached peace and tranquility in his relations with the outer world, that is, with other people, because there are not any more vices so that there may be conflicts with them.

(iii) The best relations have been established with Allahû Tealâ. Each order of our Exalted Lord has been fulfilled and each prohibition avoided. Henceforth, the virtues that the soul has possessed (that is, the good qualities of the spirit) feel a strong desire to execute the divine orders and never commit the prohibitions, because all the vices demanding to commit them have vanished. It has been thus seen that Islâm is a phase to be reached in order that an infinite happiness, a supreme delight, (hazzu'l 'azîm) should come into being.

For this reason, Allâh orders man to reach Irshad [2/Al-Baqarah – 186, 42/Ash-Shûra – 47]. Because only the person who has reached irshad has attained to Islâm, consequently to an infinite happiness. He has attained to the last rank of being a "perfect man" (Insân-ı Kâmil). He has been a perfect man from the point of view of happiness.

As this creature we name "man" is the most superior and beloved creature of Allahû Tealâ, He wishes him to live in Happiness, in Bliss. For this reason, He has created him differently from the creatures He had been creating up to that day, because we see that the man is composed of different bodies. Another creature created with the three different bodies has never been created in the Universe. His creation is out of the question, too. In the 26th verse of Hicr Sura, Allahû Tealâ makes known that our physical body was created out of soil. Allahû Tealâ wills this creature that He loves the most to be happy. For this reason, The Torah, the Book of Psalms, the Gospel and the Glorious Qur'an have been sent down as an Invitation of Happiness to the humankind. That is to say, throughout the human history, Allah always wills the human beings to be happy.

You are a human being who cannot be happy in the sight of Allahû Tealâ. You are a person who cannot apply the prescription of happiness He has granted to you and therefore who will never be able to reach HAPPINESS as long as you will not apply that prescription. But when the person fulfils the Commands of Allah, he purifies his soul. If he surrenders his spirit to Allah, fulfill the subsequent surrenders, if he keeps trying in this direction, Allahû Tealâ will absolutely direct him from unhappiness to happiness. In such a system, man will gradually experience (taste) happiness. Allah is Able to do all things. But if men provoke wrong things through their wrong behaviours, he will never be able to reach Happiness neither in this worldly life nor in the Afterlife. If we scrutinize the Commands given by Allah carefully, we will see that the aim of Allah by saying: "purify your souls" is our happiness.

We name "Zikir" the iteration of the Name of Allah by beings (mankind and jinn) possessing the free will (faculty of choice). Zikir is a volitional event. This is an act made by the consent of the person and the unique means to make our worldly works into a worship. It is only zikir that can satify the (soul's) heart. It is not possible for man to reach the happiness and the satisfaction without zikir.

The striving too is one of the means of remembering Allah. It is an occasion of zikir. That is to say, the goal is to repeat constantly Allah's Name. But just as we should repeat the name of Allah in our hearts, we should also do zikir during our apparent actions. Now, the striving also is only one of the means to remember Allah. Striving against one's soul in the Way of Allah has two meanings: Outwardly, to fight against the enemies of Islâm corporally; inwardly, to struggle against one's soul by means of zikir. Happiness will come after this fight, this struggle.

The fact that reaching Happiness is only possible by doing too much zikir has been expressed in the sacred verse below:

O you who are âmenû! When the call is made for prayer on Friday, then hasten to Allah's zikir and leave off trading; that is better for you if you did but know! Then when the prayer is ended, then disperse in the land (earth) and seek of Allah's Blessings (Virtue) and repeat Allah's name too much, that you may reach the Salvation (Felâh: the Worldly Happiness and the Bliss of Paradise).

62/Al-Jumu'ah – 9, 10

Truly, man reaches "irshad" in person at the end of this invitation. For this reason, Allah calls all the human beings to "irshad". For He wills man He loves the most to live happily in this world and in the next world. In case the person has not got rid of the tyranny of his soul through irshad, he cannot experience happiness neither in the life of this world nor in the Afterlife.

Allah sets forth a parable: There is a slave in whom are (several) partners disputing with one another, and there is another slave wholly owned by one man (master). Are the two alike in comparisoned? (All) praise is due to Allah. Nay! Most of them do not know.

39/Az-Zumar – 29

Of a certainty, the slave who will conform to a single master, obey the orders of a single master will be in a better condition. Now, we shall attain the happiness when we abandon one of the masters from whom we take orders in opposite directions and act by order of a single Master. Insha Allah (if Allah wills it), to be able to attain this happiness is possible through reaching the third servanthood.

The fact that everything has been created for man and has been subjected to him, demonstrates clearly that Allah loves mankind the most. Now on account of this boundless love that Allah has for man, He wills us to be happy. We can say briefly that Allah wishes solely the mankind to be happy. But men are unhappy, are in stress. He has been seeking happiness everywhere in vain except the place where he should search for it. The Torah, the Psalms, Gospel and the Noble Qur'ân that Allah had sent down respectively for His human servants is an Invitation to Happiness and more owe a prescription of Happiness. Allah names the state of happiness as "hazzu'l 'azîm" (the boundless delight, the greatest gratification, the boundless happiness).

8.3 Pir-O-Murshid Inayat Khan, as a Symbol of Joy and Pain

Pir Vilayat Inayat Khan details the life, work, thinking and feelings of his Sufi Master, Pir-O-Murshid Inayat Khan. Murshid, according to Khan, "in his last years carried the signature of suffering written on his face, while one would have thought that a liberated master would radiate only joy". The author further explains that while one becomes increasingly sensitive with spiritual development, one is not carried exclusively to the land of joy, while ignoring the cries of pain and despair in the world. Instead, one becomes increasingly aware of all that is, was and will be, "in the Murshid one found joy and pain simultaneously, the way of the broken heart both agonizing and jubilant, never indifferent or low key".

The Sufi Master's words, "there is an incipient suffering ingrained in the very nature of life - life's inseparable companion". Suffering is found in birth and in death. Suffering is pervasive – even in a joy too intense, or unrequited love, a loss of hope, guilt in not having given enough, or regret in having given too much.. Pir Vilayat Inayat Khan lost his sister in the Concentration Camps at Dauchau, and therefore, is deeply aware of and sensitive to global suffering, genocide, sadism, and humiliation. He has compassion for all the victims of cruelty, savagery, and natural disasters in this world. The collective Sufi consciousness is said to be aware that "everywhere and everyday there is endless bitter suffering. No matter how we may wish to protect people from it we cannot, because there must be room for the play of the forces set off by cosmic laws in motion. The only answer is to know how to harness the force that is suffering".

According to Pir Vilayat Inayat Khan we each have a certain threshold for physical pain in the human mind, with a "cut out mechanism" which is set very high for some people. Naturally, as one attempts to escape physical pain, the urgency of the pain keeps pulling one back to it and efforts to dissociate fail. The Murshid states, "The more one can bear, the more one is given to bear.

Pir Vilayat Inayat Kahn states "the more courageously you face physical suffering, the higher the threshold of suffering you can endure, and then at a moral level the more hardship one can endure". For the Sufis, accepting the situation and our suffering as part of the agony of the universe on a cosmic scale is the only way suffering can be sublimated . For us personally, the physical pain is simply pain.

According to the Murshid, it is not the detachment that is the solution to our suffering; suffering is overcome by merging with all existence. As for joy, one is never so happy as when one has no reason to be because circumstances can never be so good as to suffice in making one happy. "Happiness cannot be bought or sold, nor can it be given. Happiness is in one's own being, one's own self, that Self that is the most precious thing in life" . When one finds oneself face to face with the reality of suffering, and holds the belief that there is some intentional planning behind human affairs and destiny, we feel like storming the Universal force we perceive to be responsible. If one believes one is a victim, one feels the agony. All one can ask then is why, over and over. The Murshid points out that by blaming the cosmic planner, we become preoccupied with avoiding any suffering or bad karma that might bring more suffering upon us. We act as if happiness alone were our birth-right. It indicates that suffering is not part of left-over karma from a past life or even from this one, but is simply part of our training for life. Finding in everything its purpose, Murshid sees in pain "the lever devised by nature to make a person sincere and quickens one with life".

8.4 Essentials of Happiness in Major Sources in Sufism

The religion of Islam is accepting and being faithful to the teachings of God which He revealed to His last prophet, Muhammad. These teachings are prescribed in the Qur'an and the Sunnah (sayings and doings of the Prophet). Additional sources include analogical reasoning and the consensus of the community. In terms of belief, the Muslim should believe in One God; all of his messengers and previous books and revelations; the angels; the Last Day of Judgement; and finally, that what a human being faces in his life is God's will.

A first conclusion with regard to happiness in this system is that God is the origin of all good. He is the supplier and the Saviour. His continuous presence comforts one's life. The Qur'an describes this state by saying,

"And when My servants question thee concerning Me, then surely I am nigh. I answer the prayer of the suppliant when he crieth unto Me. So let them hear My call and let them trust in Me, in order that they may be led aright" (Qur'an, 2:186).

God metaphorically presents Himself in the Qur'an as the light of all existence, and it is that light that guides humans to true happiness. He says,

"Allah is the Light of the heavens and the earth. The similitude of His light is as a niche wherein is a lamp. The lamp is in a glass. The glass is as it were a shining star. (This lamp is) kindled from a blessed tree, an olive neither of the East nor of the West, whose oil would almost glow forth (of itself) though no fire touched it. Light upon light. Allah guideth unto His light whom He will. And Allah setteth forth for man- kind similitudes, for Allah is Knower of all things" (Qur'an, 24:35). The Qur'an promises not only Heaven after life for those who act according to the words of God but also good life on earth: "Whosoever doeth right, whether male or female, and is a believer, him verily we shall quicken with good life, and We shall pay them a recompense in proportion to the best of what they used to do" (Qur'an, 16:97).

He warns those who turn away from his remembrance unhappiness in life and after death:

"But he who turneth away from remembrance of Me, his will be a narrow life, and I shall bring him blind to the assembly on the Day of Resurrection" (Qur'an, 20:124).

Man occupies the position of God's viceroy on earth. In the Islamic narrative of the Creation of Adam, the Qur'an recounts,

"And when thy Lord said unto the angels: Lo! I am about to place a viceroy in the earth, they said: Wilt thou place therein one who will do harm therein and will shed blood, while we, we hymn Thy praise and sanctify Thee? He said: Surely I know that which ye know not" (Qur'an 2:30).

His life is then purposeful. But when it comes to his relation with the Creator, this must be of total submission. Submission to God has no prejudice to human beings but is rather presented as an act of recognition and gratefulness to all His gifts.

He challenges human's intelligence by saying,

"He it is Who hath created for you, ears and eyes and hearts. Small thanks give ye! And He it is Who hath sown you broadcast in the earth, and unto Him ye will be gathered. And He it is Who giveth life and causeth death, and His is the difference of night and day. Have ye then no sense?" (Qur'an, 23:78–80).

So, human beings, though holding the high rank of God's viceroy on earth,

"And indeed, We have honoured the Children of Adam" (Qur'an, 17:70), cannot live a peaceful and a happy life without believing in the sustaining power. Moreover, the responsibility of humans is in line with this high rank among all creatures. He is responsible of all his sayings and doings and will be questioned on everything in the Last Day of Judgement:

"Lo! We create man from a drop of thickened fluid to test him; So, We make him hearing, knowing" (Qur'an, 76:2).

8.5 The Falsafa (Philosophy) of Happiness in Sufism

Theoretical quests which are intimately linked to the Qur'an and the Hadith have accompanied the birth of Islam. They were further refined and extended as a result of Islam's meeting with other cultures. For instance, the movement of Falsafa (philosophy) continued and recreated Greek philosophical thought. Happiness and social and political conducts were among the central themes of discussion. However, the shared frame of reference was the conception of "humans as ethical beings searching for happiness through the improvement of their natures and modes of conduct". Happiness is conceived as transcendence beyond the physical or the sensual to achieve the long-lasting eternal happiness which is with the mercy of God and His heavens. So, earthly life is just a path toward the eternal home. Yet, the dichotomy between the two types of happiness is not easy to resolve as it may appear.

Big discrepancies could be noticed among Muslim scholars in approaching this issue. For instance, Al Farabi or Alpharabius (870–950) entitled one of his treaties "The attainment of happiness." It discussed lengthily how individuals and nations could reach happiness. Deeply inspired by Aristotle, he proposed four kinds of happiness: (i) theoretical virtues (knowledge naturally embedded in humans and those acquired through meditation, (ii) investigation and inference, instruction and study), (iii) deliberated virtues, moral virtues, and (iv) practical arts. Ibn Miskawayh (about 932–1030) displayed a main interest in ethics and how to reach ultimate happiness. He was deeply influenced by Aristotle and Neo-Platonism and held that happiness was the common aim for all human beings. Nevertheless, true happiness could not be found outside the boundaries of the divine word. Thus, the triumph is to succeed life tests and reach God's blessings. Ibn Misquawayh agrees with Aristotle, clearly in opposition to Pythagoras, Hippocrates, and Plato, in that man's happiness is in the perfection of both his spirit and body. Both Ibn Misquawayh and Aristotle maintain that the attainment of happiness is also possible in this world. Such things as health of body, moderation of temper and senses, wealth, good reputation, success in affaires, correctness of beliefs, moral virtues, and merited behaviour are a part of happiness, but the ultimate happiness is obtained through the accomplishment of all of the perfections related to spirit and body. Ibn Bajja or Avempace (about 1085–1139) is one of the main representatives of the falsafa in the Muslim West. In the Regimen of the Solitary, he maintained that the philosopher should isolate himself intellectually from the corrupted community, in order to attain the ultimate happiness of theoretical life. In The Conjunction of Intellect with Man, he argues that this ultimate happiness consists in the highest perfection of the human intellect.

8.6 Some Quotes / Verses on Happiness in Sufism

- "Don't Worry Be Happy" — Meher Baba

- "Happiness comes from helping others, by being with others, and by sharing, even if it's only a smile."
  — Zain Hashmi, A Blessed Olive Tree: A Spiritual Journey in Twenty Short Stories

- "Whatever happens in your life, no matter how troubling things might seem, do not enter the neighborhood of despair. Even when all doors remain closed, God will open up a new path only for you. Be thankful! It is easy to be thankful when all is well. A Sufi is thankful not only for what he has been given but also for all that has been denied."

  -Elif Shafak

- The good deed and the evil deed cannot be equal. Repel (the evil) with one which is better; then verily he, between whom and you there was enmity, (will become) as though he was a close friend. But none is made to reach it (the above quality) except those who are patient – and none is made to reach it except the owner of the great portion (of happiness in the Hereafter that is, Paradise and of the happiness in this world).

  Fussilat – 34, 35

- The owners of Belief who wish to reach Allah! Be possessed of "Takvâ" towards Allah, And seek the Means to make you reach Him, and strive hard in His Way, so that you may reach Felâh (the Salvation the Bliss of Paradise and the worldly happiness).

5/Al-Mâ'idah – 35

- Those who believed and emigrated and strove hard and fought in the Way of Allah with their property and their lives are far higher in degree in the Presence of Allah. It is those who have attained to Happiness.

9/At-Taubah – 20

- And none are made to obtain (reach) it but those who are patient, and none are made to receive (reach) it but those who are the owners of great delight (happiness, portion).

41/Fussilat – 35

- Let there arise from you a community who invite to goodness and enjoin what is right (el ma'rûf, what is ordered by Islâm) and forbid evil (el munker, what is forbidden by Islâm). Such are they who have reached the Salvation (Felâh = the happiness of the worldly life and the Bliss of Paradise).

3/Âl-'Imrân – 104

- And he has indeed reached the Salvation (the worldly happiness and the bliss of Paradise) who purifies him.

91/Ash-Shams – 9

CHAPTER NINE

HAPPINESS IN CHRISTIANITY

"Happiness is the meaning and the purpose of life, the whole aim and end of human existence." ~ Aristotle

9.1 Happiness, Well-Being, and Flourishing in Christianity

When asked what people want for themselves and their children, happiness often tops the list. Human happiness is the core business of Positive Psychology. This field has been defined as the study of the conditions and processes that contribute to the flourishing or optimal functioning of peoples, groups, and institutions.

The concept of human happiness has been debated throughout the centuries. Flourishing, thriving, wellbeing, happiness, health, and optimal functioning are often used interchangeably, and one is often used to define the other. For instance, the World Health Organization defined health as "a complete state of physical, mental, and social wellbeing, not simply the absence of disease and disability". Numerous Positive Psychology scholars have proposed wellbeing theories, which intersect and diverge according to their own worldviews. Wellbeing and happiness are often viewed as meta constructs that subsume multiple other affective, cognitive, social, physical, and spiritual dimensions. Philosophically, ancient Greek philosophers such as Aristotle and Socrates, opined that happiness aligns along two primary dimensions: hedonic and eudaimonic, as explained below.

9.2 Hedonic and Eudaimonic Happiness

Hedonic happiness is achieved through experiences of pleasure and enjoyment, while eudaimonic happiness is achieved through experiences of meaning and purpose. Both kinds of happiness are achieved and contribute to overall well-being in different ways.

9.2.1 Hedonic Happiness

Lay persons commonly associate happiness with hedonic wellbeing, which primarily refers to high levels of positive emotion (e.g., pleasure, excitement, contentment), low levels of negative emotion (e.g., sadness, anxiety, anger), and a general sense of satisfaction with life. Essentially hedonic wellbeing focuses on how wellbeing feels.

Positive emotion has been linked with numerous socially-valued outcomes, including better physical health, longer life, good social relationships, career advancement and success, lower levels of divorce, less mental illness, and greater creativity. The negative emotions narrow one's attention to the problem at hand, whereas positive emotions broaden one's psychological, social, and cognitive capacities. Evidence suggests that it is beneficial to have a greater proportion of positive emotions compared to negative emotions during the course of one's day. Positive emotions help people to connect with others and build resources, which can provide a buffer in times of stress. Positive and negative emotions can spread to others, potentially passed along through social networks.

Various interventions and exercises that can cultivate good feelings have been developed, which successfully temporarily relieve mental distress and improve self-reported wellbeing. Yet feelings are fleeting. Emotions change continuously throughout the day. We have a generally stable level of happiness, and despite good or bad experiences, we typically return to our baseline. While an entire industry of self-help books, entertainment, drugs, high-thrill activities, and the like have sprung up over the recent decades to help people 'feel good', the pursuit of pleasure often leaves a person feeling unfulfilled. Studies suggest that is possible to shift that level over time through one's activities, but it takes time and continued effort . Even while the idea of being happy sounds good, perhaps "all is vanity and a chasing after the wind".

9.2.2 Eudaimonic Happiness

Increasingly, Positive Psychology theory, research, and application has shifted its focus to eudaimonic wellbeing. Defined as "the good life", eudaimonia focuses on what makes life worth living. For example, self-determination theory suggests that humans have three core needs that drive behaviour: (i) relationships, (ii) autonomy, and (iii) competence; happiness occurs when these needs are met. Psychological wellbeing is defined across six dimensions: (i) positive social relationships, (ii) environmental mastery, (iii) autonomy, (iv) purpose in life, (v) self-acceptance, and (vi) personal growth. These phenomenological indicators capture core aspects of what it means to be human. Studies over the past 25 years suggest that psychological wellbeing reduces the risk for disease and early mortality.

An aspect of eudaimonic wellbeing that has received a growing amount of attention in recent years is the meaning in life. The meaning involves two dimensions: (i) comprehension, or an understanding of one's life (who one is, how one fits into the world, and a sense of direction), and (ii) purpose (feeling valuable, worthwhile, and that what one does matters). Studies have linked comprehension and purpose to various subjective well-being measures, active engagement in life, better physical health, and lower mortality risk. The meaningful life is not necessarily happy from a hedonic perspective, but appears to lead to a variety of valued positive outcomes.

9.3 Christian Theology (Religious Belief) and Happiness

Christian theology has always been part of the happiness discourse. Realizing that temporary happiness is not sustainable and very fragile, theologians have indeed been very cautious to enter into the terminology and even the discussion of happiness. Because of the reality of death, happiness was thought to be unattainable in this life, and theologians generally resorted to eschatological terms to express their understanding of happiness as "eternal life". In ancient Aristotelian philosophy, happiness and morality were two sides of the same coin. Severing that bond in modernity, has placed theologians in a precarious position, where it became untenable to promote happiness on a Christian basis, for fear of it being identified too closely with hedonic happiness (the boosting of momentary and sensual experiences), detached from God and the moral good. But the theology can simultaneously hold both a moral and transcendent view on happiness, and recognize material pleasure and enjoyment, in a model of mutual affirmation.

A privatized, hedonic view of happiness can thus be overcome by the realization that social happiness is inevitably linked to individual happiness, and that goodness, creating more enduring societal happiness, need to be understood as an integral constituent part of happiness. In fact, it is generally recognized today that even sadness and despair can enrich one's life. A well-designed theological response will avoid both the extremes of other-worldliness on the one side and of mere materialism on the other. Claiming the connection between the spiritual and the material and grounding it in the theology of the incarnation and of the sacraments (as material means of grace) may show a way out of the impasse. The way in which the Old and the New Testament speak of or allude to happiness is indeed consistent with an integral connection of the spiritual and the material.

The Greek terms makarios and eudaimonia are used to denote "happiness". Makarios, in Homer, is used for describing the gods' state of happiness beyond care. From the time of Aristotle, the term has become weaker, denoting any happiness, also for humans. Aristotle still uses makarios to describe the gods' happiness, and uses eudaimonia to describe the happiness of humans. Seen in its Stoic context, eudaimonia is linked to the moral purpose (proairesis) of humankind, which means to live according to nature (kata phusin). It is further related to virtue (arete) and governed by reason (logos). So, for the Stoics eudaimonia is the ultimate goal in life, and it is primarily "to act virtuously so that one's life is in accordance with universal nature." Only secondarily it is "possibly a state of exhilaration" (chara, euphrosune) as a subsequent manifestation of virtuous activity.

The New Testament does not use eudaimonia to indicate happiness. Makarios and chairo are mostly used; with less frequent use of a few other terms as well. To the early Christians, understandably, happiness was a gift from the hand of God. According to the reports in Acts, they saw themselves as a community of joy and happiness. The coming of Jesus inaugurated a new era, that is, an era of happiness. The bridegroom has arrived; the fasting is over. The blind sees, the lame walks, the dead lives, and there is good news for the poor. There was a definite positive aspect to this new view on happiness, but this happiness also included a future, where this happiness would be full and enduring. Especially in the gospel of Luke, this joyful theology was seen right from the birth narrative to the Easter accounts. With Paul this theology included joy in suffering. Happiness is "happiness in Christ", which means sharing in his suffering and his glory. Happiness in spite of suffering and happiness in suffering is possible because of the future hope of sharing in Christ's triumph. In the Johannine writings special emphasis was laid on happiness as something that is fulfilled in the present." According to Revelation, happiness is on the new earth and in the new heaven when all unhappiness is removed forever. Happiness is to be found in Christ. He is the inaugurator of happiness. In sorrow or pain, poverty or sadness, he is the reason why Christians can be happy. In Christ, God gives happiness. Happiness is both present and eschatological. In this sense, happiness appears to be a state of mind.

The "macarism" was known in both the Greek and Semitic worlds. It refers to the "life-enhancing behaviour" of the believer, e.g., coming to Zion, fearing God, studying the Torah, caring for the poor, etc. The function (appearing almost exclusively in the Psalms and Wisdom literature) is to give moral instruction, indicating that persons following these instructions will be happy. Happiness corresponds with Israel's view on well-being, which mostly concerns the present: life, security, posterity, military success, prosperity, etc.

Because happiness is a gift from God and is found in the believers' relationship with God, it seems that happiness, according to early Christianity is an inner state of the mind, a condition. Early Christians were also happy because of their conduct. Deeds have consequences, and proper conduct leads to happiness. Except for those who saw life in an apocalyptic perspective, both early Christians and Stoics had an optimistic view of life. They both accepted life as it was and tried to live happily.

To be happy is to become wise in the eyes of both Stoics and early Christians.

The New Testament also speaks of suffering. Although it is not seen in a positive light, it is not seen to destroy the road to the highest good (or the Kingdom) of the faithful, as it contrasts that road, gives it profile, emphasises the urgency of being on that road, and trains the faithful in their determination to persevere towards the goal of the highest good. The New Testament does, however, promote the concept of life, understood both in its physical and eternal sense. Not losing your "soul" or "life" by winning the (material) world and following your selfish ways, is important. Christ promises life in abundance. This life is also described in very mundane terms to be calm (1 Tim 2:2), peaceful (Jm 3:17, 1 Tim 2:2 and 1 Tess 4:11) and unselfish (1 Cor 10:33).

Linking the life-promoting God to the concept of "blessing", Westermann shows that the Christian church stood in the long tradition which distinguished them from other religions of the time in that blessing would not only denote the showering with gifts because the worshippers of the particular God have performed the right rituals to appease the divine. Blessing was seen and experienced as God's power that enabled and sustained life and flourishing. It also protected from danger and despair. The Christians understood this notion of blessing to be proprietary connected to the salvation of God in Christ. Salvation in the Jewish tradition was not primarily seen then as salvation "from", but salvation to the empowering of the people of God in their existence in God's land. It is the Creator God who also blesses, and His blessing is continuation of his life-creating love. Westermann also shows the close relationship between blessing and wisdom. Where profane wisdom was about controlling your life in order to succeed, the reciprocal relationship between wisdom and blessing in Israel meant that wisdom was received as part of the blessing of God.

9.4 How to be happy in an unhappy world?

Frequently one is asked, "Is there any such thing as 'a happy life' in a world of 'Unhappiness, sin, suffering and sorrow'? If so, what is the recipe for it?" Surely anyone would be willing to pay a big price for such a recipe. But, there are as many recipes for happiness as there are recommended cures for a cold, However, in thinking of happiness as a permanent possession only, one has an infallible recipe for it, Here is a recipe on to you because it never fails. Here it is:

"Whoso trusteth in the lord, happy is he." Proberbs 16:20.

" O, taste and see that the lord is good: happy is the man that trusteth in Him." -Psalm 34:8.

"Happy is the man that walketh not in the counsel of the ungodly, nor standeth in the way of sinners, or sitteth in the seat of the scornful. But his delight is in the law of the lord."

- Psalm l:l-2a

"Happy is that people whose God is the Lord," -Psalm 144:15.

In the light of these glorious truths, and the fact that there are two classes of people: the happy and the unhappy; let us consider three things.

9.4.1 The Pursuit of Happiness

Everybody has a desire to be happy. Happiness is one thing for which all mankind is striving. Whether young or old, rich or poor, educated or. uneducated, saved or unsaved, all are pursuing happiness. Study the faces of people as they pass by on the street. What do those faces reveal that the people are thinking about and striving for? Is it money? Is it knowledge? Is it power? No, it is something behind all of these. It is happiness. Each one is trying to achieve happiness.

Some are concentrating all their energies in the pursuit of happiness, while others seem less hopeful, and more faint-hearted in their efforts. But, if the efforts that are being made to achieve happiness were only put forth in the right direction, many of the cups of happiness would be filled to overflowing. Much of the effort to secure happiness is made in the wrong way, so happiness is never achieved although it is desired and expected.

9.4.2 Preventiveness of Happiness

While all are pursuing happiness, it must be frankly admitted that the multitudes are not happy. Very few people are satisfied with what they have, but think if they had what some other people have they would be supremely happy. They fail to realize that a covetous soul can never be happy, even if it owned the whole world. Happiness does not consist in what you have, but in what you are. There are so many things that prevent people from being happy, but let us a few of them.

i. An impossible or unattainable ambition.
ii. A self-interest which is so strong that it will not admit a social interest.
iii. An unsatisfied craving, whether it be physical, social or mental.
iv. Tormenting conscience.
v. An irritating or uncongenial environment.
vi. Uncontrolled fear and anxiety.
vii. Misdirected energies.
viii. A spirit of covetousness.
ix. An unsaved soul.

One can never experience happiness until his sins are forgiven and his soul is saved. "There is no peace, saith the Lord, unto the wicked." Isaiah 48:22. 'While an unsaved person is never happy, the Word of God says,

"Happy is he whose transgression is forgiven, whose sin is covered. Happy is the man unto whom the lord imputeth not iniquity, and in whose spirit there is no guile." Psalm 32:1-2.

x. A disobedient life:

Such people only are really happy. But one may ask, "How do you account for the fact that many Christians are not happy"? That is an easy question to answer. They are living outside the circle of God's will for their lives. Any Christian who lives inside the circle of God's will for his life will be happy. God is the fountain of life and the source of all joy. Happiness is not something that we attain through increased possessions or through the achievement of some ambition; it is an attitude of life, a spirit within our own souls. If we do not have it on a small income, neither will we have it when our income grows larger. If it is not found where we are today, it will not be found in some place we may go tomorrow or next year. It is a flower that we my grow in the secret places of our own natures, and nowhere else in all the universe.

9.4.3 The Possessors of Happiness

Since all of us are in the quest of' happiness, and the Lord wants us to be happy, let us consider the best way to come into possession of happiness. One thing is certain, happiness cannot be found merely by running after it, because the source of happiness is within instead of without. Happiness depends on what lies. between the sole of your foot and the crown of your head. “Give us everything we want, the money we want, the recognition we want, the pleasures we want, and we shall be happy. Listen ! Money and happiness are not synonymous. Neither can you buy happiness. Real and abiding happiness is dependent not upon what we have in our hands, but upon what we have in our hearts.

Happiness is not to be found in unbelief. Happiness is not to be found in pleasure. Happiness is not to be found in money. Happiness is not to be found in position and fame. Happiness is not to be found in military glory. Alexander the Great conquered the known world in his day. Having done so, he wept in his tent, because, he said, "There are no more worlds to conquer."

where, then, is happiness to be found? In Christ alone. He said,

> *"I will see you again, and your heart shall rejoice, and your joy no man take.th from you."*
>
> *-John 16:22.*

In the light of the life and teachings of Jesus Christ, if' you ever become the possessor of genuine happiness , it will come to you through the following channels.

i. Salvation from sin;
ii. Surrender to Christ;
iii. Service for Christ; and
iv. Share happiness with others.

"Lord Jesus I long to be perfectly whole; .
I want Thee forever to dwell in my soul;
Break down every idol, cast out every foe;
Oh wash me and I shall be whiter than snow.

9.5 Purpose for a Happy Life in Christianity

Positive Psychology (PP) theories focus on elements of the flourishing life, but lack a coherent purpose or outcome. Christianity adds the importance of telos – the realization of one's ultimate purpose, function, or design. The abundant theories of flourishing and happiness in the PP literature are predominantly self-driven, and interventions and activities aim to improve one's own happiness. The implied telos of PP is thus one of individual fulfillment and enjoyment. Yet the Bible suggests that such pursuits are meaningless (Ecclesiastes). In contrast, Christianity calls for a higher purpose that is defined by God. The source and meaning of happiness lie in God, rather than in the success or failure of one's own effort.

The Bible provides a specific purpose for humanity: humans were created in the image of God (the imago Dei) for the purpose of glorifying Him (1 Peter 4:11). Creation exists because God created it and humankind can only glimpse part of the full reality of God's purposes this side of heaven. Flourishing, or living the good life (i.e., a feeling of happiness and thriving), occurs when one lives in obedience to the design that God intended. This obedience is not simply a legalistic obedience confined by specific laws, but rather is a voluntary obedience to God's intentions for one's life, grounded in a close relationship with Him. As one's love for God grows, obedience to His commends becomes a natural response, and a sense of peace and happiness follow. It is a process of becoming who God uniquely intends one to be and becoming more Christ-like in one's attitudes, thoughts, and behaviour. Notably, Christ provides the ultimate example of human flourishing, demonstrating complete obedience to His design within the order of creation.

The Bible contains multiple words that in English all translate as "love". Storge refers to an empathetic bond or affection-based love, which is both need- and gift-related. It was responsible for 90% of human happiness. Philia is the love between friends, similar to that shown by Jonathan to David in the Old Testament (1 Samuel 18:1-4). Eros describes the emotional or sexual "being in love" feeling. Agape is God's unconditional love, which is extended to humankind regardless of circumstances or our response (John 3:16). These four types of love are only possible because of God's love for humankind.

9.6 Some Bible Verses About Joy and Happiness

God wants us to be happy and joyful. But what does that look like? How do we find happiness? The only way to find happiness is through Him. He created us! God knows us better than we know ourselves. Some of His ways may seem counterintuitive at first, but the verses that follow demonstrate where true contentment and joy is found—in Him!

The Bible contains many verses to provide wisdom and bring comfort in difficult times. There are also many verses about happiness to help guide you to a happy life.

You may have noticed that the Bible often uses the word joy instead of happiness. Finding happiness in the Bible isn't easy. And that's because the Bible isn't interested in making people happy. Instead, the Bible focuses on joy. These two words are often used interchangeably, but they aren't the same. The difference between joy and happiness is this: Joy is more consistent and is cultivated internally. It comes when you make peace with who you are, why you are and how you are, whereas happiness tends to be externally triggered and is based on other people, things, places, thoughts, and events.

In the modern world, joy is something we experience that is deeper and more meaningful. Happiness is something we feel because of our situation or circumstances. We are happy because something made us happy, but we are joyful because of something within us. The world tells us that we can only be happy if our situation is right. Many people that have everything they could ever want are not happy. And, on the other hand, many people have little in life but have a true joy that comes from deep within. When you study Bible verses about happiness, you will find how to experience true happiness.

Following are some of the verses in Bible about Joy and Happiness:

1 Romans 15:13 Now may the God of hope fill you with all joy and peace in believing, that you may abound in hope by the power of the Holy Spirit.

2 Hebrews 12:1-2 Therefore we also, since we are surrounded by so great a cloud of witnesses, let us lay aside every weight, and the sin which so easily ensnares us, and let us run with endurance the race that is set before us, looking unto Jesus, the author and finisher of our faith, who for the joy that was set before Him endured the cross, despising the shame, and has sat down at the right hand of the throne of God.

3 James 1:2-3 My brethren, count it all joy when you fall into various trials, knowing that the testing of your faith produces patience.

4 Isaiah 9:3 You have multiplied the nation and increased its joy; they rejoice before You according to the joy of harvest, as men rejoice when they divide the spoil.

5 Proverbs 10:28 The hope of the righteous will be gladness, but the expectation of the wicked will perish.

6 Ecclesiastes 9:7 Go, eat your bread with joy, and drink your wine with a merry heart; for God has already accepted your works.

7 Psalm 30:5 For His anger is but for a moment, His favour is for life; weeping may endure for a night, but joy comes in the morning.

8 John 16:24 Until now you have asked nothing in My name. Ask, and you will receive, that your joy may be full.

9 Psalm 34:8 Oh, taste and see that the Lord is good; blessed is the man who trusts in Him!

10. Proverbs 16:20 He who heeds the word wisely will find good, and whoever trusts in the LORD, happy is he.

11 Ecclesiastes 2:24 Nothing is better for a man than that he should eat and drink, and that his soul should enjoy good in his labour. This also, I saw, was from the hand of God.

12 Psalm 144:15 Happy are the people whose God is the LORD!

13 Psalm 16:11 You will show me the path of life; in Your presence is fullness of joy; at Your right hand are pleasures forevermore.

14 Proverbs 29:18 Where there is no revelation, the people cast off restraint; but happy is he who keeps the law.

15 Romans 5:1-2 Therefore, having been justified by faith, we have peace with God through our Lord Jesus Christ, through whom also we have access by faith into this grace in which we stand, and rejoice in hope of the glory of God.

16 Philippians 4:4 Rejoice in the Lord always. Again, I will say, rejoice!

17 Matthew 5:9 Blessed are the peacemakers, for they shall be called sons of God.

18 Matthew 5:4 Blessed are those who mourn, for they shall be comforted.

19 Matthew 25:21 His lord said to him, "Well done, good and faithful servant; you were faithful over a few things, I will make you ruler over many things. Enter into the joy of your lord."

20 Ecclesiastes 2:26 For God gives wisdom and knowledge and joy to a man who is good in His sight; but to the sinner He gives the work of gathering and collecting, that he may give to him who is good before God. This also is vanity and grasping for the wind.

21 Psalm 37:4 Delight yourself also in the Lord, and He shall give you the desires of your heart.

22 Psalms 126:5 Those who sow in tears shall reap in joy.

9.7 Happy are those who are Unhappy

The title of this message is a paradox, but so are all of the beatitudes.

Matthew 5:4 Blessed are those who mourn, For they shall be comforted.

"Blessed are those who mourn"

While this sounds more paradoxical or contradictory than others, actually it captures the spirit of all. It tells how to be happy when unhappy. It tells how to have deep joy when unhappy and things are bad enough to make you cry.

If we can only be happy when things around us make us happy, we don't have much. Our happiness is too easily taken away. The world says you can only be happy: if you have, if you get, if you join, and if you become.

Jesus says you can be happy without: having what they have, getting what they are selling, joining their group, and without becoming what they want you to be.

So that we may see Jesus' second prescription for how to have deep abiding happiness,

9.7.1 Who are Mourners?

Types of mourning – 15 words in the Bible mean to mourn.

1. Mourning over death – Abraham mourned when his wife died.
2. Mourning of discouragement – 2 Tim. 1:3-4

3. Mourning of disappointment – Jer. 9:1
4. Mourning of concern – Acts 20:31
5. Mourning of love – Mark 9:23
6. Mourning of devotion – Luke 7 (woman washes feet w/tears).

All of these in proper proportion are right and proper and some who have read this beatitude have concluded that it is just a statement of fact, "You feel better when you cry." Yes; sometimes; God designed the ability to cry to allow us to get feelings and emotions "washed out." But all of us who have mourned the loss of a loved one or mourned in discouragement or disappointment, or any other reason know that that kind of mourning does not necessarily result in marikos, the deep, pervading happiness that abides even when things are not going well!

9.7.2 The mourning Jesus describes in Matthew 5 is different – Penthos, Pentheo. Not used to describe outward display of grief though that sometimes accompanies it. But penthos itself describes the deep, inward, sorrow of the heart. Jesus is talking about spiritual mourning. Jesus is talking about mourning over what God mourns over. Jesus is talking about first and foremost mourning over our own sin. Jesus is describing a Godly sorrow over our sin that goes to the quick of the soul.

Such was the sin of David with Bathsheba and the murder of Uriah. Ps. 51:3-7 3

For I acknowledge my transgressions,
And my sin is always before me.
Against You, You only, have I sinned,
And done this evil in Your sight— ...
Behold, You desire truth in the inward parts, ...
Purge me with hyssop, and I shall be clean;
Wash me, and I shall be whiter than snow.

David fasted and prayed on ground before the Lord for seven days. Paul described this kind of sorrow in his letter to the Corinthians.14-09-07

For godly sorrow produces repentance leading to salvation, not to be regretted; but the sorrow of the world produces death. The kind of mourning Jesus is talking about is the Godly kind of sorrow for sin that turns life around. Mourning and repentance go hand in hand.

9.7.3 Mourning over sin is a necessary characteristic of those in the kingdom.

(i) You must mourn over sin to get in. "Unless you repent you shall all likewise perish." Jesus said, "Repent for the kingdom of heaven is at hand." It follows close on the heels of poverty of spirit. The poor in spirit sees his spiritual bankruptcy and own unworthiness. He sees his sin as God sees it and grieves and sorrows and mourns over his sin. No man comes into the kingdom with the attitude of "My sin is not so bad." "My sins aren't so terrible." If Jesus had to die for our sin, if it took the blood of the Son of God to wash our robes clean, then our sin is indeed ghastly.

(ii) But like poverty of spirit, mourning over personal sin is to be a continual attitude. 1 Jn. 1:5-10 5. This is the message which we have heard from Him and declare to you, that God is light and in Him is no darkness at all. If we say that we have fellowship with Him, and walk in darkness, we lie and do not practice the truth. But if we walk in the light as He is in the light, we have fellowship with one another, and the blood of Jesus Christ His Son cleanses us from all sin. If we say that we have no sin, we deceive ourselves, and the truth is not in us. If we confess our sins, He is faithful and just to forgive us our sins and to cleanse us from all unrighteousness. If we say that we have not sinned, we make Him a liar, and His word is not in us.

John testifies of five marks of kingdom citizenship.

a. Walk in light
b. Fellowship with Him
c. Fellowship with other believers
d. Confession of sins – If we continually confess
e. Forgiveness of sins – He continually forgives and cleanses.

This passage is often called the "Christians bar of soap."

Repentance and faith cleansed us in the blood. Continual repentance and confession keeps our lives cleansed.

(iii) There is a need for mourning in the church today. The Bible is not against happiness – "A merry heart does good like a medicine." Jesus is not against happiness – "Happy are" Too frequently we trade "marikos" – "abiding joy" for light-hearted frivolity.

James 4:8-10 8 "Draw near to God and He will draw near to you. Cleanse your hands, you sinners; and purify your hearts, you double-minded. Lament and mourn and weep! Let your laughter be turned to mourning and your joy to gloom. Humble yourselves in the sight of the Lord, and He will lift you up. Jesus is saying that if we want lives full of real joy and true happiness, we need to pour out some of the trivial joviality and take some time to picture our sin and failures and shortcomings and compare them to the glory and perfection and sacrifice of God so we can mourn a little bit for "Blessed are those who mourn." Blessed are those who mourn, for they shall be comforted."

CHAPTER TEN

HAPPINESS WITHIN

10.1 Story of Musk Deer and Happiness Within

As we have described in the beginning of this book that, whereas the pleasure is externally triggered and transient, the happiness is internally generated and constant. Happiness is not necessarily dependent on any external or internal pleasurable stimuli.

The greatest blessings of mankind are within us and within our reach. A wise man is content with his lot, whatever it may be, without wishing for what he has not.

Let me quote a story from Kenopanisad.

Usually found in the Himalayan regions, the deer has the musk gland underneath its skin. In the breeding season, this musk gland exudes a substance with a lovely perfume to attract the female deer. While roaming the forest, a Kasturi Mriga came across an aromatic strong musk smell. The smell intrigued the deer's most profound thoughts, and it went in search of that smell. So keen was the deer's longing for the scent that in spite of the severe cold winter it roamed about in a desperate search. It knew no fear and no rest for years and years until one day it fell from a cliff with a fatal injury. While breathing its last, the deer suddenly realized that the scent which ravished its heart, making it roam aimlessly all through life came from its own navel. Thus, the last few moments of the deer's life were moments of regrets for having chased after something, all life-long that was ultimately within itself.

Similarly, many times, we human beings too, behave like the musk deer. We search for Self-realisation(Atman/Brahman) outside, blissfully unaware that it lies within us, untapped. Kenopanisad is a quest/search for someone , who directs all our faculties from within.

We have all heard about Kabir Das–weaver, singer and saint–who lived in Benaras. In one of his evocative songs, reflecting on the same story of musk deer, he illustrates humankind's pursuit of happiness. Saint Kabir Das says the following:

Kastooree Kundalee Basai, Mrg Dhoondhai Ban Maahi.
Aise Ghatee Ghatee Raam Hain Duniya Dekhai Naanhi.

Meaning: The deer is searching for the fragrant musk in the jungles, whereas it exists within the deer itself. Similarly (Lord) Rama exists in every nook and corner, and we search for Him at all the places in the world.

This is the most perfect example for our search for happiness. We search all over the world, forgetting that happiness is resident within us and, only when it is found within us, that we derive the complete satisfaction.

Come to think of it, we are all like the musk deer. At a physical level, we search for love and happiness through family, marriage, in-laws, children and friends. In the process, we select our own poisons and seal our own fate. At a higher metaphysical level, we search for peace, self-knowledge, inner-reality and God-realisation through various books, lectures, seminars and rituals, becoming more confused than ever. All the love, happiness, peace, self-knowledge, inner-reality and God-realisation are within us if only we have the time and inclination to look for them.

We have forgotten to look 'inwards' for the illumination we crave. We are dismally ignorant and 'lost'. We run here and there but we arrive nowhere. Consider the rush-rush, go-go, hustle and bustle of modern life where God is not so much denied as merely crowded out.

There is a beautiful word in Sanskrit for completeness-***Poorna***. It means fulfilment, fullness, or completeness. The Upanishads say Poorna is the essential characteristic of one's fundamental being, the Atman-which is one's own pure consciousness that is free of all distractions.

When this Atman or the real Self is found, one reaches the state of perfect happiness. Along with this, one also realises that this state exists within every living being, although untapped. This centre and core of our consciousness is not exclusive to anybody. Everyone possesses it; it is only that they do not know it yet. The process of finding it is called Sādhana..

If there is something, there must be a way to find it. It's futile to say that there is no way to something, because if there is no way, it doesn't matter if it exists or it doesn't exist. Makes no sense. The Rishis of yore have thankfully, fortunately for us, discovered that there is a way to find this inner happiness and it can be taught and shared with other human beings.

A divine Bard once sang: "O you foolish musk deer, you sought for the fragrance everywhere but in your own body. That is why you did not find it. If you only had touched your nostrils to your own navel, you would have found the cherished musk and would have saved yourself from suicide on the rocks below."

In our everyday lives, our mundane routines, we feel lost, sad, and a plethora of emotions. We don't want to open the pandora's box, do we? Our mind wanders to areas we know we didn't cater to, and to situations we have no control over. In the end, what we sow is what we reap. We are looking for happiness outside, in other people, in those meetings, in our tiresome work, and in those material objects we don't need but end up buying anyway. And it still doesn't feel right, that sinking feeling doesn't change. It was supposed to, but it doesn't. Why not? Because you are looking at the wrong place, just like the Kasturi Mriga, you are looking everywhere, but it is actually within where you need to introspect. What we want is within us. Real happiness can only be found within and no external, outwardly situation can ever change this fact, as well as our profound happiness.

10.2 Lessons learnt from Upanishads and Vedas

The ancient Hindu scriptures–the Upanishads and the Vedas–suggest that there is indeed a way to find lasting happiness within oneself, independently of all external things. The great sages who have experienced this joy and happiness have gone on record to say-'That' happiness is an ecstasy, which is so beautiful and all-embracing that one feels like sharing it with the entire humanity.

Once, having experienced this happiness, life becomes joyful. Then, every little thing is full of joy. The dew drop in the morning, the breeze that gently blows replete with the scent of jasmines, the fragrance of the earth after the first rain, the snow-clad peak of a distant mountain, the laughter of a child, the song of the peasant. All of this, though previously unnoticed, begins to impart a superior joy.

Everything becomes a festival of joy and the root of this lies within oneself. It is when the inner being becomes happy, that the world becomes full of joy for us.

There are in us two distinct personalities: the God and the Man. While, in its very nature Godhead is unlimited and immortal, the Manhood has the experiences of limitations and death, as its birth right. Our attachment to the false negativities in us (the manhood) is the cause of all sufferings. Detach yourself from the manhood, you regain Godhead. Godhood in us being clouded, there is an imminent need to remove the shackles of manhood and understand our Atman. The Kena Upanishad makes us to realise the Truth to attain the Godhood through inquisitive dialogue among the student and the Guru to understand the Bahaman (Atman) to lead us to the path of Brahma Vidya. It forms the ninth chapter of the Talavakara Branch in the Sama Veda. The entire Upanishad is in a conversational style.

Like the Isdvdsya, this Upanishad derives its name from the opening word of the text, Kena-ishitam, "by whom directed." It is also known as the Talavakdra-Upanishad because of its place as a chapter in the Talavakdra-BrIllsmana of the Veda.

Among the Upanishads it is one of the most analytical and metaphysical, its purpose being to lead the mind from the gross to the subtle, from eject to cause. By a series of profound questions and answers, it seeks to locate the source of man's being; and to expand his self-consciousness UMW it has become identical with God-Consciousness.

Kenopnisad (3.5) says:

yanmanasā na manute yenāhurmano matam |
tadeva brahma tvaṃ viddhi nedaṃ yadidamupāsate (3.5)

Meaning: What mind does not comprehend, but what comprehends the mind— know thou That alone as Brahman, and not this that people worship here.

What is the stuff of the mind? The mind has been explained in our Sastras in different ways. According to one definition, the mind is nothing but a bundle of Vasanas (impressions). The mind is the unceasing flow of our thoughts. Subtler than the physical body are thoughts, and the flow of thoughts (the mind), is illumined for us by the intellect. Atma-Prabhava is transmitted to the mind and in that glory it functions. It is this light that illumines the mind and gives it a semblance of Reality. The existence of a state of worry, **anxiety or happiness** in our mind is understood by us under the illumination of the intelligence of the intellect. That we are living so near the Centre of truth, is not obvious to us.. For, in the secret chambers of the very obvious, resides the Lord. The Atman (Caitanya) within illumines the mind and gives out a semblance of light.

10.3 Choosing to make yourself Happy without blaming others

It is said:

"Blaming is so much easier than taking responsibility, because if you take responsibility ... then you might be to blame yourself."

Take a minute and think about people that surround you either physically or virtually. These people are clearly a reflection of the choices they have made in their life so far. They are in their current situation because of all of the choices they have made in their lifetime, and those choices have helped to contribute to where they are at today. Some of the choices they have made have most likely been good, and some of them no doubt have been bad, but they all had "choices." You are also a reflection of the accumulation of choices that you have made throughout your lifetime. The wonderful and most amazing thing about this is that you do indeed have choices. In fact, you have many choices, every, single, day. The downside is you must also take responsibility for the choices you make. The ones you have made up until this point, and the ones you continue to make, every, single, day.

Everyone has issues they need to work through, and even overcome; no one is immune to problems. It doesn't matter who you are, where you work, or if you work, it is something we all have in common as human beings. How we choose to deal with these issues, however, is what sets people apart; that is the difference.

"It's not about if you have chaos in your life, it's about how well you manage it."

When people are unhappy, they blame many other things. They blame the economy, the government, their health, their spouse or significant other, their parents, their childhood, you name it ... there is definitely something beyond their control causing their unhappiness, because they would not be in their current situation by choice! That would be ridiculous! Or would they?

There are some very successful people in the world who will settle for nothing short of success! So they work and they plan, they fail and they overcome, but they will succeed. There are also some people who never seem to be able to get it together. They self-sabotage, they are broke, they are unhappy, and they never (they believe) ever seem to be able to catch a break. They will continue to make choices over and over that will match who they believe they are, because your choices are very much a reflection of your personality.

"When working with the Universal Laws you are working with the laws of manifestation, not instant gratification ..."

People have become very spoiled. In many instances, that adults many times behave like spoiled children! As the world has become more materialistic, so have humans. Materialism has begun to overwhelm the physical senses. Materialism is a big contributing factor to people placing contingency clauses on their happiness, and the funny thing is, they do not even know they are doing it unless it is brought to their attention. However, from this day forward, understand since this has now been brought to your attention, you may no longer use this as an excuse! I hate to break the news to you, but as humans, we are a fickle people. As fickle people here is the problem: when one thing on your "I will be happy when list" gets crossed off, another item will promptly take its place, then another, then another, and so on. If you are thinking, "I don't do this!" not so fast. The tricky part here is, most of the people who do this (and it is a lot of people), do not notice that they are doing it. Because it is another "accepted" way of thinking by society today, so it has made this thought process very easily disguisable.

10.4 How to Find Happiness Within?

"Very little is needed to make a happy life; it is all within yourself, in your way of thinking."

~Marcus Aurelius Antoninus

It's worth taking a moment to consider where happiness comes from. Is it from things like having someone love you, or eating a fantastic meal, or having a great body, or relaxing on the beach, or drinking a good cup of coffee?

No, actually. Those things all are phenomena that happen outside of us ... and they don't cause the happiness. They might be correlated with happiness — they happen, and then we are happy at the same time — but it's not a cause-and-effect relationship. There's another event that's happening at the same time.

That event is what happens in our brain between the external event (a good cup of coffee) and our state of happiness.

What is this event? It's a process. Let's take a close look:

- We drink a cup of good coffee (or read a good book, eat some delicious berries, have good sex, etc.).
- We notice the coffee, pay attention to it. If we don't pay attention, and are reading on the Internet as we drink the coffee, we don't get the happiness from the coffee.
- We appreciate the goodness in the coffee that we noticed. It's not just the noticing and paying attention — we have to accept it for what it is, and appreciate the good things about it.
- This goodness we've noticed causes us to be happy about life. We are now happy about the experience of living, about life itself, because this experience is filled with goodness — even if it's just the goodness of a cup of coffee.
- So that's it: noticing and appreciating the goodness in a cup of coffee causes us to be happy about living. And the more we notice and appreciate about our lives (and ourselves), the happier we are.
- 'We tend to forget that happiness doesn't come as a result of getting something we don't have, but rather of recognizing and appreciating what we do have.' ~Frederick Keonig

Finding Happiness Within

So does this mean that happiness is really about external things, like the cup of coffee or the sex or the love from someone else? No ... it's about the process that happens within. And this process can happen no matter what's going on outside of us. It can happen even if there are no external stimuli — because there are things inside of us that we can appreciate as well.

Let us emphasize that: all the raw material we need for happiness is inside of us. The good things we can appreciate to be happy — they are always with us, already there. And the tools for turning these raw materials into happiness ... they are within us as well. We just need to develop them.

What are the things within us that we can appreciate, that can make us happy?

Some examples:

- Are you generous?
- Do you love? Can you give love?
- Do you feel compassion?
- Are you good at something?
- Are you a good listener?
- Do you empathize with the pain of others?
- Do you appreciate beauty in nature, in others?
- Do you have good ideas?
- Are you determined?
- Are you good at sports?
- Are you creative?

And so on.

These (and more) are all internal qualities you might have that you can appreciate, that can make you happy about yourself.

So the happiness process — noticing, appreciating, being happy about living — can be applied to things within us, no matter what's going on outside. We can learn to notice and appreciate the good things (and the less-than-perfect things as well!) in ourselves, and start to love ourselves.

Appreciating all that's around us

That's just the start, though. What's within us is amazing, but so is what's in everyone else, and life all around us. These might be external things, but the appreciation for them (and the happiness that results) comes from within.

So the key skill is to learn to notice, accept and appreciate everything around us, and everyone we see and interact with.

Look closely at the food you eat, and the coffee, water, tea, or wine you drink ... what can you notice? Is there good to be noticed that you can appreciate, that can make you happy to be alive?

What about the room around you? What about the book you're reading, or the blog post? What about the nature outside? Are these things there that you can notice and appreciate?

Often if we fail to see good in things or people around us (or ourselves), it's a failure to pay close attention. If the person near you seems rude or uninteresting, you're not paying close enough attention to the details: are they also funny, or talented, or shy but with hidden secrets? Are they in pain, and in need of compassion? Look closer, and see what you can find.

Once you begin to pay attention, and to look, you'll find some amazing things. All around us are examples of beauty, creativity, inspiration, triumph, pain, joy, life.

And once you get good at this, you can start to appreciate the "not-so-perfect" things as well. We judge other people's flaws, and our own flaws, as "bad" ... but what if they're just a part of being human? Then aren't the "flaws" a celebration of who we are as humans? Aren't anger and rudeness and mistakes a part of our beauty as human beings?

Appreciate the "flaws" in your children, for example, as beautiful, as part of the signature of who they are. They are different, and those differences are part of what makes each of them wonderful in their own way. If we didn't have these "flaws", we wouldn't be as wonderful.

And this is true, of course, of ourselves. We all have flaws, and we should celebrate them. Notice them, yes, but appreciate them, and use them as reasons to be happy to be alive.

Once we can do this, we can see the wonder in every little thing around us, and inside us. And then we realize that life is a true joy, in every moment, if we simply pay attention and appreciate.

10.5 Ways to Happiness Within

(i) Eat Healthy

The first steps one should take in making internal improvements is acknowledging your food choices. I know you've heard the cliche 'You are what you eat.'

Fresh fruits and vegetables will provide you with necessary vitamins and minerals to energize your body throughout the day, providing your various body systems with oxygen and energy that can greatly impact your overall mood and sense of well-being. Junk food will deplete your energy, and leave you feeling sluggish for the bulk of the day.

So often when we're busy we forget to eat, and will then grab the quickest snack available without thinking of the impending effects of unhealthy eating. Snacking on a bowl of grapes, or some refreshing watermelon can bring an amazing boost to your morale and energy level. And don't forget...along with all this healthy eating, keeping hydrated is also very important.

(ii) Exercise

Along with healthy eating comes exercise. It needn't be strenuous; this isn't about improving one's bicep ratio! A simple increase in heart rate will increase your endorphins giving you a natural feeling of happiness, and it's the endorphins that give many avid exercise enthusiasts their momentum for endurance. Physical exercise and the increase in those endorphins can naturally increase mood positivity. Just 20 to 30 minutes each day should keep your spirits right at par with your endorphin level!

(iii) Treat Yourself Well

So now that the technical stuff is out of the way, i.e., healthy eating and exercise...it's time to work on the internal stuff. During a very difficult time to wrap yourself in a comfortable blanket, make a hot tea, or hot chocolate, and keep that blanket wrapped around you and treat yourself as you would treat someone else who seems to be under the weather. Maybe when you were young, someone would make you homemade / or store bought Chicken. Well, this is similar, the comfort of the soup or hot tea and blanket provides warmth and will put your body into a relaxing mode, and therefore release certain chemicals in your brain that will give you that comfort that you once believed could only be received from a significant other. We've all heard of the book 'Chicken Soup for the Soul'.. Well this collection of 'good-feeling' books is similar in nature to sitting back and treating yourself well.

(iv) Take a Break from Social Media

As you're relaxing, you may think to yourself that it is the perfect time to check in on social media, but you might want to try and resist, and depending on your cohort, this may prove to be more difficult for some than for others! Remember, this time is about yourself and really not about your friends. It's time you dedicated solely for yourself!

When you're not at your happiest moment, seeing other's perfectly portrayed lives on social media is enough to bring even the happiest person into a non-showering, non-hair brushing, stay in bed all day slump. If you are feeling depressed or down.. avoid, avoid, avoid, social media and watch a comedy or an intriguing drama instead!

(v) Set that Movie Date Night for Yourself

A dedicated night to just yourself and a really good movie can do wonders to your morale. Prepare some healthy snacks, and settle in for the night with one of your all-time favourite 'turn-to' movies when feeling down, or a movie you've been just dying to see and never did

With the digital age the way it is now, thousands of movies are right at your fingertips, and these movies can sometimes give you a greatly needed boost that can actually carry onto the next day. Movies can be incredibly therapeutic and motivational, depending on genre.

(vi) Go out and explore

This is tip probably has always worked for many during times when they are feeling down. Select a few places that you like to walk to, and these walks lead me to places that are serene, peaceful and just down right relaxing. If you have a waterfront, seawall, beach, or just a favourite park, I recommend bringing a well-loved book or magazine and just submit to the inner peace and happiness that is lurking from deep inside. Don't allow negative thoughts or external problems to enter into your mind.

Breathe in the fresh air, appreciate the beauty that surrounds you, be it nature, trees, the sea, or an urban paradise, and treat yourself like you are dating yourself. Enjoy this time, and enjoy the fact that this is YOUR life, and you are in charge of allowing yourself to be happy. And if you don't have a time issue, then take your time there, pretend that you are taking a child or a pet to the park, you would do it for them right? Then take this time and do it for yourself. This is one of the most sure-fire ways of finding happiness.

(vii) Take Pictures of Beautiful Things

So you're taking in the beauty around you, and taking advantage of all this free enjoyment, so why don't you pull out the phone, or camera and snap a few photos? You never know.... you could find joy or even a hidden talent that you never knew you had!

Maybe you like the rainfall, or puddles, flowers, landscape, or focus on your creative side and take some unique photos of whatever you fancy from various angles, and see what you come up with. Creativity is in all of us, but sometimes we just need a little nudge to remind us to go find it. If drawing is more your thing...then draw and draw some more... really let your creativity just take over.

(viii) Write it all out

Speaking of creativity, have you ever thought of keeping a personal journal, or even a not-so personal journal, say your own blog perhaps? Writing can be cathartic, it can be a vessel to release pent up emotions, or frustration. If you write out all that is bothering you, it keeps your mind more organized and transfers your negative thoughts onto that paper, providing you the freedom to focus on positivity.

While you're at it, if you have problems that need solutions, this is also a good time to brainstorm and throw ideas onto that paper that can offer a solution.

(ix) Declutter and Purge

Lastly, if you've made it this far, then you are ready to make some serious progress. And this progress starts with completely decluttering and cleaning your home, donating or recycling anything that you don't need. A clean and clutter free home is a clean and clutter free mind.

But can you imagine how simultaneously relaxing and revitalizing a clean home can be? Pump up on those fruits, drink some water, juice or splurge on a beverage of your choice...turn on the tunes and get cleaning! You will feel better once you start, and even better once you've finished!

CHAPTER ELEVEN

HAPPINESS IS A CHOICE

11.1 Choosing to be Happy by Reacting to a Difficult Situation

According to a survey, 40% of our happiness that is determined by our own outlook, or our own choices. Happiness is a choice in a lot of scenarios.

Imagine this:

You are in a hurry after a long day at work. You need to get back home as soon as possible because you need to do groceries, cook dinner, attend to children etc.

But traffic is extremely busy, so you end up stuck in front of a red light.

You are irritated, right?!

I'm sure you've all experienced a situation like this before, but this is a very clear example of how happiness can be a choice. Let me explain.

There are a couple of things you can do here:

You can be mad at this traffic light and be pissed off. This traffic light is ruining your plans!

You can accept the fact that this traffic light is the way it is and decide to not let it influence your happiness.

Traffic is one of the best examples, as it is just so relatable. Who hasn't been frustrated at the traffic before? Road rage is real, and it's something that a lot of people have to deal with every single day. The busy traffic is a perfect example of impacting our happiness due to external factor.

We cannot control the traffic. But we can control how we react to it. And that's why it's a perfect example of how happiness can be a choice. We get to choose how we react to events, and by choosing a happy outlook, we can vastly improve our happiness when dealing with these situations.

So instead of becoming frustrated by this busy traffic, why don't you try to focus on things that actually make you happy?

Here are some of the options to be happy under this situation:

- Put on some good music and just sing along.
- Give your family or friends a call and talk about your plans for the evening.
- Send a nice message to someone you love.
- Just close your eyes and take a deep breath. Allow your mind to rest easy, instead of being focused on the busy traffic around you.

We're always making choices and doing things to be happy - choosing what to eat, what clothes to wear, who to love, where to work. Some of our choices are good and others not but they're all based on our deep and impelling desire to be happy.

Certainly genetics, your personality and nature, plays an important part in your happiness.

Then life circumstances also affect your happiness such as upbringing, health and finances.

Your personal happiness has everything to do with the conscious choices and the sincere amount of work you put into living a good life; to flourish, thrive and to be joyful even while you may be living in painful and seemingly hopeless circumstances.

Gandhi perfectly describes the solid feeling of happiness:

"Happiness is when what you think, what you say and what you do are in harmony."

- If you're in an unhappy relationship you can choose to change it and that could mean getting out.

- If you hate your job you can make a choice to change it.

- If you want to be healthier that's another choice for personal happiness.

Happiness is up to you. Your choice. Your way.

Here's how to regain and build happiness

a. Think about a time in your life when you were really happy.

b. Why were you so happy? State the facts. Write them all down.

c. What were you doing that made for such confidence, personal excitement, peace and pleasure?

Be very specific about this time in your life because once you target that time and the exact reason or reasons why you were happy you can then recreate it... and be in harmony with what you thought... and said... and did.

When you know the facts of what makes you happy you can choose to do the same things you love, choose to use your gifts and talents to be fully expressed and entirely yourself. Isn't that what happiness is about?

Happiness does take work. It takes steady practice. It's not just easy. Happiness is not something you can turn on in the midst of heart ache, profound worry or fear but at least you have the knowledge, the facts and the life experience to know what makes you happy and then you can create it, work at it and have it in your life always. I'm not saying ignore the real problems we all face in life but, think about what works well for you -- know what satisfies you -- do what gives you ultimate pleasure and practice it.

We all want to be happy. Why not make happiness a daily ritual? Choose happiness. Live it!

Remember - "Happiness is when what you think, what you say and what you do are in harmony."

11.2 Restate "Helplessness" Language into "Choice" Language

Our speech habits often reveal important underlying beliefs affecting our happiness. Our speech habits not only reveal deep, inner aspects of us, but they also change important beliefs. We may use excuses that we are too stressed, too tired, or too busy to do something, when we actually just do not want to do it. The subtle, hidden message in that excuse is that "I cannot get control of my emotions--I am too weak or helpless."

These hidden messages have two major effects. First, they will affect others' beliefs about us. Others may believe that we are weak and helpless and treat us that way. Second--and even more importantly--we may believe the hidden messages ourselves. We may become more convinced that we actually are weak and helpless--thereby undermining our self-esteem.

In addition, a belief that our emotions are out of control contributes to anxiety and depression. We can stop undermining our self-esteem and self-confidence by monitoring our language. We can stop using "helplessness" language and start using "choice" language. Choice language is based on underlying beliefs such as the following:

- "I can make choices that determine how I feel."
- "We are responsible for our own emotions."
- "I can be honest with myself and others I trust."

Sometimes we may think that a situation is hopeless. We may believe that we are in a situation for which no routes to happiness exist. Many people who feel little hope and believe that there is no way out. The problem is not that a route to happiness doesn't exist; the problem is how they view the situation.

An important underlying cause of hopelessness, powerlessness, and depression is a belief that we cannot find any possible route to happiness. Do you ever think that you have no choice except a path that will make you unhappy? The next time you feel trapped, unhappy, or depressed, ask yourself, "Am I assuming that I can't find one route to happiness in this situation?" "Am I assuming that I have no choice but to be unhappy in this situation?"

Challenge that "no choice" belief. Tell yourself that no matter what the situation is, you have many routes to happiness! Perhaps you have not yet found those routes. However, someone in this world has learned how to create happiness in a similar—or even worse--situation.

Once you believe that you can achieve happiness in that situation, that belief will give you hope. Hope will allow you to start looking for new, creative routes to happiness that you may have previously overlooked.

Seek happiness and you will find it. This is a positive self-fulfilling prophesy. It is amazing how many people have never valued their own happiness highly and have never learned how to play, have fun, or create happiness.

Seeking happiness is partly choosing to find interesting things to do, but it is mostly a mental skill--learning how to make every activity as interesting and fun as it can be. The more we begin to look for creative ways of generating interest and enjoying ourselves in difficult or unpleasant situations, the more skilled we become. There have been people who learnt how to be happy in many "impossible" situations.

Internal routes to happiness can include almost any mental activity--from appreciating a tree or enjoying music to contemplating life. We can learn new beliefs, skills, or habits which can dramatically affect our personal power and happiness. We have seen how making happiness a conscious top goal is important. Awareness that each choice we make affects our happiness is also important.

We have less control over our environment and people in our lives than over our own thoughts, actions, and emotions. Of these, the most important is our thoughts--for they have most control over our emotions and actions.

Replace all of the phrases like "should have" or "must have" with the phrase "I want." Assert that you want something based upon your choice of your ultimate concern for happiness for yourself and others.

That assertion is sufficient reason for wanting it. You do not need to justify it from any other moral code or set of "shoulds." Nor is there any moral code or set of "shoulds" that indicates you "deserve" to have it. Everything you receive in life is ultimately a gift. You would have nothing without the gift of life, the gift of your environment, and the gift of your abilities. Once you view the situation this way, everything good in life becomes a bonus: a gift you did not get because you deserved it, but a gift that you are grateful for.

To get control over inner subparts that say we are bad, we can choose to listen and to do what our healthier parts say. We can validate Higher Self empathy and love. Just keep choosing the alternative that will make you the happiest and contribute most to other people's happiness. Choosing it increases its power. Choosing the way of the negative part increases its power. Almost every choice you make empowers one or the other!

Choosing internal control often means getting far away from family or other people who have dysfunctional needs to "hold on to" and control their adult children or loved ones. It means being assertive about both how often you see them and the nature of your interactions when you are together. Structuring time together so that there is minimal opportunity for the negative interactions can help. Examples include small talk, TV, going to public places, and keeping busy.

Focus on your own choices. Take responsibility for making yourself happy for each of these situations. Be creative in finding new ways of making yourself as happy as possible with each situation. For example, spending time with a needy or demanding parent is a choice no matter how strongly you believe that you must do it (or owe it to them). It is not a must over which you have no choice.

11.3 How can you Choose Happiness?

Deep inside, we all want happiness, but how can we obtain it? Are we happy just because we're lucky enough to have the right genes or the right circumstances? What if we aren't so lucky? What if we face difficult circumstances such as rejection, failure, illness, or poverty? Can we rise above those difficulties and choose to be happy?

Once we consciously choose to make one value our top value (ultimate concern), then it becomes the ultimate test of any internal conflict. For example, if I have a conflict between spending an hour working or an hour playing, I ask myself, "Which will contribute most to my overall happiness (and the happiness of others)?" With experience, I have learned how to calculate my expected happiness quickly.

Some people believe that they cannot choose to be happy. They think that biological or environmental factors are so powerful, they cannot influence their own emotions. That belief alone can become a self-fulfilling prophesy—helping doom them to unhappiness. Our evidence strongly contradicts their belief.

No one can be happy all the time. However, we can all choose to maximize our happiness—given our unique biological and environmental situations. Thus, we can all choose to be happy and then try our best to maximize our happiness. You may truly not know how to influence your own happiness right now. However, you can learn how to maximize your happiness—as many others have. This learning strengthens your cognitive system and gives it more control over your emotions.

Even though we can choose to be happy in any situation, it is not always easy to be happy. We need the right beliefs and tools for finding happiness. No one tool will work for all situations--we need many.

Choosing to be happy is not as easy as just saying to ourselves, "Be happy" that will magically happen. However, we can choose to be happy by choosing internal and external routes that will increase our probability of being happy. We can learn from others who have been successful leading happy and productive lives, and we can learn from our own experiences.

To be happy it is necessary to accept and forgive mistakes--my own and the mistakes of others. Otherwise, we choose guilt and resentment over love and happiness. The only way to produce no waste is to think or do nothing.

Every day there are thousands of negative events occurring all over the world--people are abused, mistreated, sick, and dying. If we choose, we could focus on these events and feel miserable every minute of our life. Many of us live our lives focusing on those negative events or others closer to home. Focusing too much on these negatives creates a negative inner experience. It can lead to recurring unhappiness and depression.

If we really care about others, how else can we react? One alternative is to ignore these events. However, we cannot completely screen out all of the negative news of the world. To do so would cause us to be become hermits and turn away from responsible involvement in the world.

Entitlement to Happiness of Self: I want to be happy myself and want others to be happy not because we deserve it, but because I want it and I love myself unconditionally. It is because I have chosen to make happiness of self and others my ultimate concern (or top goal). I choose it and I assert it; I don't need to justify it or rationalize it as something I am entitled to.

The self-acceptance process is a method for accepting the parts of yourself that you may feel bad about. Think of some part or aspect of yourself that you don't like--especially some aspect that you can't change immediately. Use the following process to increase your self-acceptance of that part. Even if you do choose to change that part, gaining acceptance of it as it is now is an important first step to change.

If they are negative or controlling persons, they have us by the throat, because they can control us by giving or withholding approval. Therefore, to be internally controlled, we must consistently choose to value our own happiness and other mental or spiritual values above money, above other people's opinions, above being loved, above respect, and above any other value that is external or in the control of other people. No matter what someone does to you, you have a wide range of responses to choose from. You do not have to be aggressive or nonassertive.

We can also develop strategies to generate stimulation and interest when the input is too slow, simple, or boring. These strategies often depend upon our adding internally generated input to the situation. We can create our own thoughts or activities, which fill the gaps left by the under-stimulating activities or inputs. Choose how you feel by using one of these strategies.

11.4 Actions to Choose Happiness

"Most people are about as happy as they make up their minds to be."

-Abraham Lincoln

"Happiness is the meaning and the purpose of life, the whole aim . . . of human existence."

-Aristotle

"Success is not the key to happiness. Happiness is the key to success."

-Albert Schweitzer

One of the greatest achievements we can attain in life is leaving this world a better place than we found it. So, how can we make that a real accomplishment, and not just a hopc? For one, we may need to re-think some of our attitudes about the sources of happiness. Taking a fresh look at what we believe, can open up a world of possibilities. Ultimately, happiness boils down to small course corrections made daily. They will help us to become happier people.

There are many people who are knowledgeable and highly educated, yet who are quite unhappy in their lives. They know intellectually the steps to happiness, but knowledge without application is really just education. We can learn all the things that contribute to true, lasting happiness, like gratitude, forgiveness, love, and being of service, but if we don't apply them in our life on a daily basis, not much will change.

The good news is, we have quite a bit of control over whether we are happy or not. Although much of our natural disposition for happiness is based upon our genetic makeup, and therefore varies from person to person, it is merely an inherited tendency, not our destiny. Our destiny is, and always will be, what we work toward, what we accomplish in our lives.

Happy people are not held hostage by their circumstances and they do not seek happiness in people or possessions.

They understand that when we stop chasing the world's definition of happiness, we begin to see the decision to experience happiness has been right in front of us all along. Research in the field of positive psychology continues to reinforce this understanding.

But simply knowing that happiness is a choice is not enough. Fully experiencing it still requires a conscious decision to choose happiness each day. How then might each of us begin to experience this joy?

How to Choose Happiness Today?

Embrace one new action item, practice all of them, or simply use them as inspiration to discover your own.

Here are **12 ways to choose happiness** today:

(i) Count your blessings. Happy people choose to focus on the positive aspects of life rather than the negative. They set their minds on specific reasons to be grateful. They express it when possible. And they quickly discover there is always, always, something to be grateful for.

(ii) Carry a smile. A smile is a wonderful beautifier. But more than that, studies indicate that making an emotion-filled face carries influence over the feelings processed by the brain. Our facial expression can influence our brain in just the same way our brains influence our face. In other words, you can actually program yourself to experience happiness by choosing to smile. Not to mention, all the pretty smiles you'll receive in return for flashing yours is also guaranteed to increase your happiness level.

(iii) Speak daily affirmation into your life. Affirmations are positive thoughts accompanied with affirmative beliefs and personal statements of truth. They are recited in the first person, present tense ("I am..."). Affirmations used daily can release stress, build confidence, and improve outlook. For maximum effectiveness, affirmations should be chosen carefully, be based in truth, and address current needs.

(iv) Wake up on your terms. Most of us have alarm clocks programmed because of the expectations of others: a workplace, a school, or a waking child. That's probably not going to change. But that doesn't mean we have to lose control over our mornings in the process. Wake up just a little bit early and establish an empowering, meaningful, morning routine. Start each day on your terms. The next 23 hours will thank you for it.

(v) Hold back a complaint. The next time you want to lash out in verbal complaint towards a person, a situation, or yourself, don't. Instead, humbly keep it to yourself. You'll likely diffuse an unhealthy, unhappy environment. But more than that, you'll experience joy by choosing peace in a difficult situation.

(vi) Practice one life-improving discipline. There is happiness and fulfillment to be found in personal growth. To know that you have intentionally devoted time and energy to personal improvement is one of the most satisfying feelings you'll ever experience. Embrace and practice at least one act of self-discipline each day. This could be exercise, budgeting, or guided-learning... whatever your life needs today to continue growing. Find it. Practice it. Celebrate it.

(vii) Use your strengths. Each of us have natural talents, strengths, and abilities. And when we use them effectively, we feel alive and comfortable in our skin. They help us find joy in our being and happiness in our design. So embrace your strengths and choose to operate within your giftedness each day. If you need to find this outlet outside your employment, by all means, find this outlet.

(viii) Accomplish one important task. Because happy people choose happiness, they take control over their lives. They don't make decisions based on a need to pursue joy. Instead, they operate out of the satisfaction they have already chosen. They realize there are demands on their time, helpful pursuits to accomplish, and important contributions to make to the world around them. Choose one important task that you can accomplish each day. And find joy in your contribution.

(ix) Eat a healthy meal/snack. We are spiritual, emotional, and mental beings. We are also physical bodies. Our lives cannot be wholly separated into its parts. As a result, one aspect always influences the others. For example, our physical bodies will always have impact over our spiritual and emotional well-being. Therefore, caring for our physical well-being can have significant benefit for our emotional standing. One simple action to choose happiness today is to eat healthy foods. Your physical body will thank you... and so will your emotional well-being.

(x) Treat others well. Everyone wants to be treated kindly. But more than that, deep down, we also want to treat others with the same respect that we would like given to us. Treat everyone you meet with kindness, patience, and grace. The Golden Rule is a powerful standard. It benefits the receiver. But also brings growing satisfaction in yourself as you seek to treat others as you would like to be treated.

(xi) Meditate. Find time alone in solitude. As our world increases in speed and noise, the ability to withdraw becomes even more essential. Studies confirm the importance and life-giving benefits of meditation. So take time to make time. And use meditation to search inward, connect spiritually, and improve your happiness today.

(xii) Search for benefit in your pain. This life can be difficult. Nobody escapes without pain. At some point—in some way—we all encounter it. When you do, remind yourself again that the trials may be difficult, but they will pass. And search deep to find meaning in the pain. Choose to look for the benefits that can be found in your trial. At the very least, perseverance is being built. And most likely, an ability to comfort others in their pain is also being developed.

CHAPTER TWELVE

HAPPINESS IN FAMILY

12.1 Basis of Happiness in Family

The 20th of March is International Day of Happiness, which has been declared and celebrated by the United Nations since 2012. It's the day that recognizes that happiness is a fundamental human goal. This is a day we can really get behind! A mountain of research shows that being happy is not just a natural human desire – it is actually really good for us. Happiness makes our hearts healthier, improves our immune system, combats stress, lowers pain, is associated with improvements in long-term illness and even increases longevity, meaning that happy people live longer.

What is a Family?

All living objects – especially humans and animals are surrounded by relations. The bonding between these close groups is some time known as Family. A family is a social group characterized normally by common residence, economics, co-operation and reproduction. A joint family can also be known as a complex family, parents and their children's families often live under a single roof. This type of family often includes multiple generations in the family.

From mutual support and solidarity to a sense of belonging, there are many ways 'family' – including our own chosen tribe – can help us. So, if you're asking 'why is family important for happiness?',

Family works as a safeguard for each other family member against any possible attack. A well stitched family takes care of protection of all the members.

Family is one of the building blocks of society, and so its structure and role reflect social changes. Although family structure may have changed, its importance has not. In fact, there are many reasons why family is important for happiness.

One of the reasons why family is necessary for happiness is because it (usually) provides financial stability in our early years. Having our basic needs covered is crucial when it comes setting the basis for a happy life. But studies show that the link between family and happiness extends beyond money or possessions.

All over the world, researchers found that support is one of the reasons why family is important for happiness. And this support goes both ways: according to a study, nearly 70 per cent of parents depend on their children for emotional support. And research shows that knowing someone has your back can counter stress, depressive symptoms, and low self-esteem.

The sibling relationships is especially important to emotional well-being. In one survey, more than 60 per cent of participants said their sibling was their best friend. Evolutionary biologists say that this could be because we share half our genes, so we're predisposed to closeness and we respond positively to it. But depending on our background, there could be some differences in how family contributes to happiness.

The concept of happiness varies across cultures, and so does the "recipe" for it. Family is a central to happiness in every culture, but in some countries this is more profound. Family ties often have a stronger weight in collectivist cultures, those where the well-being of society is above the individual.

For example, in Mexico, a World Values Survey found that nearly 95 per cent of those interviewed considered family very important in life. Mexicans rank family as one of the most trust-inspiring institutions and a source of emotional, financial and practical support.

"All over the world, researchers found that support is one of the reasons why family is important for happiness."

In India, also known for its collectivist culture, many important life decisions are taken in consultation with family members. The boundaries between self and relatives are somehow blurred, so the common view is that a happy and complete individual can only exist within the family unit.

When answering the question 'why is family important for happiness?', we can also look at Western societies. In the US, a survey showed that more than 70 per cent of participants said family was crucial to their identity. The link between healthy family ties and identity is also strong in Scandinavian countries like Sweden, Denmark, and Norway, where parent-child relationships are meant to facilitate independence, individual responsibility, and promote the development of healthy identities. But, regardless of our cultural background, there are following **reasons why family is important for happiness**:

(i) Mutual support and solidarity

The people we consider family foster a sense of reciprocity, dependability and mutual reliance. Caring for our loved ones and being looked after by them brings a rewarding sense of achievement.

(ii) A shelter from the outside world

Healthy families are a place of refuge from problems and offer a safety network when things go wrong. Think about the boost you get when it's hard to cope with life's hurdles and you spend time doing something fun with your loved ones. And it's more than a feeling: studies found that quality leisure time with our family can fight off and manage stress.

(iii) Encouragement

A study showed that the encouragement of parents and grandparents was the main reason why teenagers got involved in altruistic cases. And the link between altruism and greater well-being is well documented – you probably know that it's good to be good.

(iv) Unconditional love and support

Knowing that you have a network of people you can always count on benefits our physical and emotional health. Our "tribe" accepts us for who we are, which is key to a positive self-concept. And research shows that the benefits go both ways, to those giving and those receiving love and support.

(v) Shared experiences

We're all in this together, and that helps us build stronger connections and enrich our appreciation for others. Studies show that shared experiences can amplify the effect of positive emotions. Even remembering shared experiences can give a boost to our well-being.

(vi) A sense of belonging

Here's one last reason why family is important for happiness. Researchers compared people with and without a strong sense of belonging. The results were clear: those who felt they belonged to a supportive group reported being happier. According to psychologists, belonging is a primal need, and meeting this need helps us be more resilient – and happier too.

12.2 Tips for a Happy Family Life

Here are ways we can promote happiness in our families:

(i) Create cuddle time. You can't overdose on hugs. It's important for families to spend time snuggling in bed together, reading, or talking or playing games. This kind of positive touch helps kids feel loved and secure, plus it's fun for parents!

(ii) Sing together, stay together. The happy family has the right-singing together and it is a terrific way to bond as a family. Make up your own words to your favorite tunes; dance around the living room with your children; and use music to motivate room cleaning.

(iii) Make room for fun. While it's good to encourage your children's schoolwork and extracurricular activities, too much emphasis on them can create tension and anxiety. Make time for activities that have no purpose other than to allow family members to enjoy spending time together. Play games, plot surprise parties, take long walks, explore a cave, plant a garden, or cook.

(iv) Exercise together. Take a run or a bike ride to a local park with your child. At the park, you can take time to relax while your child plays in the sandbox or on the seesaw. This kind of outing allows parents to model healthy behavior, get exercise, and spend time with their kids.

(v) Create healthy food habits. Junk food high in salt and sugar may taste appealing, but it will play havoc with your family's health and moods. Create healthy snacking habits by leaving out bowls of fruit, cut-up vegetables, nuts, or dried fruit.

(vi) Cook together. This is another way to get kids interested in healthy foods. While you're whipping up dinner with your children you are encouraging healthy eating habits as well as teaching cooking, teamwork, and improvisational skills. Also, kids who help makes meals are more likely to eat them.

(vii) Reward good behavior. It's important to reinforce your child's good behavior. But there's no need to be cxtravagant. A trip to the humane shelter, a visit to the zoo, a movie and popcorn, or a slightly later bedtime can be good motivators.

(viii) Read and write together. Make time every day for reading. Read aloud to the kids, or have the whole family spend time with their own books, or listen to an audiobook. Cuddling up on the couch can make it even cozier. It's also important for children to spend some time writing each day.

(ix) Go one-on-one. Parents with more than one child should try to spend a little time interacting just with one child each day, even if it's just for ten minutes. That special time with a parent helps the child feel special and to bond with you.

(x) Have routines. Kids thrive when they know what to expect. So bedtime routines that involve bath, stories, and songs before sleep can minimize nighttime misbehavior. A morning routine can also help you get out the door faster with little fuss.

(xi) Appreciate each other. Find little ways to show how much you value each other. One idea is to do a little happy dance every time a child returns from school or a parent from work.

(xii) Remember, sorry isn't enough. When one of your children hurts the feelings of a sibling, it's not enough to apologize. That child must also find a way to help heal the hurt he/she has caused, by helping with a chore or sharing a toy.

(xiii) Prioritize your married life. The most important thing you can do for your child is to love your spouse and to demonstrate that love. This models a good relationship for your child and helps to keep your marriage intact.

(xiv) Less stress, more sleep

The child raising years are a busy time. But, in a survey of a thousand families where kids were asked, 'if you were granted one wish about your parents, what would it be?', their number one wish was that their parents were less tired and less stressed. (The parents thought it would be more time together, but they were wrong.) More sleep and less stress will make our families happier, but it can be a big ask. Maybe we could start by dropping just one extra commitment (like saying no to social events on Sundays) or by making it a habit to go to bed earlier each night instead of watching mindless reality TV or surfing the web. Small changes can greatly increase our family's happiness.

(xv) Share your family history

Families with a strong sense of family history are the happiest. The more kids know about their heritage, the more they feel a part of a story that is bigger than themselves. They have a better sense of control over their own lives, have higher self-esteem and are even able to handle stress better. Pore over family photos. Tell your family stories often (dinner-time is a great time!). The best stories don't shy away from negative things, but talk about the family's ups and downs. They also end by emphasizing how your family always sticks together.

(xvi) Balancing work and home life

It's not easy balancing your work and home life, but how you manage it can make quite a difference to your relationship with your family. Having a balance between work and home – being able to work in a way which fits around family commitments and isn't restricted to the 9 to 5 – boosts self-esteem as you're not always worrying about neglecting your responsibilities in any area, making you feel more in control of your life. Your family will be happier to see more of you, and you'll have a life away from home.

(xvii) Look after yourself

Parents often spend all their time looking after everyone else in the family and forget about themselves. If you don't look after yourself, you can end up feeling miserable and resentful, and you won't be able to give your children the support they need. Admit to yourself that you actually have feelings and needs of your own. It's not selfish to treat yourself once in a while! It doesn't have to be expensive - but putting aside some time to do just what YOU want to do, even if it's only 10 minutes a day - is so important.

(xviii) Discipline

Rather than thinking of discipline as a punishment, you should use it as a way of teaching your children how to meet their needs without hurting or offending anyone. While you may be angry, it can help to keep calm and teach your child how he or she could have handled the situation differently, and how he or she can go about it differently next time. This way is both more positive and more constructive.

(xix) Setting Boundaries

We often use boundaries to protect children from harm or danger. But it is important that you try to explain why boundaries are there, rather than issuing orders – for instance, if you pull them away from an open fire explain why. Children may be reluctant to follow instructions if parents command them. However, an explanation as to why the instructions are important will help your child understand, and therefore cooperate.

(xx) Communication

Communication is important – during both the good and the tough times. Children often find it hard to put their feelings into words and just knowing that their parents are listening can be enough. Talk about yourself – not just about your problems but about your daily life. If they feel included in the things you do they are more likely to see the value of including you in the things they do.

(xxi) Joint Decisions

With older children, it is normal for them to test the limits of boundaries to see what they can get away with. You may need to adapt boundaries as children grow into teens – it can even help to involve your child in the negotiation of new boundaries. Too many restrictions will be hard to keep on top of, so it is a good idea to work out which boundaries are really important to you, such as the ones for your children's safety, and which boundaries are not worth fighting about. With fewer restrictions, your children will appreciate that the boundaries you do set are serious.

12.3 Vasudhaiva Kutumbakam

The Sanskrit phrase *Vasudhaiva Kuṭumbaka*consists of several words: *vasudhā* (transl. 'the earth'); *ēva* (transl. 'is thus'); and *kuṭumbakam* (transl. 'family'). Means: The whole earth is one family.

ayaṃ nijaḥ paro veti gaṇanā laghucetasām
udāracaritānāṃ tu vasudhaiva kuṭumbakam.

The original verse appears in Chapter 6 of Maha Upanishad VI.71-73. Also found in the Rig Veda, it is considered the most important moral value in the Indian society.] This verse of Maha Upanishad is engraved in the entrance hall of the parliament of India.

The world is a family

One is a relative, the other stranger, say the small minded.
The entire world is a family, live the magnanimous.

Be detached, be magnanimous, lift up your mind, enjoy the fruit of Brahmanic freedom.

—Maha Upanishad 6.71–75

Subsequent ślokas go on to say that those who have no attachments go on to find the Brahman (the one supreme, universal Spirit that is the origin and support of the phenomenal universe). The context of this verse is to describe as one of the attributes of an individual who has attained the highest level of spiritual progress, and one who is capable of performing his worldly duties without attachment to material possessions.

The text has been influential in the major Hindu literature that followed it. The popular Bhagavata Purana, the most translated of the Purana genre of literature in Hinduism, for example, calls the Vasudhaiva Kutumbakam adage of the Maha Upanishad, as the "loftiest Vedantic thought".

Dr N. Radhakrishnan, former director of the Gandhi Smriti and Darshan Samiti, believes that the Gandhian vision of holistic development and respect for all forms of life; nonviolent conflict resolution embedded in the acceptance of nonviolence both as a creed and strategy; were an extension of the ancient Indian concept of Vasudhaiva Kutumbakam.

12.4 Quotes for a Happy Family Life

1. “It didn’t matter how big our house was; it mattered that there was

love in it." -Peter Buffett

2. "Call it a clan, call it a network, call it a tribe, call it a family: Whatever you call it, whoever you are, you need one." — Jane Howard

3. "Family means nobody gets left behind or forgotten."
— David Ogden Stiers

4. "We may have our differences, but nothing's more important than family." –Coco

5. "The bond that links your true family is not one of blood, but of respect and joy in each other's life."-Richard Bach

6. "A happy family is but an earlier heaven." – George Bernard Shaw

7. "Being a family means you are a part of something very wonderful. It means you will love and be loved for the rest of your life." – Lisa Weed

8. "Happiness is having a large, loving, caring, close-knit family in another city." — George Burns

9. "A family is a risky venture, because the greater the love, the greater the loss... That's the trade-off. But I'll take it all." — Brad Pitt

10. "The strength of a family, like the strength of an army, lies in its loyalty to each other."-Mario Puzo

11. The most important thing in the world is family and love."
– John Wooden

12. "When everything goes to hell, the people who stand by you, without flinching–they are your family."– Jim Butcher

13. "To us, family means putting your arms around each other and being there." -Barbara Bush

14. "In family life, love is the oil that eases friction, the cement that binds

closer together, and the music that brings harmony."
– Friedrich Nietzsche

15. "Family is not an important thing. It's everything." –Michael J. Fox

16. "Family faces are magic mirrors. Looking at people who belong to us, we see the past, present, and future." – Gail Lumet Buckley

17. "The greatest thing in family life is to take a hint when a hint is intended-and not to take a hint when a hint isn't intended."
— Robert Frost

18. "The family is one of nature's masterpieces." – George Santayana

19. "Families are the compass that guides us. They are the inspiration to reach great heights, and our comfort when we occasionally falter."
– Brad Henry

20. "You are the bows from which your children as living arrows are sent forth."-Khalil Gibran

21. "So much of what is best in us is bound up in our love of family, that it remains the measure of our stability because it measures our sense of loyalty."
— Haniel Long

22. "The homemaker has the ultimate career. All other careers exist for one purpose only – and that is to support the ultimate career."
— C.S. Lewis

23. "Everyone needs a house to live in, but a supportive family is what builds a home."-Anthony Liccione

24. "There is no such thing as fun for the whole family." — Jerry Seinfeld

25. "You don't choose your family. They are God's gift to you, as you are to them." -Desmond Tutu

26. “Parents are like God because you wanna know they’re out there, and you want them to think well of you, but you really only call when you need something.”— Chuck Palahniuk

27. The informality of family life is a blessed condition that allows us all to become our best while looking our worst.” – Marge Kennedy

28. “Having a place to go is a home. Having someone to love is a family. Having both is a blessing.”– Donna Hedges

29. “Being part of a family means smiling for photos.” –Harry Morgan

30. “That’s what people do who love you. They put their arms around you and love you when you’re not so lovable.”— Deb Caletti

31. “There’s nothing that makes you more insane than family. Or more happy, or more exasperated, or more secure.” – Jim Butcher

32. “In time of test, family is the best.” – Burmese Proverb

33. “If the family were a boat, it would be a canoe that makes no progress unless everyone paddles.”– Letty Cottin Pogrebin

34. “I am blessed to have so many great things in my life – family, friends, and God. All will be in my thoughts daily.” –Lil’ Kim

35. “The family–that dear octopus from whose tentacles we never quite escape, nor, in our inmost hearts, ever quite wish to.” – Dodie Smith

36. “The family is the first essential cell of human society.”
– Pope John XXIII

37. “My dear young cousin, if there’s one thing I’ve learned over the eons, it’s that you can’t give up on your family, no matter how tempting they make it.” — Rick Riordan

38. “Rejoice with your family in the beautiful land of life.”
– Albert Einstein

39. “Sticking with your family is what makes it a family.” – Mitch Albom

40.“What can you do to promote world peace? Go home and love your family.”-Mother Teresa

41. “Family and friendships are two of the greatest facilitators of happiness.” –John C. Maxwell

42. “Parents were the only ones obligated to love you; from the rest of the world you had to earn it.”— Ann Brashares

43. “Nothing is better than going home to family and eating good food and relaxing.” -Irina Shayk

44. “Family and friends are hidden treasures, seek them and enjoy their riches.”-Wanda Hope Carter

45. “Other things may change us, but we start and end with the family.”
— Anthony Brandt

46. “My mother used to tell me that when push comes to shove, you always know who to turn to. That being a family isn’t a social construct but an instinct.” — Jodi Picoult

47. I think togetherness is an important ingredient of family life.”
— Barbara Bush

48. “The world, we’d discovered, doesn’t love you like your family loves you.”-Louis Zamperini

49. “My family is my life, and everything else comes second as far as what’s important to me.”-Michael Imperioli

50. “It is the smile of a child, the love of a mother, the joy of a father, the togetherness of a family.”— Menacheim Begin

CHAPTER THIRTEEN

HAPPINESS AT WORKPLACE

13.1 Introduction to Happiness at Workplace

Despite a large body of positive psychological research into the relationship between happiness and productivity, happiness at work has traditionally been seen as a potential by-product of positive outcomes at work, rather than a pathway to business success. Happiness in the workplace is usually dependent on the work environment. During the past two decades, maintaining a level of happiness at work has become more significant and relevant due to the intensification of work caused by economic uncertainty and increase in competition. Nowadays, happiness is viewed by a growing number of scholars and senior executives as one of the major sources of positive outcomes in the workplace. In fact, companies with higher-than-average employee happiness exhibit better financial performance and customer satisfaction. It is thus beneficial for companies to create and maintain positive work environments and leadership that will contribute to the happiness of their employees.

Happiness is not fundamentally rooted in obtaining sensual pleasures and money, but those factors can influence the well-being of an individual at the workplace. However, extensive research has revealed that freedom and autonomy at a workplace have the most effect on the employee's level of happiness, and other important factors are gaining knowledge and the ability to influence the self's working hours.

13.2 Factors contributing to Happiness at Workplace

13.2.1 Organizational culture

Organizational culture represents the internal work environment created for operating an organization. It can also represent how employees are treated by their bosses and peers. An effective organization should have a culture that takes into account employee's happiness and encourages employee satisfaction. Although each individual has unique talents and personal preferences, the behaviors and beliefs of the people in the same organizations show common properties. This, to some extent, helps organisations to create their own cultural properties. An employee feels satisfied not through comparisons with other peers, but through his/her own happiness and awareness of being in harmony with their colleagues. He uses a term called "carrier" to represent lack of happiness, life in constant tension and never-ending struggle for status.

13.2.2 Employee salary

There are many reasons that can contribute to happiness at work. However, when individuals are asked with regards to why they work, money is one of the most common answers, as it provides people with sustenance, security and privilege. To a large extent, people work to live, and the pecuniary aspect of the work is what sustains the living. Locke, No other incentive or motivational technique comes even close to money with respect to its instrumental value.

The income-happiness relationship in life can also be applied in organizational psychology. Some studies have found positively significant relationships between salary level and job satisfaction. Some have suggested that income and happiness at work are positively correlated, and the relationship is stronger for individuals with extrinsic value orientations.

However, others don't believe that salary, in itself, is a very strong factor in job satisfaction. Hundreds of studies and scores of systematic reviews of incentive studies consistently document the ineffectiveness of external rewards. The question regarding this subject has been recently studied by a group of people. Their research shows that the intrinsic relationship between job and salary is complex. In their research, they analysed the combined impact of many existing studies to produce a much larger and statistically powerful analysis. By looking at many previous studies, they concluded that while it is true to say that money is a driver of employee's happiness, the produced effect is transitory. Money may not necessarily make employees happy.

13.2.3 Job security

Job security is an important factor to determine whether employees feel happiness at work. Different types of jobs have different levels of job security: in some situations, a position is expected to be offered for a long time, whereas in other jobs an employee may be forced to resign his/her job. The expectation of the job availability has been related with the job-related well-being and a higher level of job security corresponds to a higher level of job satisfaction alongside a higher level of well-being.

13.2.4 Career development

The option for moving or shifting to alternative roles motivates the employee's participation in the workplace, if an employee can see the future potential for a promotion, motivation levels will increase. By contrast, if an organization does not provide any potential for higher status position in the future, the employee's effectiveness in work will decrease. In addition, the employee may consider whether or not the position would be offered to them in the future. On the other hand, not all of the opportunities for transferring into another activity are aimed to obtain the upward movement. In some cases, they are aimed to prevent the skills obsolescence, provides more future career possibility, as well as directly increasing the skill development.

13.2.5 Job autonomy

Job autonomy may be defined as the condition of being self-governing or free from excessive external control in the workplace environment. The autonomy is important to human beings because it is the foundation of human dignity and the source of all morality. Among the models of human growth and development that are centred on autonomy, the most theoretically sophisticated approach has been developed around the concepts of self-regulation and intrinsic motivation. Self-determination theory proposes that 'higher behavioral effectiveness, greater volitional persistence, enhanced subjective well-being, and better assimilation of the individual within his or her social group' result when individuals act from motivations that emanate from the inner self (intrinsic motivation) rather than from sources of external regulation. For self-determination theorists, it is the experience of an external locus of causation (or the belief that one's actions are controlled by external forces) that undermines the most powerful source of natural motivation and that (when chronic) also can lead to stultification, weak self-esteem, anxiety and depression, and alienation. Thus, health and well-being as well as effective performance in social settings are closely related to the experience of autonomy. A framework that focused attention on autonomy and four other key factors involves in designing enriched work. Work designed to be complex and challenging (characterized by high levels of autonomy, skill variety, identity, significance, and feedback) is theorized to promote high intrinsic motivation, job satisfaction, and overall work performance. It is possible to infer that the experience of autonomy at work has positive consequences ranging from higher job performance to job satisfaction and enhanced general well-being, which are both related to the concept of happiness at work.

13.2.6 Work–life balance

Work–life balance is a state of equilibrium, characterized by a high level of satisfaction, functionality, and effectiveness while successfully performing several tasks simultaneously. The non-work activity is not limited to family life only but also to various occupations and activities of which one's life is composed. Scholars have started promoting the importance of maintaining a work–life balance beginning in the early 1970s and have been increasing ever since. Studies suggest that there is a clear connection between the increase in work related stress to the constant advancements in digital and telecommunications technology. The existence of cell phones and other internet-based devices enables access to work related issues in non-working periods, thus, adding more hours and work load. A decrease in the time allocated to non-work-related activities and working nonstandard shifts has been proven to have significant negative effects on family and personal life. The immediate effect is a decrease in general well-being as the individual is unable to properly allocate the appropriate amount of time necessary to maintain a balance between the two spheres. Therefore, extensive research has been done on properly managing time as a main strategy of managing stress.

Some of the physiological effects of stress include cognitive problems (forgetfulness, lack of creativity, inefficient decision making), emotional reactions (mood swings, irritability, depression, lack of motivation), behavioral issues (withdrawal from relationships and social situations, neglecting responsibilities, abuse of drugs and alcohol) and physical symptoms (tiredness, aches and pain, loss of libido).

The condition in which work performance is negatively affected by a high level of stress is termed 'burnout', in which the employee experiences a significant reduction in motivation. When the outcomes of work performance are offset by the negative impacts on the individual's general well-being, or, are not valued enough by the employee, levels of motivation are low. Time management, prioritizing certain tasks and actions according to one's values and beliefs are amongst the suggested course of action for managing stress and maintaining a healthy work–life balance. Psychologists have suggested that when workers have control over their work schedule, they are more capable of balancing work and non-work-related activities. The reality of constant increase in competition and economic uncertainty frequently forces the employee to compromise the balance for the sake of financial and job security. Therefore, work–life balance policies are created by many businesses and are largely implemented and dealt by line managers and supervisors, rather than at the organizational level as the employee's well-being can be more carefully observed and monitored.

13.2.7 Working relationship

Feeling a sense of belonging to groups is a significant motivation for human beings. Co-workers are an important social group and relationships with them can be a source of pleasure. It suggests that people have a need for affiliation. Also, person-job fit, the matching between personal abilities and job demand, has important effects on job satisfaction.

13.2.8 Group relationship

The co-workers' relationship belongs to hygiene needs, which are related to environmental elements. When environmental elements are met, satisfaction will be achieved. Employees tend to be happier and more hardworking when they are in good working environment, for instance, being happy to work in a good working relationship.

Group relationship is important and has effects on employees' absenteeism and turnover rate. Cohesive groups increase job satisfactions. The sense of group belongingness, group pride, group solidarity or group spirit relates inversely to the absenteeism rate. Among the target groups, group with high cohesiveness tend to have low absenteeism rate while group with low cohesiveness tend to have higher absenteeism rate.

Different communication ways in groups contribute to different employees' satisfaction. For example, the chain structure results in low satisfaction while the circle structure results in high satisfaction.

13.2.9 Leadership

In relations to the work place, successful leadership will structure and develop relationships amongst employees and consequently, employees will empower each other.

There are three main **styles of leaderships:**

i. **Autocratic leaders**: control the decision-making power and do not consult team members.

ii. **Democratic leaders**: include team members in the decision-making process but make the final decisions.

iii. **Laissez-faire leaders**: team members have huge freedom in how they do their work, and how they set their deadlines.

Management plays an important role in an employee's job satisfaction and happiness. Good leadership can empower employees to work better towards reaching the organization's goals. For example, if a leader is considerate, the employees will tend to develop a positive attitude towards management and thus, work more effectively.

Feelings, including happiness, are often hidden by employees and should be identified for effective communication in the workplace. Ineffective communication at work is not uncommon, as leaders tend to focus on their own matters and give less attention to employees at a lower rank. Employees, on the other hand, tend to be reluctant to talk about their own problem and assume leaders can figure out the problem. As a result, both leaders and employees can cause repetitive misunderstandings.

13.3 Individual Actions to increase Happiness at Work

There is relatively little research on how individuals may volitionally contribute to their own happiness at work, though much of the advice on how to improve happiness in general (e.g. practice gratitude, pursue intrinsic goals, nurture relationships, find flow) could also be applied in the work setting. Momentary happiness is associated with perceptions of effective performance or progress towards goals; so setting and pursuing challenging but achievable short-term goals may enhance real-time feelings of happiness. At the more stable person-level, individuals could seek both person–job and person–organization fit when choosing employment, and adjust expectations to match reality. If dissatisfied, they might decide to leave one job and find another that suits them better, though very few studies have investigated this phenomenon by following individuals across organizations.

In research it was found that the executives who were less satisfied in a given year were more likely to change jobs and be more satisfied the following year in the new job. This was dubbed as the 'honeymoon effect'. Unfortunately, the increase in happiness was short-lived and, by the second year in the new job, satisfaction had returned to baseline levels.

It has been suggested that individuals will be more authentically happy if they feel a 'calling' or a connection between what they do at work and a higher purpose or important value. This is described as 'job crafting' by employees, which is defined as modifying the tasks to be performed, building or changing relationships with co-workers or clients, and psychologically reframing the meaning of work. Individuals are thought to craft their jobs to assert control, create a positive self-image at work, and fulfill basic needs for connection to others. For instance, nurses may redefine their work as helping patients heal as opposed to performing menial tasks as directed by physicians. Such changes should be quite effective in creating both supplementary and needs–supplies fit, and would be expected to improve happiness at work.

Another approach for individuals to improve demands–abilities fit is provided by the strengths-based view. This approach suggests that each individual has a unique configuration of personal or character strengths, talents, and preferences. Individuals should discover what their personal strengths are, and then design their job or career to allow them to cultivate these strengths and spend much of each day applying them while minimizing demands to complete activities that do not use strengths. Following this advice should improve both eudaimonic and hedonic happiness, as individuals enjoy greater competence and self-actualization.

Strengths and the means to identify them have been approached differently by the various scholars associated with this view. They advocate a process of soliciting feedback from others about times that the focal individual was at their personal best, then seeking patterns across the qualitative replies received to form a picture of the 'reflected best self'.

Creating a Space in Our Workplace

Take a few hours every day to strategically unplug and hide all electronics that are not crucial to what you are currently working on. Recent research shows that the mere presence of a cell phone can decrease your productivity and attention on cognitively demanding tasks. Reduce distractions and get your work done quicker and more efficiently by hiding your electronics until you're ready to go home.

You can even take it a step further and use your time without technology to focus on your mental and emotional health. Find a few minutes during your workday to meditate. Just sit quietly in silence and concentration. You'll be amazed at how focused you'll feel once you get back to work.

13.4 Tips for How to be Happy at Workplace

How often do you consider quitting your job and feel that you are not getting paid enough for the dedication and service you offer your organization?

Happiness and satisfaction are subjective concepts – while for some of us monetary benefits can be equated with job satisfaction, some might strive for recognition of their hard work and lose motivation on failing to achieve so.

For some people, having a friendly environment at work is an essential requisite for deriving pleasure. No matter what the standards are, being content with our careers is crucial for maintaining the 'work-life' balance.

The University of Warwick, UK, in one of their studies revealed that happy workers are up to 12% more productive than unhappy professionals. They are more likely to be the proud owner of good health, have smooth flowing professional and personal relationships, and prove to be more beneficial for the organization as a whole.

Here we shall take a look into the aspects of happiness at work, understand why it is vital to maintaining work motivation, and discuss some of the essential and cutting-edge techniques for deriving the maximum happiness at work.

"Out of each goal human beings want to attain; happiness is usually the greatest." -Tom Miles

Happiness at work is not the sum of proper investment and good returns; it is more than that. Individual factors like personality traits, level of perception, underlying psychological stressors, and emotional intelligence influence the degree to which we feel comfortable in a professional situation.

In the book, "The Happiness Advantage" author Shawn Achor (2011) stated that a company with happy employees could increase their sales by 37%, productivity by 31%, which directly contribute toward building a high-performance work environment and improves the quality of life for all people involved with the work.

The Importance Of Happiness At Work

The concept of happiness at work was not there until a few decades ago, and there is a reason for that. In the last few years, we have seen drastic changes in the industrial sector – we now work in positions that did not exist twenty years ago.

With such a wide range of complex tasks that we have to choose from today, it is only essential that we can extract the true happiness from the work we devote ourselves to. Happy employees are compulsory for a growing business.

Job Satisfaction and happiness

Being happy is the first step to anything that we want to do successfully. Going to the office, mechanically performing all the duties assigned, and coming home to spend the rest of the day with a drink in hand and the TV in front is an ideal picture of an unhappy life.

A happy worker will reach office on time because he respects his punctuality and will perform all the daily tasks because he enjoys doing it. He will work out of love, not out of compulsion.

(i) Happiness Multiplies Success

Happiness at work can spread like fire. Employees who feel pleasure in doing their work form a great example to others who are less motivated.

For example, when a team leader is happy with his position and work, he can influence his team with more positivity and maintain great functionality in the group. Happiness in the workplace is directly correlational to increased productivity and better group performance at work.

(ii) Happiness Builds Positivity

A troubled mind can be the storehouse of negative contemplations. When we work out of compulsion and don't feel passionate about the contribution we make to the organization's success, our mind starts wearing.

We become stressed, lose focus, and indulge self-deprecating thoughts like "I have to quit", "I cannot take it anymore", "I am not worth it", etc. On the contrary, a professional who has strong positive feelings about his job will undoubtedly be more enthusiastic and focus on building himself. Rather than focusing on the problems, he would look into ways of solving it.

(iii) Happiness Reduces Stress

Annie Mckee, an International Leadership advisor, and writer, in one of her publications in the Harvard Business Review, mentioned that when employees are unhappy, their brain starts to disconnect from the positive emotions, and damages their power of creative thinking and reasoning.

She further said in her article on the link between our thoughts, feelings, and actions. If any of these breaks down, it is sure to hamper the others. If we feel happy in the 8 hours that we spend at work, if somehow we can hit the strings of positivity that will keep us uplifted, it can remarkably improve our responses to stress and redirect our focus to the positive aspects of the work-life.

(iv) Happiness at Work means a Healthy Life

If we allow the work stress and disappointments to enter into our personal space, there is no way that we can get rid of them.

Successful professionals who can optimize their work are less likely to suffer from hypertension, cardiac arrests, substance abuse, and other stress-related disorders. When we are happy from inside, we get that power to fight diseases and the will to recover and get back on track.

Remaining physically or mentally sick can bring unprecedented hurdles even at work. We lose the energy to give it our best shot, become less focused on work and more focused on the woes, and consequently, kill our productive soul. Not just that, happiness at work also makes us less prone to work-related stress and burdens.

(v) Happiness at Work Increases Likeability

We all like to stay around people who have a positive attitude and look content with themselves. In a happy state of mind, people are more innovative and inspired. They are willing to improve their existing skills and contributes toward creating a fun and creative performance culture at work.

Finding happiness in work helps in building strong interpersonal relationships at work and encourage people to work together for the common welfare of the organization they are serving. It is the backbone for innovation, loyalty, responsibility, and success. Happy workers can create a pleasant environment at work that is easy for others to cope in, and the more people get into it, the better the team grows.

Science Behind Happiness At Work

Happiness is a strong positive emotion and is a fundamental human experience. Since ages, happiness has been an intriguing aspect of research and history, however, a relatively recent inclusion in the field of psychology. Positive psychology, or the science of happiness, which became popular in the past decade, was the first step by mental health professionals to gauge the importance of joy in different walks of life.

The investigation of joy, or positive brain science, is a more extensive part of regular brain research and comparatively contemporary. Until several years ago, psychological research was tied in with taking care of mental problems and taking life back to the regularity.

However, positive psychology isn't just remedial – it involves enhancing what is correct rather than correcting what is wrong. Positive Psychology ended up well known after 1998 with the spearheading work of Dr. Martin Seligman and Dr. Mihaly Csikszentmihalyi who built it up as the pathway of finding the satisfaction that we all aim to get in our lives.

Four Approaches to Life

Much like the famous saying that beauty lies in the eyes of the beholder, positive psychology propagates that the way we see life is the way it becomes. Following are four approaches to life:

(i) The Hedonic Approach – Where a person is concerned more about his pleasures and means to satisfy them. An egocentric attitude, Hedonic followers cannot refrain from guilty pleasures (for example binge eating or oversleeping) even after knowing the detriments.

(ii) The Rat Race Approach – Where we are concerned about what is good for us and continue seeking selfish goals. It is an egocentric and competitive approach in the sense that the followers may choose to overlook the benefits of others as long as they are helping themselves.

(iii) The Nihilistic Approach – Mostly seen in depressed and stressed individuals, the nihilistic approach is entirely pessimistic and caters to indulging negative thoughts. A negative person fails to divert his attention from the worries and mishaps of life and lacks the motivation to reconcile from stress.

(iv) The Positive Approach – It is believed to be the way that leads to happiness and contentment. A positive approach is where people can uncover the right balance between 'I want to' and 'I have to' and focus on building their qualities. The positive approach is in all its essence, purely solution-focused, goal-oriented, and the direct pathway to 'happiness.'

The following factors to be associated with happiness at work:

- Workplace autonomy and the freedom to decide;
- Task variations and scope for creative ideas;
- Task significance;
- Recognition for work;
- Task difficulty;
- Professional skills and specialization;
- Social support within the workplace;
- Feedback from superiors;
- Environmental conditions at work; and
- Business management and networking channels.

A Look at the Research

Making happiness a part of the performance culture, reputed organizations like Google and McDonalds have specific posts allotted for Chief Happiness Officers (CHOs). Their job is to spread positivity and work on maintaining the motivation of the workforce.

In 1999, before Google had employed their first CHO Chade-Meng Tan, a French fashion brand Kiabi hired a professional as the Happiness Officer. That was one of the earliest advancements in the field and after the massive success of Google and their motivational CHO Meng, recruiting happiness officers became a culture for companies in different sectors.

Dr. Christine Carter, a senior research associate at the University of California, mentioned in one of her research publications that happiness, whether at work or in life, is not just about deriving the feeling of satisfaction. She said that happiness is not the feeling that comes from getting or doing what we want to, instead, it is the ability to access an array of positive emotions like optimism, gratitude, etc., and consciously choosing to implement them in life. From her findings, it is evident that being happy at work doesn't mean universal acceptance or the complete absence of negative stress; it is just the power through which we can widen our perspective and bounce back from negativities.

Happy employees are an excellent investment for successful companies. Studies show that when positive individuals run an organization, it is more likely to gain financially and flourish in the long term.

Research at the University of Warwick has estimated that workplace happiness increases productivity up to 12%. Happy workers are a guarantee for more productivity, more innovation, and less conflict.

In a study carried out by Robertson Cooper Limited, it was established that the 'feel-good factor' that an employee derives from his work and workplace is by all means dependent on their persona. The study was conducted on a large sample of around 3200 employees from various organizations, and the results revealed that:

Employees who felt good at work and had better working days scored high on positive emotions and low on emotions like loneliness, hopelessness, depression, and insecurities. The percentage of employees who had high scores on positive emotions were found to be more productive, more satisfied with their jobs, and healthier than others. People who scored high on positive emotions were more compassionate and empathetic towards their colleagues and subordinates. Employees who showed traits of depression, stress, and emotional vulnerabilities were less motivated, unwilling to improve their skills, and showed signs of unhealthy interpersonal connections at work.

CHAPTER FOURTEEN

HAPPINESS IN SOCIETY

14.1 Happiness in Society

Did you ever wonder what makes a society happy? Is a happy society full of citizens who focus on their own happiness, people whose happiness then spills-over to others around them? Or, maybe, a happy society is composed of citizens who are sensitive to people around them, thereby making other people happy.

In search for the answer to the question of happy societies, some persons started from the observation that numerous cross-country studies indicate that individualism predicts societal happiness. That is, societies that emphasize individuals' needs and goals over those of the group tend to be happier. However, it has been unclear why members of individualistic societies report higher happiness. One could conclude that focusing on oneself and one's own goals—as individualistic people do—promotes societal happiness. But their research challenges this conclusion.

They analyzed data from over 100,000 individuals collected across more than 90 countries and found that societal happiness is higher in those individualistic societies where four specific attitudes are highly endorsed—tolerance, trust, civic engagement, and non-materialism. The association between these attitudes and happiness was very strong and was obtained even when other factors—such as wealth of the society—were taken into account.

But what do tolerance, trust, civic engagement, and non-materialism have in common? Why are societies in which these four attitudes are popular happier? The simple answer seems to be that each of these four attitudes benefits other people. Being tolerant obviously benefits the people around us. Likewise, trusting strangers benefits other people. Our own civic engagement may bring us personal benefits, but it also benefits other people and improves society as a whole. And being non-materialistic also makes people less focused on accumulating money and possessions and more focused on other important issues.

These four attitudes can be thought of as the "open society" attitudes, in tribute to philosopher Karl Popper, who advocated values of tolerance, trust, civic engagement and non-materialism for maintaining an open, democratic society. Popper's postulates seem to make societies not only more open, but also happier.

Interestingly, although these four "open societies" attitudes benefit society as a whole, they do not substantially promote people's individual satisfaction directly. People who endorse "open society" attitudes are not considerably more satisfied with life than people who are prejudiced, suspicious, uninvolved in civic issues, and materialistic.

To create a happy society, we need to endorse attitudes that benefit the people around us even if they don't directly benefit us personally. Happiness does not come back to us through "karma" when we behave well—it comes back indirectly when people around us share attitudes that benefit other people. In short, the happiest societies are those in which people hold and demonstrate attitudes that benefit others.

The fact that societal happiness relies on the effects of our other-benefitting attitudes has important practical implications. The direct benefits to people who adopt the open society attitudes are very weak, if present at all. Therefore, if we wish to enhance societal happiness, incentives to adopt these attitudes need to be orchestrated by governing bodies, international and local organizations, and every single person who desires a happier society.

Finally, although the open society attitudes arise in societies that emphasize individualism, in many ways, these values are quite collectivistic. Let's remember that even in individualistic cultures, the quality of the society depends on how we treat each other.

14.2 How to Create Happy Society?

A scholar on happiness suggests that the ideal type of happiness is "self-made," that is, it is something that is created entirely by oneself without relying on other people. He says that one can get a stronger sense of happiness taking things on with an independent mindset. This would enable one to come face-to-face with one's desires and emotions and to find satisfaction in the actions that one took and the results of those actions.

In recent years, the number of people that feel happy from spiritual rather than material things. Professor Takashi Maeno, from the Graduate School of System Design and Management and a director of the Wellbeing Research Center, Keio University, focuses on this change.

According to Professor Maeno, factors in providing people with a sense of wellbeing can be broadly divided into "material wealth" and "spiritual wealth."

It is mainly emerging and developing countries and regions that display a strong tendency to attach importance to material wealth. Places like these direct their interest initially to income and savings and to status symbols such as houses and cars. Water supply and sewage systems, transit services, and the building of infrastructure resilient to natural disasters are also connected to material wealth.

As these material things reach a certain level of abundance, a diversification of lifestyles and ideals for happiness starts to occur. While there are always people that attach importance to the value of material things, the number of people that feel happy in spiritual wealth or fulfillment tends to increase. According to Professor Maeno, this is a phenomenon that is seen in the entire world.

So, what is it that brings about spiritual wealth?

According to factor analysis, there are **four factors** contributing to the happiness of people in modern-day society. These are (i) "let's try it", (ii) "thank you", (iii) "it will turn out all right", and (iv) "be yourself".

Professor Maeno sees these factors as the leaves of a four-leaf clover, each of which influences the other and all of which must be satisfied. When these conditions are fulfilled, people attain a sense of wellbeing.

As an example, Professor Maeno says that, in seeking out self-realization, it is inappropriate to battle with people just to denigrate them. Happiness research also suggests that it is not desirable to "lose sight of yourself by overemphasizing harmony with those around you." When the brain comprehends the mechanism of how the four factors are linked, it naturally takes it all into account and acts accordingly. In other words, keeping the four factors in mind while putting them into practice will create a virtuous circle that will produce happiness in yourself and those around you.

The desire to live happily in a happy community

It makes the case that true happiness is the self-made happiness that each person creates on their own. Pursuing a happy life and lifestyle means happiness not only for the individual, but also for those around him or her.

In other words, happiness requires one to not simply reside and live in some community. It requires that each person living in such place involves themselves in the community with an independent mindset.

People in the modern age, however, are up against a background that inhibits such independence of mind. This background is the wave of urbanization that has surged throughout the rest of the world. Emerging nations and regions are rapidly urbanizing, a process that gradually chips away at connections between people in their communities. The fact is that, in communities lacking interpersonal connections with others, community members do not regard community involvement as a personal affair.

So, what kind of initiatives should exist to create happy communities? The following discusses two perspectives that may be our clue.

(i) Discarding compulsion and nurturing an independent mindset

A happy community, town, or city is one in which the residents involve themselves with its various local events with an independent mindset. But is this really possible?

With a hundred residents of a city having a hundred different problems and concerns, they each adopt an independent mindset to speak up on and share these with others while also having the curiosity to listen to others. Although social media may have already become a tool for realizing this kind of situation, analysis of interactions and information as data is steadily clarifying what people want to do and what they should do. It goes without saying that it is important to have such discussions in both the virtual and real worlds.

Professor Maeno states: "when starting out under such headings as 'solutions to challenges' if there is some kind of outside compulsion to act, then you aren't going to come up with any good ideas. It is better to have a diversity of people get together for dialogue and to approach things with the idea of trying something fun because this will lead to actual activities in which people retain an independent mindset and a feeling of happiness." Having everyone adopt an independent mindset and jointly contribute free ideas in a psychologically safe place can lead to finding solutions for a community's issue and has the potential to generate innovation.

Among the latest initiatives is the "Habitat Innovation" research, a project carried out by the H-UTokyo Lab, which was created jointly by Hitachi and the University of Tokyo. Aimed at realizing Society 5.0 by leveraging the strengths of both organizations, its purpose is to draw out independent-mindedness, which spurs innovation. In one of the project themes, "urban development", efforts are being made to combine the knowledge of the University of Tokyo, the technology of Hitachi, and the insight of city residents. Research is also being carried out that makes full use of various technologies, the aim of which is to enable city resident participation in city development with an independent mindset.

A sense of independence develops by interacting with diverse people, such as those with differing communication styles or different cultures. However, in recent years, the communication that existed in small towns has been lost due to the effects of urbanization, producing a tendency for more-tenuous human relations.

One example of creating a space for drawing out such independence of mind is a project run jointly by Keio University and Tokyo's Minato Ward called "Shiba-no-ie." This moniker in Japanese refers to a house with an old-style wooden veranda located in the residential district of Minato Ward. At first, it served as a place for senior residents to gather for tea. However, after a while, children began to drop by on their way home from school. Eventually, their families also began to participate, giving rise to inter-generational communication. Over time, this led to the natural springing up of events such as the Weekly Lunch Meetup.

Another example is the "Koyu-zaidan" foundation, located in Shintomi-cho, Koyu-gun, Miyazaki Prefecture. This foundation acts as a community trading company that was established based on funding by the "benefit-your-locality" tax scheme. Acting as a community business platform, it engages in the development of entrepreneurs and new industries with speedy responsiveness unattainable via conventional government administrations. Under a vision of having Shintomi-cho become "the easiest town in the world to take on new challenges," the foundation cultivates throughout the entire town a culture of free exchange, in which response to failure is support rather than resistance. Through this, the town is attracting those wanting to move to the area and start a business from all across Japan.

Although these examples of lifestyle and economic spaces appear at first glance to be small in scale, they are gradually popping up here and there and are expected to connect with each other either in the virtual or real world and to grow into a novel type of a "happy community."

(ii) Deepening Interaction and Seeking an Ideal "Space" for Innovation

Drawing out an independent mindset and creating a space to do so—technology-driven backing has considerable influence on creating mechanisms for this. Just as the internet has provided spaces for people to easily connect while making it possible to provide information with an independent mindset, the use of other technologies such as AI (Artificial Intelligence) in the monitoring of happiness also holds great potential.

Embracing the goal of providing a means of happiness management to business management, Hitachi developed "Happiness Planet", a smartphone app that quantifies the degree of happiness. In conventional organizations and work styles, people often become passive, feeling that it is better to keep one's mouth shut out of fear of how they will be judged by their boss or coworkers. These kinds of psychologically unsafe human relations inevitably give rise to losses in productivity, unforeseeable accidents, and even employee mental issues. Revitalizing organizations and improving productivity may require a new management scheme that implements reform measures based on the analysis of data acquired by visualizing the happiness.

Using a scale to visualize whether or not people are made happy will result in not only having business management, but also product and service development and the many kinds of public activities, including city planning and policymaking. Next-generation technologies will be employed to drive a cycle of measuring data related to happiness, analyzing them, and applying the results to improvement. In an age in which individuals, companies, institutions, and governments are working seriously on the question of what happiness actually is, the development of technologies and platforms that enable such a cycle has great significance.

Initiatives for using technology to "update" happiness are occurring in various areas across the world. As such initiatives spread throughout their communities, towns, and cities, these municipalities will connect with each other, leading to an acceleration of regional revitalization. This process has the potential to give birth to increasingly diverse innovation. As transportation companies, logistics companies, and other enterprises that uses Hitachi's technologies and solutions, and become involved and their mutual ties promoted, "happy communities" will further expand. It is the expansion of revitalized regions where people with independent mindsets have ties to each other in both the virtual and real worlds that will maximize the happiness of people and communities.

14.3 Can we Create a Happy Society?

"Happiness is not something ready-made. It comes from your own actions".
– Dalai Lama

Imagine two types of societies. In one society, people are stressed, unhappy, tense, irritable, and self-centred. In another, people are at ease, happy, untroubled, and compassionate. The difference between these two societies is evident and vast. People are more likely to be more content in the latter society. They are also expected to be healthier, safer, and have better relationships.

The difference between a happy and unhappy country is not a trivial thing. So how can we create a happy society? Scandinavian countries tend to do well in this matter. They generally meet the World Happiness Report prerequisites for national happiness – social support, income, healthy life expectancy, trust in their government, freedom, and generosity. No wonder they are typically at the top of the global happiness rankings.

Other countries like Bhutan, the United Kingdom, and New Zealand follow suit. Bhutan was the first country to create a policy based on the happiness of its citizens, claiming that the Gross National Happiness (GNH) is a more important measure of prosperity and progress than Gross National Product (GNP). In 2010, the UK developed a national well-being program while New Zealand introduced the 'well-being budget,' intending to improve the well-being of their most vulnerable citizens. These examples show us that it is possible to change even the most unhappy places, as long as their leaders are willing to do so.

However, not all countries are happy. Whether they are developed or not, rich or poor, some countries fail to ensure the happiness of their people. The results of the World Happiness Report and other research show that, globally, leaders of such countries fail to focus on the happiness of their people, and history teaches us that those governments that do not put happiness first risk being swept away. Ed Diener, a famous professor of psychology at the University of Utah and the University of Virginia, notes that happiness is the responsibility of both the state and the individual. Our governments and policymakers can facilitate the pursuit of happiness, but it is an individual who should follow them.

This returns us to the importance of awareness. Being self-aware allows us to identify our thoughts, actions, and behaviors. By being self-aware, we can understand who we are, how others see us, and what is our role in society. Our happiness relies on this ability, as well as the ability to be socially aware.

Social awareness is rooted in compassion and empathy. Being socially aware means understanding how our society functions, what are its problems, struggles, cultures, and norms. To be socially conscious is to step out of a personal bubble to listen and care for others. Social awareness helps us increase positivity, form healthy relationships, teaches us an appreciation of others and things we have, reduces judgment, and increases sympathy and tolerance.

Since education plays an essential role in the socialization and happiness of people, schools and universities should also have a crucial role in the effort of increasing happiness in a society. Why? Because in addition to being knowledge producers, educational institutions are responsible for developing students into productive and valuable members of society. They also help people create meaningful lives and sustainable happiness.

In addition to improving the economic and educational standard of living, policymakers should also think of ways to increase the happiness and well-being of societies by strengthening their health systems. This is a no-brainer since health is one of the most important factors of human happiness. Multiple studies have shown that happy people have a better immune system, a lower risk of diabetes and heart disease, and fewer chronic pains. Happy people also live longer. Policies focused on happiness and well-being can lead to improved health outcomes, which can ultimately enhance healthcare performance.

We also need to think of social inclusion and empowerment of people. Social inclusion is what keeps society together. Through social empowerment, people can have greater control over their lives and live as they would like. However, it requires a certain standard of health and education to be fully realized.

These elements are crucial for creating a decent, happy society. They are indicators of how we can build even better societies in the future.

A Happier Society is Possible

"What's the use of a fine house if you haven't got a tolerable planet to put it on?"– Henry David Thoreau

We are all connected to a broader world through our communities. It's common sense to want to make our community, society, and world a better place for all of us to live.

To create a happy and prosperous society, we need to develop and support incentive programs that benefit the people around us, even when they don't benefit us personally. If we want to enhance societal happiness, such incentives and programs need to be adopted by governments, local and international organizations, and everyone who wishes for a happier society.

'Happytalism' is about making this shift to a happier society, where people can lead happy, balanced, and meaningful lives. However, although the idea is clear, it requires a considerable social and cultural change. The goal of Happytalism is to bring together people who believe that we can create a better world and encourage them to do as much as they can to increase the happiness and well-being of others.

We want to help create societies that put their people's happiness first. We want to encourage people to abandon self-serving, self-centred, materialistic, and meaningless behavior and steer them towards a more loving way of living. Our goal is to inspire others to lead fulfilling lives and help them make positive changes in their homes, workplaces, schools, and communities.

The happiness we want to cultivate in people's lives is not just happiness that can be found and lost in an instant, but happiness with staying power. We may have to work hard for happiness at first, but once achieved; it becomes easier and more natural over time—a worthwhile goal.

14.4 How to make the World Happier?

There is a wind of change in our society. People are talking about feelings. Even men are doing it. Relatively recently Prince William and Prince Harry talked for the first time about their mother's death and how it affected their own mental health. All around there is a new undercurrent – a greater concern with our own inner life and with how other people feel. A new, gentler culture is emerging.

By contrast, the older culture, which still dominates, is altogether harsher. It is more focused on externals. It encourages people to aim above all at personal success: good grades, a good job, a good income and a desirable partner. This culture of striving has brought many blessings, and life today is probably as good as it has ever been in human history. But that culture also involves a lot of stress, and people wonder why – if we are now so much richer than previous generations – we are not a lot happier.

The answer is surely the ultra-competitive nature of the dominant culture. The objective it offers is success compared with other people. But, if I succeed, someone else has to fail. So we have set ourselves up for a zero-sum game: however hard we all try to succeed, there can be no increase in overall happiness. An alternative, gentler culture offers a different aim, which can lead to a win–win outcome. It says that we should of course take care of ourselves, but we should get as much happiness as possible from contributing to the happiness of others. Competition, it argues, is valuable in the right context – and that context is competition between organisations. This has been a major engine of progress. But what we need between individuals is mostly cooperation, not competition. We want people who will act for the greater good – at work, at home and in the community. This produces better results for everyone. But above all, it makes life more enjoyable. For people long to relate well to each other – as an end in itself and not just as a means to something else.

It is a fallacy to think that reputation is a sufficient motivation for good behaviour. We need people with an inner desire to live good lives, even without reward. A happy society requires a lot of altruism, and so it needs a culture which supports our altruistic side. This gentler culture has always been around, in some form or other. It is there in all the great religions. Yet for many people these religions have lost their ability to convince. As religious belief has declined, a void has been created and into that void has rushed egotism, by default. We have told our young people that their chief duty is to themselves – to get on. What a terrible responsibility. No wonder that anxiety and depression are rising among the young. Instead, people need to get out of themselves – to escape the misery of self-absorption. So there has to be a new, secular ethic, based on human need and not divine command.

This basic secular ethics goes back to the many thousands of years ago. it said, I can be happy if everyone is happy. That Happiness Principle was, I believe, the most important idea of the modern age, with powerful implications for how we should live and how our policymakers should act on our behalf.

But now the Happiness Principle is making a comeback. There are many reasons for this. One is disillusion with the dominant culture and the stress which people experience at every level of society. But the other reasons are hugely positive. Now, for the first time, we have a science of happiness, which gives us real evidence on how to create a happier society.

In modern culture the selfish strand is now legitimized as never before. The chief goal on offer to young people is success relative to others – better grades, higher pay, more friends and greater fame. Increasingly, young people compete in every possible avenue of life. These trends in youth culture have been studied intensively by many. It was found that 31% of high school students expect to be famous one day, and an increasing percentage of college entrants think they are above average.

Similar narcissistic tendencies are exemplified in the candidate whom American electors knowingly chose as their president in 2016. As Donald Trump elegantly put it: "Show me someone without an ego and I'll show you a loser."

It is easy to see how the Me-First philosophy can take root, unless constantly challenged by a more unselfish view of the purpose of life. After all, we mostly live-in large cities in which no one has any automatic position. To do anything worthwhile you have to establish your position, and this requires an element of self-promotion.

In recent years, the rise in competitiveness has been made much worse by the advent of social media, which have encouraged self-advertisement and made more young people feel inadequate, anxious, depressed and "left out". In addition it has encouraged populism, which is an increasing challenge to a cohesive and loving society.

None of these trends will be easy to alter. But there are many hopeful trends too, both among citizens and among policymakers. The first is the spectacular fall in crime of all kinds in recent decades in most advanced countries. This new degree of gentleness is one of the least noticed and least well understood changes of our time, but it is deeply significant. My own guess is that it reflects the increased influence of women in our society: women commit fewer crimes than men do, and they tend to avoid men who are criminals. Moreover, most women care more about inner feelings than men do on average, while typically men have been more focused on externals.

At the same time there are new techniques of mind-training that enable each of us to improve our own inner mental state, with evidence-based ways in which all of us can become happier. And more and more people now use age-old eastern meditation to achieve greater contentment and calm of mind.

These techniques offer the prospect of a society where we take care, more than ever, of our own inner contentment and, especially, the happiness of others.

There are two opposing strands in human nature. One stresses the differences between my own needs and wants and those of others. The other stresses the similarities and what we all have in common. The relative strength of these two influences is determined to a large extent by the prevailing culture in which we live.

In 2015, the Dalai Lama was in London launching a new course, Exploring What Matters. At one point a woman came on to the stage. She was in pain and on crutches. For years she had been mostly bedridden and often depressed. But then she enrolled on the course. It changed her life. She realized that, by helping others like herself, she could give meaning to her life. The Dalai Lama embraced her. Later on, he was asked: "What is the most important thing for a happy life?" Without hesitation, he replied: "Warm heart."

In the end it is each of us as individuals who will determine the levels of happiness in our society – by everything we do. It is not easy to live well, but it is very much easier if you are in regular contact with people who are trying to do the same. In the west this used to happen when people went to church. They were reminded that there was something bigger than them. And they were inspired, uplifted and comforted. But today people are much less likely to define ethical behaviour as conforming to the will of God.

A new culture has to be based on individuals – what we each value and how we behave. We need to address the moral vacuum which has been left by the retreat of religion. Where egotism has replaced it, we need instead the generous philosophy embodied in the Happiness Principle. And to live well, we need to cultivate the positive side of our nature which can nourish us and help us reach out to others. For many people it will help to belong to a community of people who share our outlook. Together we can build a happier society and each of us will contribute in our own unique way.

CHAPTER FIFTEEN

HAPPINESS IN DIGITAL AGE

15.1 How to Be Happy in the Digital Age?

We live in the digital age.

Some bemoan the constant interruptions and endless internet surfing. Others celebrate the new-found freedom and capabilities.

How has the digital age impacted our happiness?

According to Amy Blankson, one of the world's leading experts in creating a movement to activate positive culture change, there are five modern strategies for balancing productivity and well-being in the digital era. She says: "In recent months, I have seen a growing number of posts about how bad technology is for us. Technology is blamed for social isolation, disconnection, and corruption. But I've also heard and seen how technology can be used for good — a means to connect, to share knowledge, to empower, even to save lives. So, which is it: Is technology good for us or bad for us? Does technology make us less happy or more happy? As Shakespeare once said, "There is nothing either good or bad, but thinking makes it so." Technology is a tool, a means to an end–and WE get to decide how that story ends."

One of Ammy's favorite examples of "happytech" is the Spire stone. The Spire stone is a small wearable that clips onto your bra strap or waistband to monitor your respiration and, in turn, lower blood pressure, reduce stress, and increase the flow of endorphins in your blood stream. The

Spire uses your breathing patterns to figure out when you are tense, calm, or focused, and provides gentle notifications to guide you when you need it most.

Sometimes tech is fun just for the sake of the endorphin rush and the dopamine boost. But at what point do those focus-altering diversions cause us to lose sight over what we really care about? At what point do diversions turn into fixations that are distracting?

Sometimes we become so engrossed in our diversions that we don't notice that they are no longer making us happy anymore. We get our legs going so fast that it actually takes us a moment to realize that we have run right off the Happiness Cliff.

According to the Law of Diminishing Returns, many diversions can actually be beneficial for our productivity and happiness—up to a point. Beyond that point, the diversion simply becomes a waste of time and eventually a time sucks, that becomes harmful to our productivity. To avoid falling off the happiness cliff, start your day by setting your intention for how you want to use your time. When you start to find yourself engrossed in a task, pause to ask if your technology use is helping you tune in (helping you to achieve your intention) or causing you to zone out. If your answer is the latter, then try to set a time limit for yourself to engage in that activity so that you don't get sucked in and lose focus.

The latest research from the field of positive psychology reveals that training our brains to be more positive is not only possible, it's actually essential to striving after your full potential. Why? Because when your brain is positive, it receives a boost of dopamine, which turns on the learning centres in the brain and makes you able to see more possibilities in your environment. In fact, a positive brain has been linked to: 37% higher sales, 3x more creativity, 31% higher productivity, 40% increase in likelihood of receiving a promotion, 23% decrease in symptoms of fatigue, 10x increase in the level of engagement at work, a 39% increase in the likelihood of living to age 94, and a 50% decrease in the risk of heart disease, according to research.

Some people work in offices, while others work from home, co-working spaces, or even coffee shops. We move fluidly in and out of a nebulous internet-based "cloud," with half of our belongings in the physical world and the other half in some virtual world. As the places that we live, work, and learn become increasingly blurred, we have to reconceptualize what happiness looks like in the modern era.

Here are a few strategies for achieving happiness in such an environment:

- **Clear out digital clutter to help eliminate distractions:** Unsubscribe from the unnecessary in your life. Use services like unroll.me to help you quickly manage your inbox and then turn off as many notifications as you can on your phone and computer to limit distraction.

- **Bring meaning back into the office:** Many individuals make the mistake of just trying to slog through work until they can get home to their "real life." However, research is revealing that investing in your personal space at work is beneficial to your happiness and health, and it can also increase your productivity by 15 percent only. However, individuals who connect to their work on a deeper level are more satisfied in general with their work and their lives. Whether you have a cubicle or a shared space, take the time to find little ways to connect your home life with your work life, whether through photos and art on the walls or something more transportable like a day planner. For an extra boost, bring a plant to work to lower stress, reduce blood pressure, and feel more attentive.

- **Set invisible boundaries to guard your focus and quality time:** The average smartphone user opens and closes their phone 150 times a day, as discussed earlier It's time to get this habit under control. Download the Break Free app to see just how often you open and close your phone every day, and then use a distraction-free timer to try to get your phone addiction and email checking under control.

Often, we think of happiness as a solo pursuit. We understand that happiness is a personal choice and is something that takes diligence and effort to cultivate. However, if we stop the conversation there, we are missing out on the bigger picture. Neuroscience has taught us that we are all wirelessly connected through mirror neurons in the brain, enabling our minds to transmit emotion at lightning speed across a room. Mirror neurons explain how yawns and smiles can ripple across a room in under two minutes, but also how stress and negativity can spread as well. Knowing this, we can't think about personal happiness in a vacuum. We each play an important role in shaping collective happiness, and we each have unique skills and talents to bring that vision to life. We should, therefore, encourage everyone to be a conscious innovator–this doesn't mean that you have to be an inventor or an engineer or a coder; rather it's an invitation for you to bring your experience and ideas into a broader conversation about where we as a society are heading. The Digital Era offers some amazing new ways to brainstorm and collaborate (through crowdsourcing, open sourcing, up-sourcing and more), so let's use these resources to solve problems that we have never been able to solve before on our own.

15.2 Happiness versus Distraction in the Digital Age

It's almost incomprehensible to think about the level of distraction our technology has given to us over the last 30 years. The average person checks his or her phone 150 times every day. If every distraction took only one minute, that would account for 2.5 hours of distraction every day. That's 912.5 hours a year, or roughly 38 days of straight distraction per year.

Technology has become a necessity in our personal and professional lives, but that does not mean we have to sacrifice our happiness, success, or attention to make room for it. Moving forward in the Digital Era, we must create habitats in our homes, our workplaces, and our communities that cultivate happiness in the digital age.

Our homes of the future will seamlessly integrate our digital and physical worlds. The idea is that by automating and aggregating tasks and information in our environment, we can increase safety, save energy, and reduce anxiety. This is true to a certain degree, but as you're upgrading your systems and running out to purchase bigger screens, keep in mind that the happiest places are the ones that are connected not with physical wires but with deep personal and emotional circuitry.

We can certainly carve out moments in our day to disconnect completely, but we can also use technology to raise engagement levels together in small, inexpensive ways. For example, if everyone in your household is already on social media, find a place like Instagram where you can share family's gratitude and connect them with a hashtag to track your submissions over time. Be intentional with your technology and apps, and make sure that your usage holds some sort of deeper meaning to you than a knee jerk reaction.

Besides making time and space for ourselves, we must also create a culture of connection. Social support is just as predictive of how long you will live as obesity, high blood pressure, and smoking. From schools to community centres to local government, find ways to turn the positive aspects of technology into a benefit for everyone. A new field called civic technology is aiming to create this culture in our neighborhoods by leveraging digital tools to serve the public good. Embrace these positive technology changes and pledge to be an active member in community decisions.

Technology is not a toxin that we need to flush out of our systems. Technology is a tool that we must learn to wield effectively and live with harmoniously. Yes, it can be easy to get distracted, but we must learn to use it as a necessity, not an escape. By implementing effective technologies in the places where we live and thrive, and making sure that those technologies are only being used positively and efficiently, we can ensure our undivided attention and happiness in the digital age as we look toward the future.

15.3 Seeking Happiness in A Digital World during Pandemic

The pursuit of happiness in a digital world can be elusive, but still remains an aspiration for many.

Happiness is a profoundly human and subjective experience; and yet, the scientific study of happiness has exploded. Psychologists are interested in understanding how people feel; economists want to know what people value; and neuroscientists seek to understand how the brain responds to positive rewards. Needless to say, happiness can be measured in a variety of ways as a result.

But if there's one thing that scientific studies agree on it's the importance of social networks. We are a highly social species. The recently released 2021 World Happiness Report, highlights how one major element in Covid-19 policy has been physical distancing, which poses a significant challenge for people's social connections. According to this report, people whose feelings of connectedness fell had decreased happiness.

One factor that was identified to predict well-being during the pandemic is the use of digital media to connect. At the outset of the pandemic, companies scrambled to look for IT equipment such as laptops and IT services like Zoom to get a grip of the new digital reality that came overnight. At the individual level, some studies show the increased use of digital communications to connect. Young people, in particular, increased their digital communications usage compared to other age groups. Similarly, 2020 data from a survey demonstrated that a majority of respondents found social media to be important to remain connected during the pandemic. At the same time, the lack of access to and skills using the internet i.e., households not having access to Wi-Fi, or older adults not used to navigating technology, may have exacerbated during the pandemic which puts these individuals at risk. Digital inequality may pose risks to well-being and happiness during the pandemic.

Digital Technologies and Happiness

These findings, in the context of the pandemic, underscore the ongoing discussion on digital technologies and happiness. In short, digital technology can be a double-edged sword. For some people, the internet can offer a safe, non-threatening place to nurture and maintain social connections. At the same time, increasing evidence about user surveillance and addictive technologies underlies the harmful effects of digital technologies on happiness.

In 2018, The Pew Research Centre queried 1.150 technology experts, scholars and health specialists on the following question: "Over the next decade, how will changes in digital life impact people's overall well-being physically and mentally? The result was that some 47% of respondents predicted that digital technologies bring positive effects for well-being; while 32% believed that people's well-being would be negatively impacted. The remaining 21% predicted little change in well-being compared to now. The 2018 Pew Research Center report provides a summary of both the positive and negative relations between digital technologies and well-being that emerged.

In this report, some of the areas that digital technologies were thought to have positive effects on well-being are in helping to connect people with each other, tapping into crucial intelligence in real-time to solve health, safety and scientific problems, and in empowering people to improve and reinvent their lives. In addition to the risk of digital addiction and surveillance, digital technologies were thought to negatively impact people's cognitive capabilities in regards to their capacity for analytical thinking, memory, focus and creativity. Distrust and divisiveness could be amplified, and that information overload and poor interface design could cause an increase in stress, anxiety and sleeplessness.

Do digital technologies make us happier or not?

It is evident that technology can have both positive and negative impacts on the subjective well-being of individuals. On the other hand, digital technologies provide us with tools. And it is up to us to decide how to use them appropriately. Indeed, we have a responsibility to leverage digital technologies to mitigate potential negative impacts to well-being.

Technology-Free Sources of Happiness

In the case of Action for Happiness-a movement committed to building a happier and more caring society, the move online from in-person live events and local groups brought some larger-than-expected benefits. "We were able to reach people who are more remote, isolated or socially-anxious; and bring people from different backgrounds/countries together in a same digital space," according to Dr. Mark Williamson, CEO of Action for Happiness.

And yet, Williamson reminds us that many of the sources of happiness are technology-free.

In his article, he points to three simple non-digital actions that have been proven to make us happier:

(i) Get active outdoors - walk through the park, get off the bus a stop early or go for a "walking meeting" with a colleague.

(ii) Take a breathing space - regularly stop and take 5 minutes to just breathe and be in the moment - notice how you're feeling and what's going on around you

(iii) **Make someone else happy** - do random acts of kindness, offer to help, give away your change, pay a compliment or tell someone how much they mean to you.

15.4 Are Smartphones making People Sad?

Mobile phones have become so integral to the lives of such a large share of humanity that it's easy to lose sight of the fact that they were far from commonplace in any part of the world just 20 years ago — and internet-enabled smartphones have become prevalent in many regions in an even shorter time. A staggering 82% of adults worldwide personally had a mobile phone in 2016, according to Gallup's global surveys representing more than 99% of the world's population.

The breakneck speed with which mobile phones and other mobile IT devices have swept across the planet is a testament to their usefulness and versatility. They now influence billions of lives, changing the way people live and work, giving people access to vast social networks and providing new ways to deliver essential information and services. But the remarkable ascent of mobile phones raises an important question that can't be addressed simply by listing their various uses: Do they actually make their owners happier?

New psychological research in 2018 from the University of Virginia has found that smartphones are having a chilling effect on human relationships.

Face-to-face interactions make people happy. Your smartphone is probably getting in the way of that age-old social interaction, the researchers found.

Working with partners at the University of British Columbia, a psychology post-doctoral student used the dinner table as his testing ground.

The team randomly selected 304 diners in a British Columbia café, with an average age of 30, to enter one of two conditions. In the first, they were asked to keep their phones on the table. In the second, they were asked to put their phones away.

Rather than tell them the study was testing the effects of smartphone use during meals, the participants were told they were part of a study about people's experience dining out with friends.

"To manipulate the phone use, we told one, randomly assigned group to keep their phones out on the table, under the pretext that halfway through them having food, we would be sending them one question over text message,"

In the other condition, the participants were told that researchers would give them a paper survey midway, so they would not need their phones.

After the meals, each group was given a longer questionnaire asking how they enjoyed the food, the conversation and the experience. Participants also reported how much they used their smartphones.

Diners whose phones were tucked away, reported having had a happier experience than those whose devices were on the dining table. In essence, distractions by smartphones reduced the enjoyment of people sitting together.

They found a pretty substantial effect on how distracted people felt, with people in the phone condition feeling substantially more distracted.. The effect was pretty significant.

Smartphones have both positive and negative effects. Maybe you are texting somebody and you feel connected to them, but at the same time you feel distracted and you feel less connected to the people around you.

How is this changing fundamental human behaviors that have been central to human society and human well-being throughout history.

Similarly sharing food is a traditional way of bonding with others.

When you go on a date, you usually have some food, or maybe a drink, at a table, what is really important about this study is that it shows that these social-connecting devices might actually potentially disconnect us from people in our immediate social environment and that might have some negative consequences for our well-being.

This research is important because today's younger users can barely remember a time when they didn't have a smartphone in the palms of their hands.

Today, smartphone users send emails, texts, Snaps, Tweets and Facebook posts anytime they want, from almost everywhere they go, and that is dangerous.

Going forward, designers should be thinking about how the devices can be less distracting and allow human well-being to flourish.

The researcher said most companies like Facebook, say they are interested in well-being. "But the bottom line is that they want to grab as much attention as possible from users," he said.

"That is where their money comes from. The more frequently you go to Facebook, the better for them."

This global analysis suggests that having a mobile phone alone (the absence of internet access) provides a modest boost with regard to people's daily emotional experiences. However, it does not appear to influence people's overall ratings of their own lives. Given the near-universal rates of mobile penetration in many countries, basic mobile access may be something that is taken for granted — and thus not a consideration in people's life evaluations, even if its absence would be greatly disruptive.

The results suggest that when mobile access is complemented by internet access, the well-being potential of information technologies is more fully realized, and clearly reflected in both life evaluations and emotional affect metrics. This is particularly the case in regions such as sub-Saharan Africa and South Asia, where mobile information technologies have been increasingly used to deliver vital information and services in disadvantaged rural areas. Given the innumerable ways the internet has expanded human capabilities, it is perhaps no surprise that the most substantial well-being gains are associated with online access. Mobile devices improve happiness largely by bringing that access to so many around the world who would otherwise not have it.

15.5 Quitting this bad habit can improve your happiness and productivity

Not getting a good night's rest is a surefire way to sabotage your productivity, mood and overall well-being. Yet 63 percent of Americans keep their phones close to bed, so it's the last thing they look at before they got to sleep and the first thing they check when they wake up, according to Gallup.

A new scientific study shows that simply leaving your smartphone outside of the bedroom at night can improve your happiness, mental well-being and quality of life in just a week's time.

"There is a deep resistance from people to put their phones away and this study shows how deeply ingrained technology is in our lives," the study's co-author Nicola Hughes tells CNBC Make It. "We wanted to look at what the consequence of no longer being connected and available to work all the time."

University of East London psychology senior lecturer Jolanta Burke and Hughes, a master's candidate at the time, delved into the relationship people have with their phones on a daily basis in their study, "Sleeping with the frenemy: How restricting 'bedroom use' of smartphones impacts happiness and wellbeing," published in the "Computers in Human Behavior" journal in March this year.

Hughes tells 'Make It' that the experiment was based on her own experience: up until four years ago, she had a Blackberry cellphone which she mainly used for emails, texts and "well, phone calls." As everyone around her got iPhones and other advanced smartphones, she noticed they also became hooked to their phones.

"Now, you look down at your phone, you open Instagram, which then leads to an article and suddenly 40 minutes have gone by," Hughes says. "You're getting information that you didn't seek out and going down mental and emotional journeys that you did not choose or intend to go down."

In the study, Hughes and Burke split their 95 participants — a majority of them millennials — into two groups: a control group which could use their smartphones as usual and an experimental group which was not allowed to use their phone in their bedroom for one week.

Hughes says the initial sample size group was made of 200 people, but once she shared the requirements of the experiment, people dropped out. She noted this may have been a sign of how attached people can be to their phones.

The study concluded that those who didn't use their phones in their bedrooms showed a statistically significant increase happiness and overall quality of life.

To Hughes' surprise, the study also found that the week-long experiment made people less likely to be addicted to their phones.

These **tips** will help you overcome work stress to get some sleep:

"If you break that cycle, if you don't check the phone at night or morning, you actually are less likely to show addictive behaviors in other ways of your life as well," Hughes says.

The participants also reported improved personal relationships, quality of sleep, well-being and reduced anxiety. With their phones out of reach, they also had more time on their hands.

The researchers want to make it clear, though, that they aren't completely demonizing the use of your smartphones: "Since social connectedness and feeling like part of a community have been shown to correlate with positive affect and subjective well-being, it's evident that smartphones and social media platforms can bring about positive effects for users, if used in community building and enhancing ways," they wrote in the paper.

For those looking to try this experiment on their own, Hughes says to challenge yourself for a week to keep your phone out of your bedroom.

"Think about it: do you really need to check your email right now? Do you need to be on social media first thing in the morning?" Hughes says.

You can also take a few pointers from some of today's top leaders: billionaire media mogul Arianna Huffington takes a hot bath, literally tucks her phone into bed every night and reads a physical book. Like Huffington, Microsoft co-founder Bill Gates also dedicates an hour to reading before bed.

"Keep the bed a tech-free place. Read a book, meditate, talk to your partner," Hughes says. "You don't need to be constantly contacting people."

CHAPTER SIXTEEN

HAPPINESS IS CONTAGIOUS

16.1 Is Happiness Contagious?

A Facebook friend sent me this post:

Happiness does the opposite of standard arithmetical logic. More you share it with other people, the more it gets multiplied: a simple (and obvious) statement but a strong one to take note of. So, spread happiness and multiply your happiness.

Imagine a birds-eye view of a party: "You may see some people in quiet corners talking one-on-one. Others would be at the centre of the room having conversations with lots of people. According to the study findings, those in the centre would be among the happiest.

We think the reason why is because those in the centre are more susceptible to the waves of happiness that spread throughout the network. Of course, it's true that emotions can be fleeting; happiness is elusive and sometimes it's situational. For these reasons, emotional states are difficult to measure, says a professor of psychology at the University of Maryland. "There are lots of challenges."

Dr. Jonah Berger and Dr. Katherine Milkman from the University of Pennsylvania examined 7,000 articles from the New York Times. The Drs found that positive articles were shared more often than negative ones. "Stories about newcomers falling in love with New York City," wrote Dr. Berger, were more likely to be e-mailed than "pieces that detailed things like the death of a popular zookeeper." Similar studies of online behavior show that we're more likely to use words like "happy, love, nice and sweet" online than "worried, hurt, sad and ugly."

Besides your inner circle, you should take the reins yourself and share your happiness with the world. You want to give back, be supportive, boost morale, or creating a piece of content for your brand. The reason? It's been found that when you share positive experiences, it heightens the impact of that moment because it allows you to re-live and re-savour the experience. That may sound difficult to do, but it's really not that difficult to make your happiness go viral if you do the following.

Activate The Hidden 31

Shawn Achor is New York Times best-selling author of "The Happiness Advantage" and "Before Happiness." Michelle Gielan is an expert on the science of positive communication.

Achor and Gielan suggest in Live Happy magazine that you can get optimism to go viral by activating the "Hidden 31." Achor and Gielan came up with this name after a survey in Training magazine that found 31 percent of respondents stated that they are "positive but not expressive of it at work."

This was expressed in these three-steps:

- Identify,
- Acknowledge, and
- Activate.

"While this strategy works well for companies and business teams, it works at the family dinner table, too. Customers can also become "enthusiasts," spreading the word about the product or service they appreciate. And sports teams can recruit and develop the Hidden 31, thereby tipping balances to winning mindsets," writes Achor and Gielan.

"If you identify, acknowledge and activate the Hidden 31 by giving people clear ways to express their positive mindsets, you can inspire optimism and happiness to go viral. And that makes it much easier for us all to live happy."

Activate High-Arousal Emotions

"If your content activates a high-arousal emotion, you're set. The likelihood of people sharing and talking about your content will increase drastically," writes Derek Halpern of Social Triggers. This idea was already found to be true through Jonah Berger's research, as well as the experiences of Halpern.

Halpern explains that "a high arousal emotion can be either positive or negative (both types work)," such as awe, anger, anxiety, fear, joy, lust, and of course, surprise.

"But this is where things get a little more complicated. While it's simple to activate these emotions, it's not easy. You've got to think about which emotion you want to target, and hit it perfectly."

Since we're currently focused on happiness here, let's go over the positive high-arousal emotions.

- Awe.
- Joy.
- Lust.
- Surprise.

16.2 Research on Contagion of Happiness

According to research reported from Harvard Medical School and the University of California, San Diego, it suggests that happiness is influenced not only by the people you know, but by the people they know.

The study showed that happiness spreads through social networks, sort of like a virus, meaning that your happiness could influence the happiness of someone you've never even met.

Sadness spreads too, but much less efficiently.

The researchers have known for a long time that there is a direct relationship between one person's happiness and another's,. But this study shows that indirect relationships also affect happiness. They found a statistical relationship not just between your happiness and your friends' happiness, but between your happiness and your friends' friends' friends' happiness.

Three Degrees of Separation

These researchers have been studying social networks for several years, using data from the ongoing Framingham Heart Study. Last year they reported that obesity seems to spread through social groups, so that your chances of becoming overweight are greater when your friends and their friends gain weight.

A related study, published earlier this year, found that smokers were more likely to give up cigarettes when their family, friends, and other social contacts stopped smoking

Their latest research, published online, was designed to determine whether happiness spreads through social networks in a similar way.

The researchers were able to recreate the social networks of 4,739 Framingham participants whose happiness was measured from 1983 to 2003. A standard test for assessing happiness was used, which included questions like "I felt hopeful about the future," and "I was happy."

Important family changes for each participant -- such as a birth, death, marriage, or divorce -- were also recorded. The participants were also asked to name family members, close friends, co-workers, and neighbors.

Because many of these contacts were also study participants, the researchers were able to identify more than 50,000 social and family ties and analyze the spread of happiness through the group.

Happy Friends make you Happy

They concluded that the happiness of an immediate social contact increased an individual's chances of becoming happy by 15%.

The happiness of a second-degree contact, such as the spouse of a friend, increases the likeliness of becoming happy by 10%, and the happiness of a third-degree contact -- or the friend of a friend of a friend -- increases the likelihood of becoming happy by 6%.

The association was not seen in fourth-degree contacts (the friends of friends of friends of friends).

Having more friends also increased happiness, but having friends who were happy was a much bigger influence on happiness.

These findings do not mean that you should avoid unhappy people, but that you should make an effort whenever you can to spread happiness.

We need to think of happiness as a collective phenomenon. If we come home in a bad mood, we may be missing an opportunity to make not just our wives and children happy, but their friends too.

As mentioned above, according to another research conducted at the University of Pennsylvania, making yourself and those around you happy is not only possible, but really quite easy. All you have to do, quite literally, is spread the word.

Titled 'What Makes Online Content Viral?', the study tracked the circulation of almost 7000 articles from the New York Times over a three-month period and found that positive articles were shared more often than negative ones.

Similar studies of online behaviour also suggest we're more likely to use words like "happy, love, nice and sweet" online than "worried, hurt, sad and ugly" and that we share our positive daily experiences 70% of the time.

These studies form part of a veritable swathe of research into the way moods and emotions spread between people linked through online social networks. According to a two-decade long study conducted by researchers at University of California, San Diego, happiness is not only highly contagious but online communities may actually "magnify the intensity of global emotional synchrony".

In research carried out at Tübingen University, scientists who tracked the emotional responses of Facebook users in Germany and the US found that reading other people's positive posts triggered happiness in 64% of people.

Think of it this way: Your good news positively influences your friends, who in their turn positively influence their friends. With one positive post you can brighten up the day of someone you have never met.

On the flip side, however, negative emotions spread through networks too. In an online social network study in the US using data from millions of Facebook users, rainfall was found to negatively affect the emotional content of people's status updates, and this influenced the negativity of posts made by friends in other cities who were not experiencing rainfall. Negativity, it showed, begets negativity.

Sharing your positive news also, research suggests, has direct perks for you. Communicating a positive experience you have had with another person heightens the impact of the positive experience itself because you get to re-live and re-savour the experience.

When researchers from four universities across the United States partnered with e-harmony they found that sharing positive news between partners boosted happiness and life satisfaction. As Virginia Wolf so eloquently states: "Pleasure has no relish unless we share it".

Understanding the impact good – and bad – news can have on our moods is important for many reasons. In the midst of a 24/7 news cycle dominated by stories about violence, war, natural disasters and corruption – think of the old media adage "if it bleeds, it leads" – it is little wonder people report depression and worry after watching nightly news bulletins.

The reaffirming aspect of this research is that it shows we want to hear good news and we are using social media as a medium to create and disseminate it.

Further evidence for this desire for uplifting news can be found in the burgeoning of websites such as Positive News, which has become the world's first crowdfunded global media cooperative. The paper is now owned by 1526 readers, journalists and supporters.

Another example is the Real-Life Heroes series by KST TV on YouTube, along with sites including Good News Network, Joy News Network, Daily Good, HuffPost Good news, Oh My Goodness, Positive News, Sunny Skyz and Gimundo.

So, how can you go about sharing good news? You can visit the sites above and share their positive stories with others. You can commit yourself to writing more positive posts on Facebook, Twitter, Instagram and sharing more good news in person. You can start your own way to share and spread positive news.

Sharing your good news might seem like a small gesture but it can have a big effect and provide people with a life raft in the sea of negativity that is often mainstream media. Isn't it time we steered our own boat?

So what does bring us happiness? Research shows that our relationships with others, rather than what we see in the mirror or find in our wallets, may be what matter most. It's a concept that held true for our cave–dwelling ancestors, who formed elaborate social structures to increase their odds of survival. These days, our connections are more about building a family, gossiping in the living room, and adding to our list of Facebook friends than outsmarting saber–toothed tigers. But results of the long–running Grant Study of Adult Development suggest that the emotional benefits of connectedness remain. These researchers have found, for instance, that only the capacity for loving relationships predicted life satisfaction in older men.

In turn, being happy can have its own advantages. More than three decades ago, Grant Study data showed that good mental health in men slowed the deterioration of their physical health, even after adjusting for genetics, obesity, and tobacco and alcohol use. Although it has been found that after age 50 vascular risk factors such as smoking, elevated diastolic blood pressure, diabetes, obesity, and alcohol abuse appear to play a far greater role than mental health in subsequent health and longevity, other research still supports a link to mental health. Research in Brigham and Women's Hospital, found a strong correlation between happiness and good health, both in individuals and within communities.

And there's more good news: Happiness may be limitless. Just as someone's bad mood can rub off on you, positivity, too, may spread, says a researcher who has worked on the contagion of emotions within the larger context of social networks. His findings have shown that happiness may be a collective phenomenon: Having a happy friend who lives within a mile of you, for example, appears to increase the probability that you will be happy as well. In collaboration with the University of California at San Diego, another researcher found similar effects for the spread of happiness between next–door neighbors, siblings that live nearby, and spouses—so that good feelings continue to move from person to person, even when there's no longer a direct connection to the original Pollyanna.

"Just as some diseases are contagious, we found that many emotions can pulse through social networks. And unlike the flu, happiness is a gift you can actually enjoy," asserts a researcher.

Happiness isn't just one big event but the accrual of smaller, incremental steps, such as feeling gratitude and helping others. Rather than asking how we can get happier, we should be asking how we can increase happiness all around us. When you make positive changes in your own life, those effects ripple out from you and you can find yourself surrounded by the very thing you fostered.

Happiness, in other words, is not merely a function of individual experience or individual choice but is also a property of groups of people. Indeed, changes in individual happiness can ripple through social networks, giving rise to clusters of happy and unhappy individuals. These results are even more remarkable considering that happiness requires close physical proximity to spread and that the effect decays over time.

No one knows exactly how happiness spreads. Happy people might share their good fortune (for example, by being pragmatically helpful or financially generous to others), or behave in different ways toward others (for example, by being nicer or less hostile), or merely exude an emotion that is genuinely contagious (albeit over a longer time frame than previous psychological work has indicated). Another possibility is that being surrounded by happy individuals has beneficial effects on the interaction between our psychological processes and our nervous and immune systems.

The findings suggest that policies that increase the happiness of one person might have 'cascade' effects on others, thereby enhancing the efficacy and cost effectiveness of the intervention. For example, illness is a potential source of unhappiness for patients and for those individuals surrounding the patient. Providing better care for those who are sick might not only improve their happiness, but also the happiness of numerous others, thereby further vindicating the benefits of medical care or health promotion.

16.3 Is Generosity linked with Happiness and is it Contagious?

Generosity appears to have especially strong associations with psychological health and well-being. For example, a meta-analysis of studies of older adults found that those who volunteered, reported greater quality of life; another study found that frequent helpers reported feeling greater vitality and self-esteem (but only if they chose to help of their own accord).

Other studies have shown a link between generosity and happiness. Some studies have found that people are happier when spending money on others than on themselves, and this happiness motivates them to be generous in the future. And even small acts of kindness, like picking up something someone else has dropped, make people feel happy. Generosity is also associated with benefits in the workplace, such as reducing the likelihood of job burnout, and in relationships, where it is associated with more contentment and longer-lasting romantic relationships.

Individual Factors Linked to Generosity

There are several intrapersonal factors that can influence generosity. Feelings of empathy, compassion, and other emotions can motivate us to help others. Certain personality traits, such as humility and agreeableness, are associated with increased generosity, and a person's tendency to engage in prosocial behavior may be considered a personality trait in itself. A person's values, morals, and sense of identity can also modify how willingly they engage in generous acts. In addition, research suggests that gender and religion may influence generosity, although the findings from different studies have sometimes shown conflicting or nuanced results.

Social and Cultural Drivers

A host of social and cultural factors also influence generosity. Many studies suggest that people often act generously out of an expectation that their generosity will be reciprocated or because they feel it will help their reputation. A person's generosity is also influenced by cultural norms, such as standards of fairness. Strong social networks may also influence generosity. For example, people with more friends engage in more volunteering, charitable giving, and blood donations. What's more, **generosity is contagious**; it can propagate within social networks and workplaces.

16.4 Emotional contagion through social networks, like Facebook

Emotional states can be transferred to others via emotional contagion, leading them to experience the same emotions as those around them. Emotional contagion is well established in laboratory experiments, in which people transfer positive and negative moods and emotions to others. Similarly, data from a large, real-world social network collected over a 20-year period suggests that longer-lasting moods (e.g., depression, happiness) can be transferred through networks as well.

The interpretation of this network effect as contagion of mood has come under scrutiny due to the study's correlational nature, including concerns over misspecification of contextual variables or failure to account for shared experiences, raising important questions regarding contagion processes in networks. An experimental approach can address this scrutiny directly; however, methods used in controlled experiments have been criticized for examining emotions after social interactions. Interacting with a happy person is pleasant (and an unhappy person, unpleasant). As such, contagion may result from experiencing an interaction rather than exposure to a partner's emotion. Evidence that positive and negative moods are correlated in networks suggests that this is possible, but the causal question of whether contagion processes occur for emotions in massive social networks remains elusive in the absence of experimental evidence. Further, others have suggested that in online social networks, exposure to the happiness of others may sometimes be depressing to us, producing an "alone together" social comparison effect.

Some studies have laid the groundwork for testing these processes via Facebook, the largest online social network. This research demonstrated that (i) emotional contagion occurs via text-based computer-mediated communication; (ii) contagion of psychological and physiological qualities has been suggested based on correlational data for social networks generally; and (iii) people's emotional expressions on Facebook predict friends' emotional expressions, even days later (although some shared experiences may in fact last several days).

On Facebook, people frequently express emotions, which are later seen by their friends via Facebook's "News Feed" product . Because people's friends frequently produce much more content than one person can view, the News Feed filters posts, stories, and activities undertaken by friends. News Feed is the primary manner by which people see content that friends share. Which content is shown or omitted in the News Feed is determined via a ranking algorithm that Facebook continually develops and tests in the interest of showing viewers the content they will find most relevant and engaging.

An experiment manipulated the extent to which people (N = 689,003) were exposed to emotional expressions in their News Feed. This tested whether exposure to emotions led people to change their own posting behaviors, in particular whether exposure to emotional content led people to post content that was consistent with the exposure—thereby testing whether exposure to verbal affective expressions leads to similar verbal expressions, a form of emotional contagion. Two parallel experiments were conducted for positive and negative emotion: One in which exposure to friends' positive emotional content in their News Feed was reduced, and one in which exposure to negative emotional content in their News Feed was reduced. In these conditions, when a person loaded their News Feed, posts that contained emotional content of the relevant emotional valence, each emotional post had between a 10% and 90% chance (based on their User ID) of being omitted from their News Feed for that specific viewing. It is important to note that this content was always available by viewing a friend's content directly by going to that friend's "wall" or "timeline," rather than via the News Feed. Further, the omitted content may have appeared on prior or subsequent views of the News Feed. Finally, the experiment did not affect any direct messages sent from one user to another.

The experiments took place for one week (January 11–18, 2012). Participants were randomly selected based on their User ID, resulting in a total of ~155,000 participants per condition who posted at least one status update during the experimental period.

For each experiment, two dependent variables were examined pertaining to emotionality expressed in people's own status updates: the percentage of all words produced by a given person that was either positive or negative during the experimental period. In total, over 3 million posts were analyzed, containing over 122 million words, 4 million of which were positive (3.6%) and 1.8 million negative (1.6%).

If affective states are contagious via verbal expressions on Facebook (our operationalization of emotional contagion), people in the positivity-reduced condition should be less positive compared with their control, and people in the negativity-reduced condition should be less negative. As a secondary measure, we tested for cross-emotional contagion in which the opposite emotion should be inversely affected: People in the positivity-reduced condition should express increased negativity, whereas people in the negativity-reduced condition should express increased positivity. Emotional expression was modeled, on a per-person basis, as the percentage of words produced by that person during the experimental period that were either positive or negative.

As such, direct examination of the frequency of positive and negative words would be inappropriate: It would be confounded with the change in overall words produced. To test their hypothesis regarding emotional contagion, they conducted weighted linear regressions, predicting the percentage of words that were positive or negative from a dummy code for condition (experimental versus control), weighted by the likelihood of that person having an emotional post omitted from their News Feed on a given viewing, such that people who had more content omitted were given higher weight in the regression.

The results showed emotional contagion. For people who had positive content reduced in their News Feed, a larger percentage of words in people's status updates were negative and a smaller percentage were positive. When negativity was reduced, the opposite pattern occurred. These results suggest that the emotions expressed by friends, via online social networks, influence our own moods, constituting, to our knowledge, the first experimental evidence for massive-scale emotional contagion via social networks, and providing support for previously contested claims that emotions spread via contagion through a network.

CHAPTER SEVENTEEN

HAPPINESS MOLECULES

17.1 Happiness Hormones

Hormones are chemicals produced by different glands across your body. They travel through the bloodstream, acting as messengers and playing a part in many bodily processes.

Certain hormones are known to help promote positive feelings, including happiness and pleasure.

These “happy hormones” include:

(i) Dopamine

Also known as the “feel-good” hormone, dopamine is a hormone and neurotransmitter that’s an important part of your brain’s reward system. Dopamine is associated with pleasurable sensations, along with learning, memory, motor system function, and more. Nearly all pleasurable experiences — from eating a good meal to having sex — involve the release of dopamine.

That release is part of what makes some things addicting, such as: (i) drugs, (ii) gambling, and (iii) shopping etc.

Experts evaluate something’s potential to cause addiction by looking at the speed, intensity, and reliability of the dopamine release it causes in the brain. It doesn’t take long for a person’s brain to associate certain behaviours or substances with a rush of dopamine.

Over time, a person's dopamine system may be less reactive to the substance or activity that used to cause a big rush. For example, someone might need to consume more of a drug to achieve the same effects that a smaller amount used to provide.

Dopamine (DA) is a catecholamine neurotransmitter, biogenic amine and an adreno-medullary hormone. It is the principal neurotransmitter of several pathways in the Central Nervous System (CNS) starting in the midbrain and significantly involved in motivation, learning, and motor activity, any disturbances of which have been associated with several disorders, including Parkinson's disease and schizophrenia. Dopamine is catecholamine secreted from the medulla of adrenal glands. It belongs to the phenethylamine family and functions as both a hormone and neurotransmitter in several parts of the body. Normal plasma dopamine levels are very low, i.e., 0.13nmol/L. Its effect as a catecholamine includes renal and mesenteric vasodilatation, vasoconstriction of other parts of the body. Dopamine has positive inotropic effects on the heart mediated via β_1 receptors. It causes an increase in systolic Blood Pressure and do not affect Diastolic Blood Pressure significantly. In the proximal tubules, it inhibits the sodium-potassium pump and causes natriuresis. Also, highly intervened for the treatment of traumatic and cardiogenic shock.

(ii) Serotonin

This hormone (and neurotransmitter) helps regulate your mood as well as your sleep, appetite, digestion, learning ability, and memory.

Dopamine and serotonin are both neurotransmitters. Neurotransmitters are chemical messengers used by the nervous system that regulate countless functions and processes in your body, from sleep to metabolism.

While dopamine and serotonin affect many of the same things, they do so in slightly different ways.

Also known as 5-hydroxytryptamine (5-HT), serotonin is a complex neurotransmitter. It is distributed in various body tissues like CNS, GI tract etc. and known as enter-amine due to its increased concentration in the intestine. It is a derivative of the branched- chain amino acid, tryptophan and is metabolized to 5-Hydroxyl Indole Acetic Acid (5-HIAA). It performs several functions in the body, that is, it causes generalized vasoconstriction, bronchoconstriction, increases gastric secretions and motility, causes platelet aggregation, is anti- diuretic in nature, important component of the endogenous analgesic system, acts as anorectic agent, suppresses sleep and is a strong anti- depressant.

(iii) Oxytocin

Often called the "love hormone," oxytocin is essential for childbirth, breastfeeding, and strong parent-child bonding. This hormone can also help promote trust, empathy, and bonding in relationships, and oxytocin levels generally increase with physical affection like kissing, cuddling, and sex. Oxytocin is referred to as the "bonding molecule" or "hug hormone" because its levels go high during feeding the baby, skin- skin contact, intercourse, orgasm, and hugging. It is also a hormone involved in increasing the trust and loyalty as per recent studies and is known to cause romantic attachment. In other words, it is known to facilitate social interaction and is also linked with positive social behaviour. Such a significant correlation between social bonding and satisfaction, then indeed brought about by the effects of oxytocin can in turn lead to a happier life. It has been recently showed that Oxytocin causes a huge scale of physiological and behavioural effects controlled via certain receptors in the brain, mainly, social, sexual and maternal behaviours. Being associated with positive social behaviours and known to increase the relationship or bonding with others, it is assumed that the hormone brings about happiness. Because relationships have a strong impact on life satisfaction and as there is a strong association between happiness and relationships; oxytocin can be a method of producing happiness by stimulating or strengthening social relations. Low levels of oxytocin is associated with depression, poor communication, increased fear and anxiety, sleep disturbances, irritability and cravings for sugar. Gifting can increase the release of the hormone established by increasing the bonding between the receiver and giver.

Oxytocin is an oligo-peptide hormone with 9 amino acids and is released from the neurohypophysis. It is synthesized mainly in the paraventricular nucleus and partly in the supra-optic nucleus of hypothalamus and is released into the posterior pituitary via the hypothalamo- hypophyseal tract. It is released in response to 2 stimuli, suckling during breast feeding, and dilatation of the cervix during parturition.1 It is thus an important hormone in the regulation of uterine spasms and milk ejection.

(iv) Endorphins

Endorphins are your body's natural pain reliever, which your body produces in response to stress or discomfort. Endorphin levels also tend to increase when you engage in reward-producing activities, such as eating, working out, or having sex.

Endorphins or endogenous morphine are opioid neuropeptides, are naturally produced in the body. Endorphins function not only as neurotransmitters but also as peptide hormone. It is known to be derived from repeated cleavage of its precursor molecule, pro-opiomelanocortin (POMC) polypeptide, synthesized in the pituitary gland and in some amounts by the immune system of the body . There are 3 functional sub-types based on the process of cleavage named alpha-endorphins, beta-endorphins and gamma-endorphins. They are known to be an endogenous analgesic that blocks the perception of pain, involved in pleasure sensations.

Endorphins or "pain-killing molecules" or "pain relievers" have been found to be linked with pleasure states like emotions brought about by love, laughter, sex, and even appetite. Even though functions mainly in blocking pain, they are also a reason for our pleasure feelings and it is for this reason is one of the 4 major hormones of happiness or pleasure hormones. It's believed that the feelings of pleasure persists to make us realize at what time we have had that sort of a good experience and also to boost us to go behind that experience so that pleasure associated with the older one can be felt. Also, happiness expressed as laughter or even the expectation of something funny is known to cause the further release of these chemicals. Clinically, endorphins have been associated with conditions of autism, depression, and depersonalization disorder and physiologically known to be related with activities like laughter and vigorous aerobic exercise

(v) Estrogens

Estrogens are certain ovarian steroid hormones secreted from the granulosa cells of follicles of ovary, corpus luteum and placenta. It is also indirectly released from adrenal glands as the androgens are converted to estrogen by the enzyme aromatase. The naturally synthesized estrogens include 17β-estradiol, estrone and estriol, the former being 15 and 80 times potent than the respective latter ones. It is mainly synthesized from cholesterol and its mechanism of action is through transcription of mRNAs. The major action of estrogens includes, promotion of growth of all components of female reproductive system including ovary and ovarian follicles, stimulation of smooth muscle contraction in fallopian tube, increases uterine size, its blood flow, causes proliferation of uterine endometrium etc. Under the presence of estrogen, cervical mucous becomes abundant, watery and clear and male female secondary sexual characters develop. Estrogen stimulates libido by acting on the limbic system neurons and can also help in bone growth. On kidneys it regulates salt and water retention and activates Renin-Angiotensin- Aldosterone system. Estrogen also acts as a cholesterol lowering agent, promotes more fluid secretion from sebaceous gland and thus prevents acne.

Role of Estrogens in Happiness

Estrogen is known to be a happy hormone due to its indirect effect in stimulating the formation of serotonin. This can protect the body from conditions of irritability and anxiety, thereby keeping the mood constant. it is also known to cause increased secretion of endorphins both of which are chemical messengers linked with positive states of mood. Estrogens can cause mood disruptions in women, failure of synthesis or low levels of which can result in mood swings, anxiety and depression. High levels of estrogen can also be dangerous. Estrogen has also a role in regulating the levels of hormones like serotonin, endorphins and nor-epinephrine by causing a decline in the level of the enzyme mono-oxidase that deactivates these hormones hence referred to as „positive mood hormone".

(vi) Progesterone

Progesterone is a C-21 steroid hormone secreted by corpus luteum and placenta during pregnancy period. A small amount is also released from adrenal cortex and testes. The normal plasma levels of the hormone vary with different phases of the female cycle, although reaches its peak in the luteal phase, that is, 18ng/ ml. Progesterone has both reproductive and non-m reproductive actions on the body. Reproductive actions are primarily focused on the reproductive organs mainly uterus, endo- cervix, vagina, fallopian tubes and breasts. Other systemic actions are on kidney, CNS, Respiratory system, fat metabolism and thermo-genic effects.

Role of Progesterone in Happiness

Progesterone alters the secretion of several neurotransmitters in the brain affecting appetite and sleep. It causes the effect of somnolence, that is helps to sleep well and thereby prevents anxiety, feelings of irritability and mood swings. This can help in maintenance of a peaceful or calm state of mind. Progesterone due to its Valium-like effect of its metabolite named allopregnanolone (ALLO), is known to soothe the mood. ALLO interacts directly with the receptors of GABA promotes sleep. Progesterone also has a control on the DAO enzyme and therefore relieves the symptoms of anxiety in the condition of histamine intolerance. Progesterone also seems to activate the activity of amygdala, the chief alert system of the brain.

(vii) Endo-Cannabinoids

Endocannabinoids (ECs) are defined as the endogenous ligands of cannabinoid receptors (CB1 and CB2) and a growing body of evidence has emerged on the role of the endocannabinoid system (ECS) in the regulation of several physiological conditions and numerous conditions. These are certain lipid metabolites and has both juxtacrine and paracrine roles in intercellular communications. These are self- produced cannabis and works on the CB-1 and CB-2 receptors of the cannabinoid system and Anandamide is the most known among them.2The endocannabinoid system is another protective system of the body that regulates many physiological functions. This includes endocannabinoids, cannabinoid receptors, and enzymes that synthesize and degrade endocannabinoids.

Role of Endocannabinoids in Happiness

Cannabis compounds are actually called as "bliss molecules" that enhances the subjective concept of well-being by activating the endocannabinoid system (ECS), and modulates almost all of the response to stress, reward, and also the interactions between them. There are much evidences that endocannabinoids control mood, emotion, memory, motivation, perception of pleasure, metabolism, and appetite and so on. The association between cannabinoids and different states of emotion has empirically and scientifically been established for long. The first active ingredient of the system was discovered from the cannabis plant (Cannabis sativa) and is delta9-tetrahydrocannabinol (delta9-THC), and even it tends to produce euphoria and enhancement of sensory perceptions. The discovery of endocannabinoids opened a new pathway to the biochemistry of happiness for previously it was named after serotonin and dopamine. The name of the well-known endocannabinoid, anandamide itself (ananda - Sanskrit word meaning "joy, bliss or happiness") reveals its role in mood states. Recent researches also show a strong association between the serotonergic and endocannabinoid systems. The connection between depression, anxiety, mood disorders, emotional states and cannabinoids is an established fact, and a lot of research is currently focusing on it. The genes that code for these receptors also determine their role in bliss for CB-1 genes exhibit polymorphisms bringing about a variety of differences. Also, an individual with a specific genetic code for CB-1 receptor tend to be much happier and responds better to positive stimuli. They are also known to play an important role in response to stress, that is, they are compounds released in response to diverse stimuli of stress and thereby protect the body and helps in stress management.

17.2 Difference between Dopamine and Serotonin

Dopamine plays a big role in motivation and reward. If you've ever worked hard to reach a goal, the satisfaction your feel when you achieve it, is partly due to a rush of dopamine.

Some of the main symptoms of depression include:

- low motivation;
- feeling helpless;
- a loss of interest in things that used to interest you.

These symptoms are linked to a dysfunction within your dopamine system. They also think this dysfunction might be triggered by short- or long-term stress, pain, or trauma.

Besides Parkinson's disease, experts also think that a dysfunction of the dopamine system may be involved in: (i) bipolar disorder, (ii) schizophrenia, and (iii) attention deficit hyperactivity disorder (ADHD).

Researchers have been studying the link between **serotonin** and depression for more than 5 decades. While they initially thought that low serotonin levels caused depression, they now that isn't the case.

The reality is more complicated. While **low serotonin** doesn't necessarily cause depression, increasing serotonin through the use of selective serotonin reuptake inhibitors (SSRIs) is one of the most effective treatments for depression. However, such medications do take some time to work.

In a 2014 review, serotonin was also linked to several other conditions, including: (i) anxiety disorders, (ii) autism spectrum disorder, (iii) bipolar disorder.

More specifically, the researchers found low serotonin binding in specific brain areas among people with obsessive-compulsive disorder (OCD) and social anxiety disorder.

In addition, they found that people with autism spectrum disorder are more likely to have lower levels of serotonin in certain areas of the brain.

Bipolar disorder was also associated with altered serotonin activity, which may influence the severity of someone's symptoms.

Among people with moderate to severe depression, 40 to 60 percent of people report an improvement in their symptoms only after they've taken SSRIs for 6 to 8 weeks. This suggests that simply increasing serotonin isn't what treats depression.

Instead, research Source has suggested that SSRIs increase positive emotional processing over time, resulting in an overall shift in mood.

Another factor:

Researchers have found that depression is associated with inflammation in the body. SSRIs have an anti-inflammatory effect.

The main difference:

Dopamine system dysfunction is linked to certain symptoms of depression, such as low motivation. Serotonin is involved in how you process your emotions, which can affect your overall mood.

17.3 How to increase your Dopamine and Serotonin Levels?

(i) Get outside in the Sun

Looking to boost your endorphins and serotonin levels? Spending time outdoors, in sunlight, is a great way to do this. According to 2008 Source, exposure to sunlight can increase production of both serotonin and endorphins. Start with at least 10 to 15 minutes outside each day. If you're tired of the same old sights, try exploring a new neighbourhood or park.

(ii) Take time for exercise

Exercise has multiple physical health benefits. It can also have a positive impact on emotional well-being. If you've heard of a "runner's high," you might already know about the link between exercise and endorphin release. But exercise doesn't just work on endorphins. Regular physical activity can also increase your dopamine and serotonin levels, making it a great option to boost your happy hormones.

(iii) Maximize your workout

To see even more benefits from exercise:

- **Include a few friends.** A small study looking at 12 men found evidence to suggest group exercise offers more benefits than solo exercise.
- **Get some sun.** Move your workout outdoors to maximize your serotonin boost.
- **Time it.** Aim for at least 30 minutes of aerobic exercise at a time. Any amount of physical activity has health benefits, but research associates endorphin release with continued exercise rather than short bursts of activity.

(iv) Laugh with a friend

Who hasn't heard the old saying, "Laughter is the best medicine"?

Of course, laughter won't treat ongoing health issues. But it can help relieve feelings of anxiety or stress, and improve a low mood by boosting dopamine and endorphin levels.

According to a study looking at 12 young men, social laughter triggered endorphin release.

So, share that funny video, dust off your joke book, or watch a comedy special with a friend or partner. An added bonus? Bonding over something hilarious with a loved one might even trigger oxytocin release.

(v) Cook (and enjoy) a favourite meal with a loved one

This tip could — in theory — boost all 4 of your happy hormones.

The enjoyment you get from eating something delicious can trigger the release of dopamine along with endorphins. Sharing the meal with someone you love, and bonding over meal preparation, can boost oxytocin levels.

Certain foods can also have an impact on hormonc levels, so note the following when meal planning for a happy hormone boost:

- spicy foods, which may trigger endorphin release;

- yogurt, beans, eggs, meats with low-fat content, and almonds, which are just a few foods linked to dopamine release;

- foods high in tryptophan, which have been linked to increased serotonin levels; and

- foods containing probiotics, such as yogurt, kimchi, and sauerkraut, which can influence the release of hormones.

(vi) Listen to music (or make some)

Music can give more than one of your happy hormones a boost.

Listening to instrumental music, especially music that gives you chills, can increase dopamine production in your brain.

But if you enjoy music, simply listening to any music you enjoy may help put you in a good mood. This positive change in your mood can increase serotonin production.

Musicians may also experience an endorphin release when creating music. According to research, creating and performing music by dancing, singing, or drumming led to endorphin release.

(vii) Meditate

If you're familiar with meditation, you might already know of its many wellness benefits — from improving sleep to reducing stress.

A study links many of meditation's benefits to increased dopamine production during the practice. It also suggests that meditation can spur endorphin release.

(viii) Plan a romantic evening

Oxytocin's reputation as the "love hormone" is well-earned.

Simply being attracted to someone can lead to the production of oxytocin. But physical affection, including kissing, cuddling, or having sex, also contributes to oxytocin production.

Just spending time with someone you care about can also help boost oxytocin production. This can help increase closeness and positive relationship feelings, making you feel happy, blissful, or even euphoric.

If you really want to feel those happy hormones, note that dancing and sex both lead to endorphin release, while orgasm triggers dopamine release.

You can also share a glass of wine with your partner for an added endorphin boost.

(ix) Pet your dog

If you have a dog, giving your furry friend some affection is a great way to boost oxytocin levels for you and your dog.

According to research, dog owners and their dogs see an increase in oxytocin when they cuddle. Even if you don't own a dog, you might also experience an oxytocin boost when you see a dog you know and like. If you're a dog lover, this might happen when you get a chance to pet any dog at all. So, find your favourite canine and give it a good ear scratch or lap cuddle.

(x) Get a good night's sleep

Not getting enough quality sleep can affect your health in multiple ways. For one, it can contribute to an imbalance of hormones, particularly dopamine, in your body. This can have a negative impact on your mood as well as your physical health.

Setting aside 7 to 9 hours each night for sleep can help restore the balance of hormones in your body, which will likely help you feel better.

If you find it difficult to get a good night's sleep, try:

- going to bed and getting up around the same time every day;
- creating a quiet, restful sleeping environment (try reducing light, noise, and screens);
- decreasing caffeine intake, especially in the afternoon and evening.

(xi) Get a Massage

If you enjoy massage, here's one more reason to get one: massage can boost all 4 of your happy hormones. According to research, both serotonin and dopamine levels increased after massage. Massage is also known to boost endorphins and oxytocin.

You can get these benefits from a massage by a licensed massage therapist, but you can also get a massage from a partner for some extra oxytocin.

17.4 Ways to Increase Dopamine Levels Naturally

Dopamine is an important chemical messenger in the brain that has many functions. It's involved in reward, motivation, memory, attention and even regulating body movements.

When dopamine is released in large amounts, it creates feelings of pleasure and reward, which motivates you to repeat a specific behaviour. In contrast, low levels of dopamine are linked to reduced motivation and decreased enthusiasm for things that would excite most people.

Dopamine levels are typically well regulated within the nervous system, but there are some things you can do to naturally increase levels.

Here are the ways to increase dopamine levels naturally:

(i) Eat Lots of Protein

Proteins are made up of smaller building blocks called amino acids.

There are 23 different amino acids, some of which your body can synthesize and others that you must get from food. One amino acid called tyrosine plays a critical role in the production of dopamine.

Enzymes within your body are capable of turning tyrosine into dopamine, so having adequate tyrosine levels is important for dopamine production. Tyrosine can also be made from another amino acid called phenylalanine.

Both tyrosine and phenylalanine are naturally found in protein-rich foods like turkey, beef, eggs, dairy, soy and legumes.

Studies show that increasing the amount of tyrosine and phenylalanine in the diet can increase dopamine levels in the brain, which may promote deep thinking and improve memory.

Conversely, when phenylalanine and tyrosine are eliminated from the diet, dopamine levels can become depleted.

While these studies show that extremely high or extremely low intakes of these amino acids can impact dopamine levels, it's unknown whether normal variations in protein intake would have much impact.

(ii) Eat Less Saturated Fat

Some animal research has found that saturated fats, such as those found in animal fat, butter, full-fat dairy, palm oil and coconut oil, may disrupt dopamine signalling in the brain when consumed in very large quantities.

Some researchers hypothesize that diets high in saturated fat may increase inflammation in the body, leading to changes in the dopamine system, but more research is needed.

Several observational studies have found a link between high saturated fat intake and poor memory and cognitive functioning in humans, but it's unknown whether these effects are related to dopamine levels

(iii) Consume Probiotics

In recent years, scientists have discovered that the gut and brain are closely linked.

In fact, the gut is sometimes called the "second brain," as it contains a large number of nerve cells that produce many neurotransmitter signalling molecules, including dopamine.

It's now clear that certain species of bacteria that live in your gut are also capable of producing dopamine, which may impact mood and behaviour.

Research in this area is limited. However, several studies show that when consumed in large enough quantities, certain strains of bacteria can reduce symptoms of anxiety and depression in both animals and humans.

It's likely that dopamine production plays a role in how probiotics improve mood, but more research is needed to determine how significant the effect is.

Interestingly, these changes occurred even without differences in weight, body fat, hormones or blood sugar levels.

Some researchers hypothesize that diets high in saturated fat may increase inflammation in the body, leading to changes in the dopamine system, but more research is needed.

(iv) Eat Velvet Beans

Velvet beans, also known as Mucuna pruriens, naturally contain high levels of L-dopa, the precursor molecule to dopamine.

Studies show that eating these beans may help raise dopamine levels naturally, especially in people with Parkinson's disease, a movement disorder caused by low dopamine levels.

One small in those with Parkinson's disease found that consuming 250 grams of cooked velvet beans significantly raised dopamine levels and reduced Parkinson's symptoms one to two hours after the meal. Similarly, several studies on Mucuna pruriens supplements found that they may be even more effective and longer lasting than traditional Parkinson's medications, as well as have fewer side effects.

Keep in mind that velvet beans are toxic in high amounts. Make sure to follow dosage recommendations on the product label.

(v) Exercise

Exercise is recommended for boosting endorphin levels and improving mood. Improvements in mood can be seen after as little as 10 minutes of aerobic activity but tend to be highest after at least 20 minutes. While these effects are probably not entirely due to changes in dopamine levels, animal research suggests that exercise can boost dopamine levels in the brain.

In one study, a 30-minute session of moderate-intensity treadmill running did not produce an increase in dopamine levels in adults. However, one three-month study found that performing one hour of yoga six days per week significantly increased dopamine levels.

(vi) Get Enough Sleep

When dopamine is released in the brain, it creates feelings of alertness and wakefulness. Animal studies show that dopamine is released in large amounts in the morning when it's time to wake up and that levels naturally fall in the evening when it's time to go to sleep. However, lack of sleep appears to disrupt these natural rhythms.

When people are forced to stay awake through the night, the availability of dopamine receptors in the brain is dramatically reduced by the next morning.

Since dopamine promotes wakefulness, reducing the sensitivity of the receptors should make it easier to fall asleep, especially after a night of insomnia. However, having less dopamine typically comes with other unpleasant consequences like reduced concentration and poor coordination.

Getting regular, high-quality sleep may help keep your dopamine levels balanced and help you feel more alert and high-functioning during the day.

(vii) Listen to Music

Listening to music can be a fun way to stimulate dopamine release in the brain. Several brain imaging studies have found that listening to music increases activity in the reward and pleasure areas of the brain, which are rich with dopamine receptors.

A study investigating the effects of music on dopamine found a significant increase in brain dopamine levels when people listened to instrumental songs that gave them chills.

Since music can boost dopamine levels, listening to music has even been shown to help people with Parkinson's disease improve their fine motor control.

(viii) Meditate

Meditation is the practice of clearing your mind, focusing inward and letting your thoughts float by without judgment or attachment. It can be done while standing, sitting or even walking, and regular practice is associated with improved mental and physical health.

New research has found that these benefits may be due to increased dopamine levels in the brain. One study including eight experienced meditation teachers found a 64% increase in dopamine production after meditating for one hour, compared to when resting quietly.

(ix) Get enough sunlight

Seasonal affective disorder (SAD) is a condition in which people feel sad or depressed during the winter season when they are not exposed to enough sunlight.

It's well known that periods of low sunshine exposure can lead to reduced levels of mood-boosting neurotransmitters, including dopamine, and that sunlight exposure can increase them.

One study in 68 healthy adults found that those who received the most sunlight exposure in the previous 30 days had the highest density of dopamine receptors in the reward and movement regions of their brains.

While sun exposure may boost dopamine levels and improve mood, it's important to adhere to safety guidelines, as getting too much sun can be harmful and possibly addicting. One study in compulsive tanners who visited tanning beds at least two times per week for one year found that tanning sessions led to significant boosts in dopamine levels and a desire to repeat the behaviour.

17.5 Ways to Increase Serotonin Levels Naturally

(i) Tweak your diet

Depending on what you eat, you could be replenishing the serotonin in your brain—or depleting it. Nutritional deficiencies can directly lead to problems with replenishing serotonin. We now have real evidence to back up what's good common sense: that eating well doesn't just benefit your body, but it also benefits your brain. The Mediterranean diet, for example, is especially beneficial for boosting happiness because omega-3 fats, vitamin B-12, zinc, magnesium, and iron boost brain health while lowering inflammation.

(ii) Get consistent, sound sleep

People who are depressed or have other mental health problems are often not sleeping enough or sleeping too much. And this could affect your body's ability to use or make serotonin. One should aim to get between seven to eight hours of good sleep a night.

(iii) Go outside for some sunshine

One way to get enough vitamin D is by spending some time outdoors, which is why many people tend to feel a drop in mood during the winter months. If you're feeling down, try making fresh air a priority to up the amount of vitamin D you're getting, which may help boost your serotonin levels.

(iv) Get creative and crafty

Doing something you enjoy—crafting, gardening, playing music—has mood-boosting rewards. In addition to just feeling really good, it has been reported that doing these things can boost serotonin and dopamine level, positively impacting your mood.

(v) Get a massage

It's no secret that massages are, in most cases, pretty relaxing, right? Well, According to one study, a 60-minute massage lowers the stress hormone, cortisol, by 30 percent and increases serotonin levels by 28 percent.

(vi) Take steps to lower stress

Stress is messing with your serotonin. Stress is a chronic inflammatory condition, both in the brain and in the body itself. It can indirectly result in damage to neurons that produce serotonin or the other parts of the brain that are involved and the serotonergic pathways that make the system work less effectively. In other words, stress causes inflammation, which is bad news for your brain. Prioritizing self-care, therapy, and other stress-reduction tactics could go a long way towards better health, including better serotonin levels.

CHAPTER EIGHTEEN

HAPPINESS AND LONGEVITY

18.1 Introduction to Happiness and Longevity

When people list the key characteristics of a good life, they are likely to include happiness, health, and longevity. Her we describe the evidence that subjective well-being (SWB) causally influences both health and longevity. Early research on SWB and health established a correlation between the two. But because the studies were largely cross-sectional, often with small samples of convenience, it was impossible to determine the causal direction between SWB and health. However, there are now a number of converging lines of evidence based on diverse methodologies supporting the conclusion that SWB influences health and longevity:

(i) Long-term prospective studies in which participants are followed over time, and initial levels of SWB are related to later health and longevity. These studies were most powerful when baseline levels of health were controlled, and socioeconomic status (SES) was often controlled as well. Survival in ill populations has been studied, as well as morbidity and mortality in initially healthy populations.

(ii) Studies in which natural levels of SWB were related to specific physiological processes that can affect health and longevity, as well as studies where changes in SWB were related to changes in physiological measures.

(iii) Studies in which moods and emotions were experimentally manipulated, and effects on physiological variables that could affect health were assessed.

(iv) Animal studies in which there is experimental control over the environment of the animals, and physiological and health measures were assessed in animals likely to differ in SWB, for example, in stress

(v) Quasi-experimental studies in natural settings, in which natural events can be examined for their effects on health outcomes.

(vi) Experimental intervention studies in which treatments are administered that can influence people's long-term SWB. The treatment groups were compared to control groups in terms of both SWB and physiological measures.

(vii) Studies on how quality of life factors such as pain and mobility were related to SWB.

In terms of additional life-years, Veenhoven it was estimated that the effects of SWB on longevity might be 7.5 to 10.0 years, based on a small number of studies that reported effect size in life-year units. For example, the 10-year figure comes from a study of nuns—one of the largest longitudinal studies—and is a comparison of the happiest versus unhappiest quartiles.

Another researcher found that famous psychologists who used positive emotion words in their autobiographies lived 4.2 years longer than those who did not, while the use of negative words did not predict longevity. Further, it was that estimated a 14 per cent longevity difference between happy and unhappy individuals based on a meta-analysis of 24 studies. Using the average correlation in the analysis and converting to standard deviation units, this could amount to 6 years' difference in the USA between individuals who are two standard deviations apart on SWB, or 75 years versus 81 years life expectancy. Based on the age effects estimated from several reviews and studies, an unhappy person in an economically developed nation might live 4–10 years less than a very happy person, recognising that such an estimate depends on many factors. There is no underlying universal effect size for the association of SWB with health and longevity. Effect sizes depend on the amount of variability of SWB in a population, exposure to virulent pathogens, the length of the study, at what ages participants are observed, the reliability of the SWB measures, types of SWB assessed, and many additional factors. This variability was clearly demonstrated in a study on the effects of smoking, in which British physicians were assessed over a period of 40 years. Death rates due to smoking were double in the second 20 years compared to the first 20 years. Had the investigators followed participants for 10 years and controlled for initial health at the start of the study, the effects would have been much smaller. Thus, the effects found in studies rarely give the full lifelong effects of lifestyle and personality factors.

Many people seem older than they are. Research into the causes of premature aging has shown that stress has a lot to do with it, because the body wears down much faster during periods of crisis. The American Institute of Stress investigated this degenerative process and concluded that most health problems are caused by stress.

To summarise, the high subjective well-being (SWB) is a state that many desire, some achieve, and a few despise as an unnecessary luxury or even a detriment. Given its clear and compelling relation to physical health and longevity, we need to begin thinking of societal SWB as something that is indeed desirable and beneficial.

18.2 Subjective Well-Being (SWB) Aids Health and Longevity

Subjective wellbeing, often called —happiness, in layperson terminology, refers to peoples' sense of wellness in their lives – in both thoughts and feelings. The physiological pathway by which subjective well-being influences health are important for establishing the causal connection going from subjective well-being to health and longevity.

Reviewed above, are seven types of evidences that point to a causal connection going from subjective well-being to health and longevity. The researchers reviewed longitudinal studies with adults, animal experiments, experiments in which participants' moods were manipulated and biomarkers are assessed, natural quasi-experiments, and studies in which moods and biomarkers and tracked together over time in natural settings. It was concluded that the evidence is —clear and compelling‖

that positive feelings are causally related to health. Not only do negative emotions predict mortality, but positive emotions predict longevity.

Even in animals happiness can affect longevity. It was found that the orang-utans who were rated as happier by their caretakers lived longer. Indeed, the difference between the apes that were one standard deviation above versus below the mean in happiness was 11 years. Because these animals often live about 50 years in captivity, happiness accounted for a very large increase in longevity.

We now have initial evidence about the processes that mediate between happiness and the beneficial outcomes. For instance, happiness produces greater cooperation, energy, motivation, and creativity, which in turn are instrumental to business success. Conversely, depression creates problems such as illness, quitting one‘s job more frequently, and alcohol abuse that all lead to less success in the workplace. Similarly, positive feelings are associated with a stronger immune system and fewer cardiovascular problems, whereas anxiety and depression are associated with poorer health behaviours and problematical physiological indicators such as inflammation. Thus, the causal role of happiness on health and longevity can be understood with the mediating mechanisms that are now being uncovered.

18.3 Do happy people live longer?

For the last thousands of years, people have been looking for ways to reverse aging and prolong life. Each generation has eagerly sought out the path to immortality. While humanity continues its fruitless search for an anti-aging panacea, sensible doctors admonish patients to quit smoking, exercise regularly and follow a low fat diet.

Based on mounting research, such a premise isn't too far off. Happiness, loosely defined as satisfaction and appreciation for one's life, appears to be the psychological equivalent of Vitamin C. In ways that aren't yet completely understood, a positive outlook on life helps to protect against the negative effects of stress, safeguarding people from becoming sick.

Not only are happy people less likely to send out surges of stress hormones like cortisol that contribute to heart disease, but they're also more likely to follow good self-care and have better social networks -- both reliable indicators of good physical health. Chronic unhappiness, on the other hand, leads to increased blood pressure and decreased immunity. Unhappy people lacking emotional support also don't tend to take very good care of themselves.

Scientific Studies

Perhaps one of the most convincing studies linking happiness to longevity is based on -- of all people -- a group of nuns. This particular study involved having each nun write an autobiographical sketch upon their acceptance into the convent. Six decades later, the contents of those sketches proved to be surprisingly strong indicators of whether the author was still alive and how healthy they were.

What makes this particular study so convincing is that by following a group of people with nearly identical life histories, it eliminated practically all of the possible confounding variables such as diet or socioeconomic background. Yet despite their similar habits, some of the nuns experienced long, illness-free lives, while others succumbed to death at an early age. It turns out that those nuns who had expressed the most positive emotions in their journal entries were the same ones who were still around. A full 90 percent of the most cheerful quarter of nuns were still alive at age 85, while only 34 percent of the least cheerful quarter were. The happiest nuns lived a full 10 years longer than the usually expected age.

When combined with other indicators of longevity, happiness can have an even more pronounced effect. In a test of 50 variables thought to have an effect on a person's lifespan, satisfaction ranked as one of the strongest predictors, right up there with expected indicators like genetics, intelligence, socioeconomic status, tobacco use and overall health. Coupled with one or more of these other factors, the tests indicated that happiness adds a total of 16 years to the life of a man and 23 years to the life of a woman.

The mechanism for happiness's impressive effects on health can perhaps partly be explained by research showing that people with positive emotions tend to have higher levels of Immunoglobin-A, a key immune system protein and one of the body's primary defences against respiratory illness.

Even short-term gaiety may boost your body's defences. In a Tufts University study, researchers separated subjects into two groups of people: one group watched comedic films while the other suffered through stressful ones. The group who spent their time laughing saw their circulation improve as though they'd been exercising while the other group experienced reduced flow. In addition, when subjected to stressful events afterwards -- sending stress hormones skyrocketing -- the people who spent their time laughing recovered much more quickly, their heart rates fast returning to normal.

18.4 IKIGAI: The Japanese Secret of Long and Happy Life

"Only staying active will make you want to live a hundred years." -A Japanese Proverb

This Japanese concept, of IKIGAI which translates roughly as "the happiness of always being busy." It also seems to be one way of explaining the extraordinary longevity of the Japanese, especially on the island of Okinawa, where there are 24.55 people over the age of 100 for every 100,000 inhabitants—far more than the global average. It was further discovered that one place in particular, Ogimi, a rural town on the north end of the island with a population of three thousand, boasts the highest life expectancy in the world—a fact that has earned it the nickname the Village of Longevity. Okinawa is where most of Japan's shikuwasa—a limelike fruit that packs an extraordinary antioxidant punch—comes from. Could that be Ogimi's secret to long life? Or is it the purity of the water used to brew its Moringa tea? When a survey was conducted by interviewing the eldest residents of the town, it was realized that something far more powerful than just these natural resources was at work: an uncommon joy flows from its inhabitants and guides them through the long and pleasurable journey of their lives. It turned out that one of the secrets to happiness of Ogimi's residents is feeling like part of a community. From an early age they practice 'yuimaaru', or teamwork, and so are used to helping one another.

In Japanese, ikigai means "life," "to be worthwhile." IKIGAI is the art of staying young while growing old. One surprising thing you notice, living in Japan, is how active people remain after they retire. In fact, many Japanese people never really retire—they keep doing what they love for as long as their health allows. There is, in fact, no word in Japanese that means retire in the sense of "leaving the workforce for good" as in English. Having a purpose in life is so important in Japanese culture that our idea of retirement simply doesn't exist there.

Certain longevity studies suggest that a strong sense of community and a clearly defined ikigai are just as important as the famously healthful Japanese diet—perhaps even more so. Recent medical studies of centenarians from Okinawa and other so-called Blue Zones—the geographic regions where people live longest—provide a number of interesting facts about these extraordinary human beings:

- Not only do they live much longer than the rest of the world's population, they also suffer from fewer chronic illnesses such as cancer and heart disease; inflammatory disorders are also less common.

- Many of these centenarians enjoy enviable levels of vitality and health that would be unthinkable for people of advanced age elsewhere.

- Their blood tests reveal fewer free radicals (which are responsible for cellular aging), as a result of drinking (green) tea and eating until their stomachs are only 80 percent full.

- Women experience more moderate symptoms during menopause, and both men and women maintain higher levels of sexual hormones until much later in life.

- The rate of dementia (a chronic or persistent disorder of the mental processes) is well below the global average.

One of the most common sayings in Japan is "Hara hachi bu," which is repeated before or after eating and means something like "Fill your belly to 80 percent." Ancient wisdom advises against eating until we are full. This is why Okinawans stop eating when they feel their stomachs reach 80 percent of their capacity, rather than overeating and wearing down their bodies with long digestive processes that accelerate cellular oxidation. The way food is served is also important. By presenting their meals on many small plates, the Japanese tend to eat less. A typical meal in a restaurant in Japan is served in five plates on a tray, four of them very small and the main dish slightly bigger. Having five plates in front of you makes it seem like you are going to eat a lot, but what happens most of the time is that you end up feeling slightly hungry. This is one of the reasons why Westerners in Japan typically lose weight and stay trim.

Moai: Connected for life

It is customary in Okinawa to form close bonds within local communities. A moai is an informal group of people with common interests who look out for one another. For many, serving the community becomes part of their ikigai.

The moai has its origins in hard times, when farmers would get together to share best practices and help one another cope with meagre harvests.

Members of a moai make a set monthly contribution to the group. This payment allows them to participate in meetings, dinners, games of go and shogi (Japanese chess), or whatever hobby they have in common.

The funds collected by the group are used for activities, but if there is money left over, one member (decided on a rotating basis) receives a set amount from the surplus. In this way, being part of a moai helps maintain emotional and financial stability. If a member of a moai is in financial trouble, he or she can get an advance from the group's savings. While the details of each moai's accounting practices vary according to the group and its economic means, the feeling of belonging and support gives the individual a sense of security and helps increase life expectancy.

CHAPTER NINETEEN

HAPPINESS VERSUS COMPASSION

19.1 Happiness and Compassion go hand-in-hand

"If you want others to be happy practice compassion; and if you want yourself to be happy practice compassion." -Dalai Lama

Compassion is defined as a feeling of deep sympathy for another who is stricken by misfortune, accompanied by a strong desire to alleviate the suffering. Compassion is about letting the other person know: I understand you and I empathize. It is a mental attitude based on the wish for others to be free of their suffering and is associated with a sense of commitment, responsibility, and respect towards the other. Compassion is passion with a heart. The sages already know it for ages: Helping others leads to more happiness.

Researchers often wonder about the causal sequence between compassion and happiness. They ask: Is it the case that compassionate people are happier or are happy people more compassionate? In Buddhist tradition, numerous mental trainings are offered to systematically cultivate greater compassion and well-being. There is an inextricable link between one's personal happiness and kindness, compassion, and caring for others. And this is a two-way street: increased happiness leads to greater compassion, and increased compassion leads to greater happiness. This is stated in the above-mentioned quote by H.H. Dalai Lama. In other words, studies have found not only that happier people tend to be more caring and more willing to reach out and help others, but that by deliberately cultivating greater kindness and compassion, a person will experience increased happiness. Today such evidence exists, showing that the practice of kindness and compassion is a powerful strategy to increase personal happiness.

In one of the experiments, a researcher brought a French Tibetan Buddhist monk into his lab to study the effects of compassion. This monk was a highly trained adept who had spent many years in the Himalayan region, meditating on compassion (and who acted compassionately, as well, dedicating his life to charitable activities in the region). The researcher began by monitoring the monk's brain function in a resting state to measure baseline brain activity; then he asked him to perform an intensive Buddhist meditation on compassion. The results showed that during his meditation on compassion, there was a dramatic leftward shift in his prefrontal function, lighting up the "happiness region" of the brain. This researcher concluded: "The very act of concern for others' well-being creates a greater sense of well-being within oneself." What could be more conclusive evidence of the link between personal happiness and compassion?

In conclusion. cultivating positive mental states like kindness and compassion definitely leads to better psychological health and happiness." It is clear that feelings of love, affection, closeness, and compassion bring happiness. Our physical structure seems to be more suited to feelings of love and compassion. We can see how a calm, affectionate, wholesome state of mind has beneficial effects on our health and physical well-being. Conversely, feelings of frustration, fear, agitation, and anger can be destructive to our health.

Reaching out to help others may be as fundamental to our nature as communication. One could draw an analogy with the development of language which, like the capacity for compassion and altruism (selfless concern for the well-being of others), is one of the magnificent features of the human race. Particular areas of the brain are specifically devoted to the potential for language. If we are exposed to the correct environmental conditions, that is, a society that speaks, then those discreet areas of the brain begin to develop and mature and our capacity for language grows.

In the same way, all humans may be endowed with the "seed of compassion." When exposed to the right conditions—at home, in society at large, and later perhaps through our own pointed efforts—that "seed" will flourish. With this idea in mind, researchers are now seeking to discover the optimal environmental conditions that will allow the seed of caring and compassion to ripen in children. They have identified several factors: having parents who are able to regulate their own emotions, who model caring behaviour, who set appropriate limits on the children's behaviour, who communicate that a child is responsible for her or his own behaviour, and who use reasoning to help direct the child's attention to affective or emotional states and the consequences of her or his behaviour on others.

In conclusion, we must develop basic good human qualities—warmth, kindness, compassion. Then our life becomes meaningful and more peaceful—happier. Once you encourage the thought of compassion in your mind, once that thought becomes active, then your attitude towards others changes automatically. If you approach others with the thought of compassion, that will automatically reduce fear and allow an openness with other people. It creates a positive, friendly atmosphere. With that attitude, you can approach a relationship in which you, yourself, initially create the possibility of receiving affection or a positive response from the other person. And with that attitude, even if the other person is unfriendly or doesn't respond to you in a positive way, then at least you've approached the person with a feeling of openness that gives you a certain flexibility and the freedom to change your approach as needed. That kind of openness at least allows the possibility of having a meaningful conversation with them. But without the attitude of compassion, if you are feeling closed, irritated, or indifferent, then you can even be approached by your best friend and you just feel uncomfortable. So, approaching others with the thought of compassion in your mind is the best way to do this.

Within all beings there is the seed of perfection. However, compassion is required in order to activate that seed which is inherent in our hearts and minds.

If one is seeking to build a truly satisfying relationship, the best way of bringing this about is to get to know the deeper nature of the person and relate to her or him on that level, instead of merely on the basis of superficial characteristics . And in this type of relationship there is a role for genuine compassion.

In recent years there have been many studies that support the idea that developing compassion and altruism has a positive impact on our physical and emotional health and consequently, happiness. In one well-known experiment, for example, a psychologist at Harvard University, showed a group of students a film of Mother Teresa working among Calcutta's sick and poor. The students reported that the film stimulated feelings of compassion. Afterward, he analysed the students' saliva and found an increase in immunoglobulin-A, an antibody that can help fight respiratory infections. In another study done at the University of Michigan Research Centre, investigators found that doing regular volunteer work, interacting with others in a warm and compassionate way, dramatically increased life expectancy, and probably overall vitality as well. Many other researchers in the new field of mind-body medicine have demonstrated similar findings, documenting that positive states of mind can improve our physical health.

In addition to the beneficial effects on one's physical health, there is evidence that compassion and caring behaviour contribute to good emotional health. Studies have shown that reaching out to help others can induce a feeling of happiness, a calmer mind, and less depression. In a thirty-year study of a group of Harvard graduates, researcher George Vaillant concluded that adopting an altruistic lifestyle is a critical component of good mental health. Another survey conducted with several thousand people who were regularly involved in volunteer activities that helped others, revealed that over 90 percent of these volunteers reported a kind of "high" associated with the activity, characterized by a feeling of warmth, more energy, and a kind of euphoria. They also had a distinct feeling of calmness and enhanced self-worth following the activity. Not only did these caring behaviours provide an interaction that was emotionally nourishing, but it was also found that this "helper's calm" was linked to relief from a variety of stress-related physical disorders as well.

19.2 Path of Happiness is through Compassion

When you are grateful, you open up, you sprout, you blossom, you bloom, and then you spread fragrance. The next principle, besides being grateful, is to be compassionate. Karuna is the word in Sanskrit for Compassion. If we have no compassion in us, then we are of no use to Nature. Nature's only focus is to survive. If you look at how evolution has panned out, everything is based on survival. The emotion of fear is such that you can be afraid, runaway, protect yourself, and survive. So, when you do something for others, you are helping Nature grow. However, to expect compassion and acknowledgement from those towards whom you are compassionate is a mistake. Do not have that expectation. Everyone has their Karmic account. The person you are exercising compassion for, may not even regard it as such; may not even respect it. But, that is not a good enough reason to abandon compassion.

There is a story about a scorpion and a saint. A saint was taking a dip in the river, and there was a scorpion there that was drowning. The saint took the scorpion in his hands to save it, but the scorpion stung him. The saint immediately let it go. The saint again attempted to save it, and the scorpion stung him again. In his third attempt, the saint took the scorpion out swiftly, and hence the scorpion was saved.

A man was watching the saint and said, "I don't understand. I can understand why you were trying to save the scorpion, but one time was enough. If it doesn't want to listen, then let it go. Let it die. Why do you care? The scorpion stung you twice, and you still saved it a third time. This does not make sense to me. It is OK to be compassionate but you don't have to be foolish." The saint said, "This creature here is at the lowest end of the food chain, and I am at the highest. Such a creature did not let go of its basic tendencies in my presence. Should I, a saint, let go of my basic tendencies in the presence of a mere scorpion?"

When your circumstances and when those around you are able to shape you the way they want, they have won and you have lost. That means they are stronger than you. If you are stronger than them, you would know how to stand your ground. Compassion is a matter of choice. Compassion is about forgiving the other person. But forgiveness does not mean that you accept what they have done to you. It is not reconciliation.

It is an affirmation that 'I am not going to hold anything against this person in my heart.'

By any stretch of imagination, there is no suggestion that you become a doormat and let anybody walk over you. But compassion is a divine emotion. You are of use to the world and Nature when you exercise compassion. Nature is then interested in you. It is interested in what you want. It is interested in making sure that you are taken care of.

It is easy to just move away, but compassion requires great strength. Any time you are not able to exercise compassion, all you have to think is ,'Am I so weak that I cannot even be compassionate towards my siblings, towards my parents, towards my friends, towards this society, towards this world?'. Compassion has a calming effect on the mind. If there is only one virtue that you could have, then have compassion. A life without compassion is as good as an animalistic life.

Scriptures state that there are 8.4 million species on the planet. These are just different forms of consciousness. Even within human beings, there are 8.4 million types. Some live like wolves, some like lions, some like crows, some like scorpions, some like cows, some like bulls etc. If you behave in a certain way, then ask yourself what type of consciousness is prevalent in you? Are you behaving like a human being or a bull or something else?

A lot of the times this query where people wish to know if there is a mantra that they can chant, some meditation that they can do, some temple they can visit, or a Guru who will bless them and suddenly they will feel compassionate. It will never happen that way. Never. It is entirely in your hands. It is a conscious choice. Neuro-scientifically speaking, the same part of our brain gets activated when we make others happy as when we ourselves are happy. The brain makes absolutely no distinction between whether I'm making another person happy or making myself happy.

Everything that happens around us is very much our problem. When somebody is in trouble, it is our problem. There was once a farmer, who lived with his wife, and in his barn, he had a goat, a cow, and a hen.

There was a mouse in that house that used to go around in the house, nibbling on everything that it could get its hands on. The farmer's wife was really bothered by this. She said, "I am going to set a mousetrap so that this mouse stops bothering us." So, they set up a mousetrap.

The mouse sees the trap and is very anxious. He thinks, "I can see the cheese hanging in there, and I know I will not be able to resist it for long. It is only a matter of time before I get caught in the trap." He goes to the hen and says, "Can you save me? Can you do something? There is a trap there." The hen says, "Well, what can I do? It is not my problem. Why do I have to worry about a mousetrap? You should be careful. There is nothing I can do."

The mouse then goes to the goat and says, "Could you just stomp on the trap and crush it because I am going to get trapped and get killed?" The goat says, "It is not really my problem. I don't care about the mouse trap." Then the mouse goes to the cow, "You are the biggest one around here, and there is a trap set in the house. Please crush it and get rid of it." The cow says, "It is not my problem, it is your problem. You go figure out a solution."

This is what is happening in the world all the time. We are so concerned about our own problems all the time that we do not want to take time out to solve anybody else's. But you always have the time to solve it. Out of twenty-four hours in a day, you give eight hours to your employer, and they pay you for it. However, sometimes you even give nine or ten hours to your work. You take time out for things that matter to you. The same thing goes for compassion. If it matters to you, nature will give you adequate resources, so that you can exercise it.

So, the mouse is very worried and he is praying for its life. That night, a snake gets trapped in the mousetrap. As soon as the trap closes, the wife goes running to the trap thinking it is the mouse. She accidentally steps on the tail of the snake, and the snake bites her. The farmer rushes her to the hospital. It was a small village hospital, and she had no medical insurance. The doctor asks the farmer, "How will you pay me my fee?" The farmer says, "Look I am a poor farmer, I have already invested money in my farm, and I can only pay you after the harvest." The doctor says,

"This is not good enough. Surely there is something that you can do for me now." The farmer says, "Could I give you some food?" The doctor says, "Okay, what can you give me?" The farmer says, "I can give you some rice."

"I am not interested in rice, but I do love chicken", says the doctor. The farmer says, "I have a hen, and I will happily give it to you." The doctor takes the hen, and the hen is now dead. The mousetrap was not the hen's problem but now, it became its problem. The farmer takes his wife back home, and the wife is still not well. The farmer takes his wife to the local Shaman. The Shaman says, "If you sacrifice a goat, I am sure your wife would be absolutely fine." The farmer says, "I have a goat, I could do that much for my wife." The goat is sacrificed but the wife still dies. All the relatives come to the house for the funeral. The farmer sells the cow in order to feed all the relatives and neighbours. So, in the end, in that house, only two creatures are left- the farmer and the mouse. Almost everyone else ends up dead.

In the equation of this life, we do not know whether we are the farmer, the mouse, the goat, the cow or the hen. It doesn't matter who we are. It helps to be responsible. It helps to take care of those around us.

Somebody wrote a letter to Mahatma Gandhi. When the letter was delivered, a person was sitting next to him. Mahatma Gandhi read the two-page letter. After reading, he took out the pin that was holding the two pages together and put it aside. He then crumpled the letter and threw it in a trash can. The person sitting next to him said, "I don't understand. Somebody sent you a letter. That person gave time, and you so cruelly crumpled it and threw it in the bin."

Gandhi said, 'Well, it was all full of abusive language. The person was hurling abuses at me. There was nothing nice in the letter.' The person said, 'In that case, why did you take all the time and go through the effort of taking the pin out? Why didn't you throw the whole thing away?' Gandhi said, 'Well, I have kept what I will reuse. The thing that matters to me, the only useful thing in the letter, I have kept. What I did not want to use, I have thrown away.' When the world is writing you 'letters,' it is a choice whether you accept it or reject it. Sometimes, compassion is in rejection. Sometimes, ignoring the other person is compassion. Because if you accept what they say about you, then you might feel agitated.

Sometimes, compassion is simply that, "I have opened both my ears – in through one and out through the other." Compassion is not about preaching the other person or trying to change them. In fact, the only person you can really change is yourself. That too, if you are very lucky and very persistent, because the hardest to change is ourselves. A life of compassion is always going to be meaningful. If you have compassion, you may not have as much money or you may, you may not have amenities or you may, but you will have one thing for sure, and that one thing is peace. You will not struggle to sleep.

19.3 How can compassion boost your happiness?

Compassion is your ability to experience others' feelings — from joy to sorrow — with a desire to help. Not only does compassion decrease suffering by helping those in need, but also it can boost your bond with others. Plus, you may find that the pursuit of compassion makes you happier than the pursuit of happiness.

Why? Giving or receiving compassion can:

- Make you healthier. The reason: The happier you are, the easier it is to commit to healthy habits.
- Improve your mental health by decreasing your stress levels.
- Temporarily shift your attention away from your own challenges and put things into perspective.
- Enhance your spiritual well-being.

Want to experience the joy of compassion? Try any of these random acts of kindness:

- Pay for a stranger's toll or bill.
- Let someone go ahead of you in the checkout line.
- Spend time with people in a nursing home.
- Volunteer at a free medical clinic or children's hospital.

- Join a group to adopt a cause.
- Pray for a stranger or loved one.

The joy you'll feel after committing a random act of kindness will give you a sense of elation that money just can't buy.

19.4 Money doesn't buy you Compassion and Happiness

As riches grow, our feelings of compassion and empathy for others seem to decline. 'A higher social class also negatively influences a person's ability to pay attention in interactions with other persons' circumstances. Two Berkeley psychologists conducted several studies in which they looked at whether social class (as measured by wealth, occupational prestige, and education) influences how much we care about the feelings of others. According to their research, individuals of a lower social class are better at recognizing the emotions of others and more emphatically accurate in judging the emotions of other people, compared to upper-class individuals.

Some researchers suspect that wealth can lead to a feeling of independence from others. Having to rely less on others, we can become more self-focused, caring less about the feelings of others.

From which you could conclude that the degree of (inter) connectedness — whether there is a common connection with the other person — might be of influence here. These researchers also found that wealthier people are more likely to agree with statements that greed is justified, beneficial, and morally defensible. An attitude that is not likely to lead to a feeling of compassion.

Does being wealthy or having money mean you cannot be compassionate or happy? Of course not. But it does mean that you run the risk of becoming less compassionate and emphatic and therefore less happy if you don't cultivate your ability to be compassionate and emphatic.

19.5 Self-Compassion to Boost Your Happiness

Most people think of self-compassion as being kind to yourself. Although that is certainly a part of the concept, self-compassion involves a way of relating to yourself in a way that allows you to become more emotionally flexible, able to navigate challenging emotions, and enhance your connection to self and others. The ability to relate to ourselves in a compassionate way may sound easy enough but, in fact, it can be quite a challenge

You may find it easy to be compassionate toward a friend or loved one when they come to you with a personal struggle or a challenging situation. Your response to them may be one of understanding, hope, guidance, help, and encouragement.

However, when we are faced with our own life challenges, we tend to be a little more harsh or critical with ourselves. We examine our thoughts and behaviours in a way that can leave us feeling unworthy, ashamed and frustrated with ourselves. In an effort to keep moving forward, we may tell ourselves to "buck up," or "get over it." Although the intent is to help move us forward during times of emotional challenge, this way of relating to ourselves can create an extraordinary amount of stress and become a significant obstacle in our ability to experience happiness within ourselves and with others.

Three Elements of Self-Compassion:

(i) Self-kindness: When people who practice self-compassion find themselves in challenging situations, they recognize that being imperfect or falling short at times is a part of living. The ability to navigate these experiences without putting yourself down is an element of self-compassion.

(ii) Common Humanity: When we are faced with challenges, it can be easy to feel alone in our experience, as if others would not be able to relate to what we are going through. People who practice self-compassion understand that some of these challenges are part of the shared human experience.

(iii) Mindfulness: Practicing self-compassion involves being able to observe our uncomfortable emotions without exaggerating them or ignoring them. This mindful and balanced stance helps us to not become emotionally reactive.

How to Practice Self-Compassion?

(i) Imagine how you would talk to a friend. We can often extend kind words, hope and encouragement to friends or loved ones. When going through a difficult time, take a moment to consider how you might respond to a close friend if they were going through a similar situation.

(ii) Become an observer. During times when we feel challenged or struggling emotionally, it can feel like we are simply reacting and trying to emotionally survive the moment. By slowing down, we can take a small step back to observe our experience. Looking at the bigger picture can help us keep things in perspective and help us see important information that may have been missed otherwise.

(iii) Change your self-talk. Notice how you talk to yourself in moments when you are experiencing negative emotion. Work to reframe your critical self-statements in a more positive, nurturing way. This new tone may sound more like a mentor or advocate, rather than a critic or judge.

(iv) Keep a journal and write it out. Take time each day to write out some of the challenges you are experiencing. Note moments as your mind tends to wander into critical statements or you begin to feel alone in your experiences. As you would with self-talk, intentionally reframe any critical statements with a softer, more understanding tone to see how it might feel different.

(v) Become clear about what you want. As you practice ways to reframe critical thoughts into more nurturing self-talk, you can start uncovering clues as to what you are needing and wanting. Take a moment to consider what you want, need or long for in your life. Clarifying these needs will help you focus on where you want to go and what you are working toward, helping to increase motivation and happiness.

(vi) Care for yourself. Sometimes we take care of others and overlook, or completely ignore, the need to take care of ourselves. When practicing self-compassion you are recognizing that you have needs to be met as well and are worthy of engaging in those self-care behaviours. The ability to establish self-care practices can help lessen the desire to engage in unhealthy coping behaviours when faced with challenges and stress.

CHAPTER TWENTY

MANTRAS FOR HAPPINESS

20.1 Difference Between Mantras and Affirmations

A mantra is any word(s), sound(s) or collection of words or sounds designed to promote focus, aid concentration or increase confidence. Many people use the word mantras interchangeably with affirmations. While all affirmations are a form of mantras, not all mantras are affirmations. The main difference between affirmation and mantras is that a mantra can be sounds and phrases (like Omm... in yoga & meditation) designed to aid concentration, but affirmations are centred around positive thinking phrases mainly used to build confidence. Translating a mantra gives you an affirmation where the words have the additional benefit of imparting a sense of confidence with time when repeated.

Following are some of the mantras/affirmations and their meanings in English:

- Shanti – Peace
- Dharma – Righteous path
- Ananda – Bliss
- Prasada – Radiance or happiness
- Prajna – Wisdom
- Bhakti – Devotion, faith, love

While mantras are often thought of in reference to eastern religions, by no means is this the only place you have mantras. Often repeated Catholic and Christian prayers are also mantras. As are many Latin phrases in common use today, such as, "caveat emptor", "carpe diem" and "semper fidelis".

Finally, all repeated and spoken phrases in the English (or any) language are also mantras. Commonly known as "affirmations" these mantras are repeated for the purpose of building confidence, quieting anxiety or trying to take advantage of the neuroplasticity of the human brain.

20.2 Mantras and Affirmations for a Happy Life

These daily mantras can help quiet anxiety. They can help to boost happiness. And finally, they will help to inspire self-confidence. Repeat one (or all!) of these mantras daily to yourself for the best results.

20.2.1 Ten Daily Mantras for Happiness and Self-Confidence

(i) All is well mantra

All is well, right here, right now. All is well, right here, right now - mantra for peace and calm. All is well, right here, right now.

This mantra reminds us that no matter how chaotic life can seem. Things are not that bad. This phrase calms us with a positive reminder that life is good. This mantra helps you feel peaceful and calm.

(ii) I am enough positive mantra

I am enough. Who I am is enough. What I do is enough, and what I have is enough.

This is a simple mantra. But a powerful one. "I AM ENOUGH".

It is important to know what you have all the tools you need for happiness, confidence, and self-esteem. You do not need the approval of others. Everything you need is within yourself.

(iii) Don't be afraid to give up the good

Don't be afraid to give up the good and go for the great. Don't be afraid to give up the good and go for the great.

This mantra teaches an important life lesson. While it is good to be happy and comfortable, it can sometimes be better to strive for something great.

Don't let complacency lull you into a life of average. Sometimes it is time to set aside comfort and try for something better. Motivate yourself to achieve more.

All it takes is perseverance and you might achieve things you never imagined you could. That spirit is why we love to repeat this mantra to ourselves now and again. To remind ourselves that now and then, we need to break out of our comfort zone and try for the "brass ring".

(iv) Laughter lightens my load

The power of laughter is well known in positive psychology. Laughing has many benefits. Both short term and long term. Laughter:

- Increases oxygen intake. Stimulating the heart, lungs, muscles and many other organs.
- Releases endorphins to the brain.
- Relieves stress.
- Decreases heart rate.
- Improves immune system.
- Reduces pain.
- Improves mood.
- Increases personal satisfaction.

(v) Be a warrior, not a worrier

Anxiety can get the best of us.

Sometimes we need to fight back and stand up for ourselves. This mantra gets us looking to the warrior spirit that is inside of us all to fight back against the anxiety. As the turn of phrase so clearly brings about to be a warrior rather than a worrier.

(vi) I choose to be calm and at peace

- I choose to be calm and at peace.
- I choose to be calm and at peace.

This is a very calming daily mantra. If you are an anxious person, suffer from anxiety. Or simply feel a little bit stressed our having some tools to calm yourself down is important to minimize this negativity. This calming mantra is great to achieve that sense of calm when you are feeling stressed.

(vii) My Life is Good

- My Life is Good - daily mantra.
- My Life is Good.

Gratitude is essential for our happiness. Due to hedonic adaptation many of the good things in life quickly become normal and do not increase our happiness. But when we express gratitude it also reminds of these good things in life.

No matter what is happening in your life, it is therefore important to take a few moments to remind yourself that life is good.

It is important to remember that your life is good and that there is so much to be grateful for! This simple mantra helps boost happiness and calm you down.

(viii) I am blessed with an incredible family and wonderful friends

- Family & friends mantra.

For many of us, our family and friends are the most important things in our lives.

But, ironically we forget about them and their support very quickly when we need them the most.

This mantra is designed to remind you of the family and friends and how important they can be in your life. Particularly when you feel sad, depressed or feeling lonely.

(ix) I let go of anything not for my highest good

- I let go of anything not for my highest good.
- I let go of anything not for my highest good.

In life, it is important to let go of the past and focus on the present, future and the things that you can change.

When you fail to forgive yourself for past mistakes you are only hurting yourself. The same is true when you are still bitter over things others have done to you in the past.

A good example of letting go and focusing on the "highest good" is after a breakup with someone you love. You could sit around angry and hurt about a failed relationship or you could go out and try to find someone new (and better). Always choose to strive for that higher good.

(x) Love radiates out from me in all directions and returns to me multiplied

- Love radiates out from me in all directions and returns to me multiplied.
- Love radiates out from me in all directions and returns to me multiplied.

We all want to be loved. Even if you have many who love you it is natural to want more. It is just human nature.

This mantra is a wonderful reminder to both give love and be willing to receive love, The love in the universe is infinite. Sometimes you just need to open yourself up to experience the love. This love mantra is a great reminder of that.

20.2.2 Time-tested Famous Mantras

These mantras have been used for centuries. They are tried and tested and many people discover great enlightenment and focus when they use these mantra's regularly in their lives and mindful daily practices.

Om or Aum – This is probably the most famous mantra around. It has been used for centuries in the practice of Yoga and Meditation. This sound is said to be the first sound made when the universe was created. Although I am not sure who was around to record that sound....

Shanti Mantra, a chant for peace – "sarvesham svastir bhavatu — sarvesham shantir bhavatu — sarvesham purnam bhavatu — sarvesham mangalam bhavatu" translation: May there be well-being for all, may there be peace for all. May there be wholeness for all, may there be happiness for all.

Yoga Mantra – May we together be protected; may we together be nourished. May we work together with vigour, may our study be illuminating. May we be free from discord.

Mangala Mantra – May the rulers of the earth protect the well-being of the people, with justice, by means of the right path. May there always be good fortune for all living beings. May all the inhabitants of the world be full of happiness

Gayatri Mantra – Earth, Heaven, the Whole Between. The excellent divine power of the sun. May we contemplate the radiance of that god, may this inspire our understanding.

Pema Condron Mantra –You are the sky, everything else is just the weather

Hebrew Mantra "Elohim" – meaning "who to turn to when need of guidance in life"

Buddhist mani mantra –"Om Vasudhare Svaha," This mantra is a prayer to the earth goddess. Traditionally for this chant to have success. Doing this will have the earth goddess shower you with abundance.

Laura Silver Mantra – "Every day in every way I'm getting better and better."

Lokah Samastah Sukhino Bhavantu – Sanskrit Mantra -Translation – May all beings everywhere be happy and free. May our thoughts, our words, and our actions, contribute in some way to that happiness and freedom.

So Hum Mantra – The translation of So Hum (Sanskrit) is 'I AM'.

Famous Gandhi Mantra -"Be the change you wish to see in the world."

Serenity Prayer – God, grant me the serenity to accept the things I cannot change, the courage to change the things I can, and wisdom to know the difference.

20.3 More Daily Mantras for Happiness

- I'm worth it.
- I love myself. No matter what!
- I am in complete control of determining my emotions.
- My body is good.
- I choose me.
- I am in control of my own emotions.
- I believe in my skills and abilities.
- I surround myself with loving people.
- I have everything I need.
- Where I am right now is exactly where I need to be.
- I choose to be happy.
- Every day is a new beginning.
- Suffering is temporary. It gets better.

- All I need comes to me when I need it.
- I am blessed.
- I am worthy of good things.
- I am not just a drop in the ocean. I am the ocean in one drop.
- I am thankful for all life has given me.
- I will not take for granted the people who love me.
- A river of compassion washes away my anger and replaces it with love.
- Look back at your happy and humble past. Marvel at how far you have come.
- The grass looks greener on the other side. Stop looking at the other side. Stop comparing. Stop complaining. Begin to water the grass you're standing on.
- The true measure of success is not how many times you fall down, but how many times you get back up.
- One bad chapter does not make the book of your life.
- Worry is a waste of time. It has no benefits and takes away time and resources better spent on doing.
- Good riddance to decisions that don't support self-care, self-value, and self-worth.
- No one has ever been blinded by looking at the bright side of things.
- I have the power to shape my ideal reality.
- I create the life I desire with my good feelings.
- Everything is always working out well for me.
- When I feel happy I manifest more reasons to be happy.
- I am willing to be happy now.
- I accept that happiness is my true nature.
- I am worthy of feeling happy.
- My happiness comes from within me.
- I create my happiness by accepting every part of myself with unconditional love.
- Joy is the essence of my being.
- I see so many positives in my life.
- I am constantly creating everything my heart desires.
- I experience joy in everything I do.
- I feel happy with myself as a person.
- I give myself permission to enjoy myself.
- I allow myself to feel good.
- The life I've always dreamed of is created by my choice to be joyful now.

- Following my joy reveals the path to my best life.
- My choice to be happy keeps me in perfect health.
- The happiness I feel is felt by everyone around me.
- I create the possibility of happiness for others by being happy.
- I am meant to live a happy life.
- My inner joy expands when I share it with others.
- All the good in my life comes to me as result of my willingness to find happiness in each moment.
- My happiness is reflected back to me in everything I attract.
- My inner joy is the source of all the good in my life.
- I experience joy in everything I do.

Mantras and affirmations are not the be-all and end-all of achieving your dreams. You will still need to go out and put in the work. But mantras can be a great way to "get your head on straight", boost your confidence and help you focus.

20.4 Keys to Happiness

Following are some of the keys to happiness:

- Live beneath your means.
- Return everything you borrow.
- Stop blaming other people.
- Admit it when you make a mistake.
- Give clothes, but not worn, to charity.
- Do something nice and try not to get caught.
- Do not let your charitable works become an opportunity for publicity.
- Listen more, talk less.
- Take a 30-minute walk every day.
- Strive for excellence, not perfection.
- Be on time. Don't make excuses.
- Don't argue. Get organized.
- Be kind to unkind people.
- Take time to be alone.
- Cultivate good manners.
- Be humble.

- Realize and accept that life isn't fair.
- Know when to keep your mouth shut.
- Donate To The Poor Online, without publicizing it.

CHAPTER TWENTY-ONE

MEASUREMENT OF HAPPPINESS

21.1 Introduction to Measurement of Happiness

Happiness is defined as the subjective enjoyment of one's life as a whole, also called 'life-satisfaction.' Two components of happiness are distinguished; an affective component (how well one feels most of the time) and a cognitive component (the degree to which one perceived to get what one wants from life). Individually people seek ways to a more satisfying life and in Western societies this quest is manifest in the soaring sales of 'how-to-be -happy books', such as 'The art of happiness' (Dalai Lama & Cutler 1998). It is also reflected in the development of life-coaching businesses. Citizens in western societies also call on their governments for greater happiness and 85% of the British agree with the statement that 'a governments prime aim should be achieving the greatest happiness of the people, not the greatest wealth'. Consequently, interest in happiness is rising among policy makers; happiness is a new topic on the political agenda, next to sustainability.

To be able to measure happiness, some premises need to be met: (i) We need to know what happiness actually is, thus, we need a clear definition of this construct. (ii) We need measures that capture the defined concept of happiness validly and reliably. The available measures of happiness in the sense of life-satisfaction, drawing on measures and findings are gathered in the World Database of Happiness. A next question is which measures are most appropriate in what context.

(i) Hedonic level of affect

Hedonic level of affect is the degree to which various affects that someone experiences are pleasant in character. The concept of hedonic level concerns only the pleasantness experienced in affects, that is, the pleasantness in feelings, in emotions, as well as in moods. So a high hedonic level may be based on strong but passing emotions of love, as well as on moods of steady calmness. A person's average hedonic level of affect can be assessed over different periods of time: an hour, a week, a year, as well as over a lifetime. The focus here is on 'characteristic' hedonic level. That is so to say: the average over a long time-span such as a month or a year. The concept does not presume subjective awareness of that average level.

(ii) Contentment

Contentment is the degree to which an individual perceives his/her aspirations are being met. The concept presupposes that the individual has developed some conscious wants and has formed an idea about their realization. The factual correctness of this idea is not at stake. The concept concerns the individual's subjective perception.

21.2 Techniques for Measurement of Happiness

21.2.1 Self-report

Happiness as defined above is something on our mind and can for that reason be measured using self-reports. In this respect, happiness differs from many concepts in psychology that do not require subjective awareness, e.g. 'neuroticism'; neurotics mostly do not know how difficult they are, since excessive ego-defence is part of the syndrome. Hence neuroticism is mostly measured using observations of symptoms from which an expert infers the degree of neuroticism. These symptoms are often measured using self-reports and as such self-reports can be used to measure neuroticism indirectly. Direct questions such as 'How neurotic are you?' are not appropriate for this subject.

Direct self-report is possible in the case of happiness and is the only suitable technique in the cases of 'overall happiness' and 'contentment'.

Happiness cannot be measured using peer ratings; friends cannot look into your head and can at best guess how much you like your life.

Self-reports are typically made in response to single direct questions, which respondents answer by ticking one of several pre-given answer options.

21.2.2 Rating by others

The case of hedonic level of happiness is different. Hedonic level can be measured using time sampling techniques in which an investigator aggregates repeated self-reports of momentary affect. Since hedonic level reflects in non-verbal behaviour it can also be measured using observation techniques, such as time-sampling of smiling, and using ratings by parents or peers.

These measures quantify how much people like the life they live. This is typically not assessed in qualitative studies on happiness, which focus on what people like or not. A few studies have estimated the degree (quantity) of happiness on the basis of content analysis of qualitative data such as life review interviews and ego-documents.

Of the many measures claimed to assess 'happiness' about half tap something else than happiness as 'the subjective enjoyment of one's life as a whole'. The measures that do fit this concept are gathered in the 'Collection of Happiness Measures' of the World Database of Happiness. To date this collection contains about 2000 measures, most of which are single direct questions that differ slightly in phrasing and response format.

The strength of each of these selected measures is that it is clear what they measure; there is no doubt about their validity. A strong point of the World Database of Happiness collection is that investigators can choose a variant that fits their research needs best.

One weakness of most of these measures is that they are not very precise. While corrections can reduce this reliability deficit, they cannot entirely solve it. A further weakness of this family of indicators is that the many small differences between measures reduce comparability across studies. New transformation techniques will improve comparability, though it will remain a problem in happiness research.

21.3 Can You Test and Measure Happiness Scientifically?

Self-reports allows us to take the assessment over and over, especially after specific interventions. The specific self-report test gives us a way to measure our happiness and find out if the changes we have implemented in our lives have made an impact. It also gives us an idea of specific times when we are doing well and how we can continue to do well.

Another way of scientifically measuring happiness can be done by specifically looking at biological factors. As the happiness doctor focuses on studying happiness by looking at different biological indicators. They take samples of **saliva and urine** from their participants so that they can study changes in neurotransmitters and hormones.

Happiness can also be measured by studying our different behaviors. More obvious behaviors would be smiling and laughing. The **Duchenne smile**, meaning smiling with your eyes, is said to be a sign of a genuine smile. Studying the presence of a Duchenne smile is also another behaviour that can be observed and it has previously been connected with good thoughts and happiness.

Behaviors that involve **gratitude**, acts of kindness or generosity, and appreciation, may be other ways to measure happiness as these have been found to positively correlate with our wellbeing.

Psychology Behind How Happiness is Measured

Meik Wiking, CEO of the Danish Happiness Research Institute, states that happiness can have many different meanings among different people. Happiness is also a subjective experience and is often interchangeably referred to as subjective-well-being. Because of this, some measures may look at our overall wellbeing and not just one aspect of happiness. Wiking further explains that in order to measure happiness, it is important to look at the various parts that contribute to the concept of happiness.

Wiking shares that before diving into these factors, we must first differentiate between momentary happiness and overall happiness. Momentary happiness takes into consideration our current state and emotions. On the other hand, overall happiness considers our experiences, such as positive affect and life satisfaction, over a given time.

Now that we know the difference between momentary and overall happiness, we can consider the three main factors that contribute to it, namely a person's genetics, situation, and behavior as Wiking stated. Among these three factors, psychologists have found that our behavior can account for 40% of our happiness. It is also possible to consider three different constructs, that are involved when talking about happiness: more positive emotions, high-life-satisfaction, and less negative emotions.

These three, mean that, when we are happy, we are likely to experience more positive emotions such as pleasure, contentment, and joy. We are also more likely to report that we are highly satisfied with our lives. High life satisfaction usually means that we have a good number of positive experiences in the different aspects of life, such as in our relationships, at work, and in our own personal development. Lastly, as happy people, we infrequently experience negative emotions, like anger, guilt, and fear.

Studies have shown that we can positively impact our own happiness by focusing on the way we interpret situations and experiences, how we perceive our own lives, and what we choose to think and do on a daily basis.

Happiness, more than anything, is a state of mind, a way of perceiving and approaching ourselves and the world in which we reside.

The Secrets of Happiness Survey

There are many surveys available to help us discover the secrets to happiness. These questionnaires make use of different questions, items, and scoring systems. A good number of these surveys were created by psychologists who recognized that there was a need to be able to measure happiness.

The True Happiness Scale

Is there a test that we can consider as the true happiness scale?

Happiness, with its many different definitions, tends to be a highly subjective topic. The different tests available measure happiness in many ways. These tests also look at various factors that contribute to happiness. Even the manner of how these surveys assess happiness can greatly differ from each other. Some assessments are lengthy with different types of questions while others are so short you can possibly memorize them.

One thing these happiness surveys have in common is that they aim to help you identify what happiness looks like for yourself. These happiness tests can also guide you to work on specific areas of your life.

Here are a few surveys to help you find the secrets to your own happiness:

The Penn Authentic Happiness Survey and Test

This survey is also known as the Authentic Happiness Inventory, which can be accessed through the University of Pennsylvania Authentic Happiness website. The survey was developed in 2005 by Christopher Peterson, who was a psychologist and professor at the University of Michigan.

This inventory is one of Peterson's many contributions to the field of Positive Psychology. This self-assessment looks at how you experience positive emotions, how engaged you are in your day-to-day tasks, and how you feel towards your life's meaning and purpose.

There is a total of 24 item groups in the inventory. Each group consists of 5 statements which refer to how you view different aspects of life. The assessment requires that you choose a statement, from each group, that best describes your past week.

Your score is presented to you at the end of the inventory and is shown on a scale of 1 to 5, with 5 being the highest in terms of happiness. The Authentic Happiness site only shows scores in relation to other people who have taken it. The site also explains that scores on this assessment do not indicate exactly what your happiness looks like.

This inventory is recommended if you want to track your own happiness. You can take the assessment every so often and see how your scores fluctuate on a weekly basis. The movement of your scores can likely help you to better understand what contributes to your own happiness.

The Yale Happiness Test

Laurie Santos, a psychology professor at Yale University, opened her Psychology and The Good Life class in January 2018. It received an incredible amount of attention with over 1,200 students registering for the class.

At the start of the course, students were asked to take a happiness test. Santos uses the University of Pennsylvania Authentic Happiness Inventory to help her participants gain a clearer idea of their own happiness.

By the middle of 2018, Santos launched her course online through Coursera and is free to take. It is reported that there have been over 130,000 people who have enrolled in the course since its launch.

The Oxford Happiness Questionnaire

This questionnaire received its name because it was created by Michael Argyle and Peter Hills at Oxford University. Argyle and Hills stated that the questionnaire is an improved version of its predecessor, the Oxford Happiness Inventory.

This happiness questionnaire consists of 29 statements. The items are a combination of positively and negatively phrased statements and pertain to different areas of well-being. This ensures that the respondent takes time to carefully read each item before answering. The survey asks you to evaluate each statement and rate it according to how much you disagree or agree with the statement. It uses a 6-point Likert scale with 6 being the highest as "strongly agree".

The Subjective Happiness Scale

The Subjective Happiness Scale (SHS) is a short and straight-forward survey. It was created by Lyubomirsky and Lepper. This scale is also often referred to as the General Happiness Scale.

The SHS consists of only four items, each rated on a 7-point Likert scale that differs per item. The items were validated through 14 different studies with over 2,700 participants and were found to be correlated with other well-being scales.

To interpret your score, consider which group you belong to. If you are a working adult and your score is higher than a 5.6, you can consider yourself happier than most people. It is recommended that you seek professional help or find interventions to help you if your score is lower than a 4.

The SHS is really easy to use since it is short. You can use the items as a guide and complete them mentally. Some practitioners also use the items during an interview.

The 1-10 Happiness Scale

The 1-10 scale is likely the most popular one among all the happiness surveys out there. This is because there are quite a number of them. The most common among all of the happiness scales is that it aims to help you assess your current happiness in life. It can even be more specific by asking you about a particular area of your life. Here is an example of the 1-10 Happiness Scale.

Happiness scales can range from 10 to around 20 items. Each item is usually a category related to a specific part of your life. An example of this would be family, work, spirituality, communication, sleep, health, and even sobriety.

The scoring system is the same across all scales. You are asked to rate each item on a 10-point Likert scale, 10 being the highest. A score of 10 indicates that you are "very happy" with that area, while a score of 1 shows how "very unhappy" you are.

This scale is convenient to use since you can measure your own happiness. One way of doing this is to ask yourself "On a scale of 1 to 10, How happy am I with...?" and ask yourself this question for various parts of your life.

The Happiness Test by Psychology Today

Psychology Today, a popular magazine and website, devotes itself to providing you with the most recent updates and studies in the field of Psychology. They created their own Happiness Test which can be taken for free on their website. The free version gives you a snapshot of your results. You can also opt to pay their fee to gain access to your full report.

The test consists of 47 items and takes around 20 minutes to complete. Items are a combination of hypothetical and self-assessment statements. Each item is rated on a 5-point scale with various meanings depending on the item being answered.

There are 11 items that are rated based on how often the statement describes you – 1 being "most of the time" and 5 being "almost never". The next 23 items are rated on how much you agree with each statement, 1 being "strongly agree" and 5 being "strongly disagree. The last 12 items offer a scenario and ask a question at the end. You are asked to choose one out of the five answers provided.

Results of the Happiness Test gives you an idea of how pessimistic or optimistic you are. The free version gives your score on a scale of 1 to 100 and provides a paragraph that explains what your score means. You will be asked to pay their fee to see more than that.

Measuring happiness: unifying the methodologies

Of course, if one academic study into subjective well-being uses a particular questionnaire, then the results found in that sample group can only inform us of that group of people and of other groups which have been subject to assessments using the same methodology.

If academics use their own questionnaires, then no matter how carefully the data they collate has been analysed, it's not possible to pool such datasets. Therefore, relatively simple questionnaire formats have been developed so that researchers can use the same scales and the same form of wording around their questions in order to obtain results which can be used together.

The Subjective Happiness Scale is a good example of this sort of approach. The questionnaire can be downloaded by anyone so long as it's for academic research and not commercial use. It uses a simple scoring system of one to seven which cleverly allows people to place themselves in the middle of the scale, at number four, if they feel that's appropriate for them – not all scales allow for this.

Additionally, it allows researchers to ask negative questions, like those about being unhappy. All the researcher needs to do is to reverse the scoring system to continue to obtain viable and simple-to-understand results. Another questionnaire that does this is the 'Better Life Index', the sophisticated survey from the Organization for Economic Co-operation and Development (OECD).

"Happiness is rather like physical well-being: multiple measurements and assessments must be made to understand the body's well-being in the round." With small sample groups, this approach works very conveniently. For mass observations surveys, such as those which measure and compare happiness in every country of the world, it's essential.

21.4 More on Methods for Measuring Happiness

21.4.1 Measurement of Happiness in Social Science Research

Happiness in this context is defined as `the degree to which an individual judges the overall quality of his life-as-a-whole positively', or in short: how well one likes the life one lives. In this way, happiness belongs to a wider class of subjective appraisals of life, which is usually referred to as 'subjective well-being' (SWB) or 'life satisfaction'.

Given the above definition of happiness, the obvious way to measure it is to ask the individual to give his or her opinion on one's own happiness situation. The measurement of the happiness of a particular person as such is the objective of measurement in exceptional cases only; it occurs in psychological practice incidentally.

Sociologists, however, are always interested in the happiness of (members of) collectivities, e.g., of the citizens of a nation, but yet they cannot get away from starting their study with measuring happiness at the individual level. Moreover, they are usually hardly interested in happiness as such, but only in the association of happiness with one or more other variables. These other variables are usually referred to as "correlates" or as "conditions"; the latter term is in particular in use if the observed association with happiness is supposed to be a causal one. In the case the investigation concerns "trends", the other variable is time.

21.4.2 Standard method of measuring happiness in practice

Survey studies

Measuring happiness for social scientific purposes is usually realized as a part of a 'survey' in which a lot of people answer the same questions, either in face-to-face interviews or on questionnaires presented on the web. The way questions are presented to the respondents is adjusted to this technique, and that means typically that question are answered selecting from a limited number of response options (so-called 'closed' questions). We will refer to this method as the standard method, which implies that also non-standard methods exist.

Survey questions

To all members of a sample that is considered to be representative for the target population of the study, one or more closed questions are presented with a limited number of response options. This combination of the question and all response options together is referred to as a primary scale of happiness measurement. In the World Database of Happiness (further abbreviated as WDH), some one thousand such scales have been gathered in the so-called "Measures of Happiness" collection.

In the Happiness Research literature they are often referred to as "items".

Examples of survey questions on happiness:

An example of such a primary scale is the combination of the single question: "Taking all things together, would you say you are ...? " with four response options:

- very happy
- quite happy
- not very happy
- not at all happy

These options are ordered either in ascending or – as in the above example – in descending order of (subjective) happiness intensity; this order should be unambiguous. The respondent is asked to tick the one out of the four response-options he feels to be the most appropriate, or sometimes the least inappropriate.

21.4.3 Happiness measured as a discrete variable at the ordinal level of measurement

Happiness, when measured as described in the above Section, is a discrete variable at the ordinal level of measurement, not only if verbal scales are used, but also for numerical scales. The digits of numerical scales are code numbers in principle; e.g., progress report marks in Dutch schools, where usually "6" is defined as a code number for "satisfactory progress". A variable is called discrete if it can adopt a very limited number of values only, four in the example.

21.4.4 Happiness research at the individual vs. the collective level

Happiness can be measured at two levels, the individual and the collective one. This distinction has consequences for the way the measured responses are treated in the further analysis.

Individual level

In studies at the micro-level of individuals the researchers link the responses for both happiness and the correlate of the study of each respondent separately. In this way one can investigate whether, e.g., very happy people are living more frequently in a rural than in an urban environment or whether the reverse is true.

Collective level

At the macro level of nations this is usually not possible. A scientist who wants to compare the happiness situation of the Dutch population to the French is not interested in all individual responses, but only in the statistical distribution of the happiness intensity in both nations separately. 'Measuring happiness at the collective level' is a short-hand term for measuring this statistical distribution of individual responses of the members of this collectivity. The researchers want to characterize these distributions with one of more index numbers. We use the term "index number" in this context as it is in use among statisticians and economists, i.e. as a number that quantifies a property of a phenomenon in a standard way, so not for the sum score of a number of indicators, as it is used by sociologists.

The next step will be to look for a possible relationship between these index numbers and the index numbers that characterize potentially interesting correlates in both nations. Such correlates do not necessarily bear on individual inhabitants, but can also pertain to living conditions such as, e.g., the climate or the way the government operates in one or more specific respects.

21.4.5 Cumulative frequency distribution of happiness in a sample

The result of measurement of happiness as described in 21.4.2 can be summarized completely in a cumulative frequency distribution, which is characterized by the "cumulative distribution function" (abbreviated as "cdf") of the measured happiness in a sample. This cdf is a step function with the same number of steps as the number of response options of the primary scale of measurement. We will denote this number with the symbol "k". If we give a hypothetical example of a sample with size N=200 and the four-point verbal primary scale (k=4), and so on.

21.4.6 Index numbers for the statistical distribution of happiness

As has been pointed out in Section 21.4.4, happiness research requires the characterization of the happiness distribution by index numbers, in particular of the distribution of happiness in the population. These index numbers are so-called statistics. 'Statistics' in this context are defined as 'variables, the value of which can be calculated from observed data', in our case the sample size, the happiness ratings and their observed frequencies.

Usually two such index numbers are defined. One is for the general happiness level, also referred to as the "central tendency of the distribution", for which the average or mean value is the usual choice; most statisticians make a distinction between "average" for the sample distribution and "mean" for the population distribution. The other index number is to characterize the dispersion, the scatter around the central value, in other words the inequality or disparity within a distribution. A conventional choice for this statistic is the standard deviation of the distribution. The most frequently used symbols for these sample statistics are m and s respectively.

Contrary to a wide-spread belief, not only the standard deviation, but also the average value is to be considered as a statistic that characterizes the happiness inequality. Whereas the standard deviation characterizes the inequality within a distribution, the average value of the latter has, from a sociological point of view, no other meaning than to characterize the inequality between distributions of different nations or other collectivities.

CHAPTER TWENTY-TWO

BENEFICIAL EFFECTS OF HAPPINESS

22.1 Benefits of Happiness

Over the past several decades the science of subjective well-being, or happiness, has been developed and the findings help us understand many of the factors that lead to this positive state. Importantly, it was discovered that happiness is more than a measure of individual welfare. It has a generative capability that brings about a host of beneficial effects. When people are happy they are more likely to be productive, creative, helpful, and have good health. Happiness does not merely feel good; it benefits both the person and the society. More importantly, happiness functions as a psychological and societal resource that is beneficial for achieving a wide variety of desirable outcomes, helping citizens to be better friends, neighbors.

employees, and citizens. In light of this, happiness is not synonymous with selfish hedonism, which can work against other values such as good citizenship and altruism. Instead, it is a characteristic that helps people achieve their values. Religion, self-help books, and accumulated wisdom point to the belief that the practice of happiness brings about benefits.

Science has now analyzed the specific ways in which happiness generates tangible benefits. The experience of well-being encourages individuals to pursue goals that are resource-building to meet future challenges. In line with this, a sense of wellness helps individuals engage in new goals that promote gains rather than goals that only emphasize preventing losses. At the physiological level negative emotions have been found to hurt immune, cardiovascular, and endocrine functioning. In contrast, positive emotions improve them.

This discovery makes it imperative that societies monitor happiness, and consider happiness scores when deciding on new policies. Some have argued that measures of economic development are all we need to assess the progress of societies. Although economic progress can be desirable, it can produce some negative outcomes, such as environmental pollution, a reduction in social capital, inequality, and higher rates of major depression. Thus, it is important to balance economic measures with measures of subjective well-being, to ensure that economic progress leads to broad improvements across life domains, not just higher incomes. By assessing subjective well-being as well as economic variables, the society can gauge whether overall net progress is positive.

It was Aristotle who once said "Happiness is the meaning and purpose of life, the whole aim and the end of human existence" – a sentiment that is still true today. While Aristotle had a philosophical notion of the importance of happiness for human well-being, today we have a range of science and research to back it up.

Scientific studies have begun to reveal a host of physical health benefits surrounding happiness including a stronger immune system, stronger resilience in the face of stress, a stronger heart and less risk of cardiovascular disease, alongside quicker recovery times when overcoming illness or surgery. There is even a body of research that indicates being happy may help us to live longer lives.

Across all of the research, there is a conflict between whether feeling happier directly leads to better health outcomes, or whether it is merely a correlation.

Some researchers have hypothesized that feeling happier and more positive leads to greater participation in activities that are healthier including exercise, eating healthy, socializing and good sleeping habits. Either way, the two are connected, and researchers are continually seeking to explore the link further.

22.2 Physical Health Benefits of Happiness

The benefit of being happy is not limited to psychological aspects alone. Happiness also plays a big role in physical health. Happiness can provide benefits not only to an individual's mental health but also physical health. If you want some inspiration to get a happier life, take a look at these ways happiness has been linked to good health:

(i) Happiness Lowers the Risk of Cardiovascular Disease

A happy life means you are less prone to develop heart disease. Basically, spending some few minutes each day relaxing and enjoying yourself is definitely good for your mental health, which can improve your physical health as well.

(ii) Happiness Strengthens Immune System

There are a lot of people who deal with a wide range of conditions, and many of the observable symptoms as a result of stress and more. Constructive thinking and attitude are able to prompt changes in your body that reinforce your immune system, improve positive emotions, reduce pain and chronic disease, and provide stress relief.

When it comes to the immune system, many people believe that it's all natural. Whilst that may seem to be true, it's not 100% exact. What you have to appreciate is that you can actually enhance your immune system through happiness.

(iii) Happiness Fights Stress

A brief exposure to high anxiety levels can harm the brain and obstruct good cognitive functioning. As a part of a brain-healthy way of life, it's important to manage stress successfully and effectively.

The following may help you combat stress:

- Exercise;

- Recreation;
- Socialization (can do this with group classes);
- Self-empowerment;
- Getting a good laugh; and
- Having an optimistic belief.

(iv) Happiness Leads to Fewer Aches and Pains

Positive emotions also lessen the feelings of constant pain.

Unhappiness can be literally painful. Aching and negative symptoms like muscle strain, faintness, and indigestion and even arthritis and prolonged pain seem to be less painful when we are happy mainly as we have more of endorphins in our bloodstream effectively acting as the natural painkillers.

(v) Happiness Combats Disease and Disability

Happiness leads to improvements with long-term conditions as well. In a study of 10,000 Australians in the 2008 American Journal of Health Promotion, those who were happy and fulfilled 'most of the time' were 1.5 times less likely to have a long-term health condition.

Another study written in 2008 BMC Cancer showed that females with breast cancer were less happy and positive before their diagnosis as compared to females without breast cancer.

(vi) Happiness Lengthens Life Expectancy

Happiness leads to a long life. In a famous long-term study of Catholic Nuns researched by Deborah Danner et al, the happiest lived 7-10 years longer than the least happy. IKIGAI is another technique to conclude that some citizens in Japan live more than 100 years.

Whilst happiness can make you live longer, keep in mind that it can't perform miracles. It is in a sense that happiness and long life do not extend to people who are ill.

(vii) Improved Heart Health

Several studies have linked happiness with improved heart health and lower risk of heart disease by 13-26%

22.3 A Look at the Research on Happiness

Below is an overview of some of the research exploring the physical health benefits of happiness:

(i) A researcher asked participants to rate their happiness at 30 different points in one day. Participants were asked to repeat the exercise three years later. Their findings showed that individuals who rated themselves as the happiest at both the first and later exercise were also those with a lower heart rate and blood pressure. People with lower heart rates and blood pressure are less likely to suffer from cardiovascular disease. This suggests that feelings of happiness contribute positively to these physical measurements.

(ii) A group of researchers found a link between happiness and heart health. The researchers studied individuals who already had, or were suspected of having coronary heart disease. They asked participants to rate their happiness, and their hearts were then tested for symptoms. Those who rated the highest for happiness on the day also had the healthiest heart patterns. This suggests that happiness can still have health benefits, even when illness or disease is already present.

(iii) Happiness has also been linked to reducing the risk of a stroke. Strokes occur when the blood flow to the brain is disrupted, resulting in a loss of physical control and responsiveness. Depending on the severity and longevity of the disruption, a stroke can have dire consequences for the individual. Some researchers found older adults with a higher reporting of positive well-being, had a reduced likelihood of experiencing a stroke by 26%.

(iv) Some of the earliest studies in this area have focused on the immune system. A researcher explored the persistence of the human immune system when participants reported positive moods by having them ingest a pill that caused an immune response. Participants were asked to rate their mood across different days and then their saliva was tested for antibodies in response to the pill. Those who rated themselves the happiest had a higher level of antibodies. The results suggest that feeling more positive can help support the immune system to defend against foreign bodies.

(v) Two studies further explored the impact of positive emotions on the immune system. One group asked participants to rate their experience of positive emotions over a two-week period. They then exposed them to the common cold virus and checked in five days later to see who had developed a cold. Those who rated themselves as experiencing the most positive emotions in the preceding two weeks were less likely to have fallen sick. A similar study exposed participants to the hepatitis B vaccine and asked them to rate their positive emotions. Those who rated highest for positive emotions were twice as likely to have a high antibody response.

(vi) Three researchers found that happier people are better able to mitigate pain when experiencing chronic illness. Participants with chronic pain, such as arthritis, were asked to rate their positive emotions across a three-month period. Their personal experiences of pain relating to their illness were also measured. Those who reported higher ratings of positive feelings also reported fewer increases in pain. Similar studies also found these results to be consistent with participants with chronic pain.

22.4 Some Interesting Scientific Findings about Happiness

(i) Some researchers explored the impact of happiness on 32,000 participants and their survival rate over a 30-year period. Participants who were rated the least happy had a 14% higher chance of death than their happiest counterparts.

(ii) A quantitative review of 70 observational studies explored the link between positive affect (well-being) and life expectancy, in both healthy participants and participants who had already been diagnosed with a health condition. Healthy participants who were rated as having a higher positive affect reduced their risk of death by 18%, and by 2% for those with a pre-existing condition.

(iii) A further study exploring this connection also indicates that it is the consistency of life satisfaction (or happiness) that has an impact on life longevity. Some researchers found that participants who reported a low sense of life satisfaction with a high level of variability (meaning they went through high and low phases) were more likely to die earlier than participants who reported a consistently low sense of satisfaction.

(iv) Researchers have speculated over why this link seems to exist, and why it is so prominent for participants who rate the highest for happiness and positive emotions. Many believe it is because individuals who are happiest, are also more inclined to engage in activities and behaviors that are positive for their overall health, including physical exercise, eating healthy, not smoking, sleeping well, and even meditation.

22.5 Other Benefits of Happiness

(i) Happiness Boosts Productivity

Consider a study which measured people's initial level of happiness, and then followed their job performance for the next 18 months. Even after controlling for other factors, people who were happier at the beginning received higher pay and better evaluations later on.

A similar study measured college freshmen's happiness levels. 19 years later, it predicted how high their income was, regardless of their initial financial situation.

Happy workers, in general, are more productive, perform more effectively as leaders, generate more sales, take fewer days off due to sickness, and receive higher pay and higher performance ratings across the board. Happy people make more money and are more productive at work.

(ii) Happiness and Relationships

Happiness is good for our relationships. Happy people are more likely to get married and to have fulfilling marriages, and they have more friends.

(iii) Happiness and Generosity

Happy people are more generous.

(iv)Happiness Primes You to Perform at Your Best

Happy people are more creative and are better able to see the big picture. One experiment asked four-year-old kids to complete a series of learning tasks, such as putting together blocks of different shapes. One group was told to put together the blocks as quickly as possible. The other group was given the same instructions, but were told to first think of something that makes them happy.

The results? Children "primed" — meaning researchers evoked a certain emotion or mindset before an experiment — for happiness significantly outperformed the other kids, completing the tasks faster and with fewer errors.

Another experiment yielded even more impressive results. A common med school exercise for doctors in training is to make a diagnosis based on a rundown of a patient's symptoms and history.

In this experiment, the doctors in training were put into three groups. One group was primed to feel happy before making the diagnosis. Another was asked to read neutral material, and a control group wasn't given any special instructions prior to the exercise.

The happiness-primed doctors ended up being twice as fast at making the right diagnosis compared to the other groups. They were also less likely to fall prey to something called anchoring — a phenomenon that occurs when a doctor has trouble letting go of an initial diagnosis (the anchor point), even in the face of updated information that contradicts the initial diagnosis.

Priming the brain for happiness doesn't just work for kids and doctors. Another study showed that students who were told to think about the happiest day of their lives before taking a math test outperformed their peers. And people who expressed more positivity while negotiating business deals did so more effectively than those expressing more neutral or negative emotions.

The message is clear: Sacrificing happiness for success will result in, well, less success. Instead, why not capitalize on happiness and bring about more success that way?

(v) Happiness Creates Success (Much More than Success Creates Happiness!)

Society preaches a simple success/happiness model: If you work hard, you'll become successful, and once you're sufficiently successful, you'll be happy.

Don't even worry about happiness right now. First, become a success, and then happiness will follow.

Once you earn enough money, drive a nice car, own a lovely house, and are successful in your career, then you'll be happy. And if not, maybe lose those last five pounds, earn some more money, upgrade your wardrobe, and then you'll be happy.

Keep chasing after success, and once you've made it, then you'll be happy.

But don't try to be happy right now! That's futile, if you're not yet successful enough. First, you need to work hard, sacrifice your health and friendships, and then you'll automatically be happy.

Don't worry about happiness; double down on becoming a success instead.

The only problem with that model? It's broken.

There's always more success to be chased after. More money, more fame, more power — it never ends. Once you get your promotion, you'll set sail for another goal. Once you achieve that goal, another one follows. Most of us pursue one unfulfilling goal after another, hoping success finally comes with accomplishing the next one. Before we know it, life has passed us by and we're no happier than before.

Even if we "make it" and become out-of-this-world successful, what then? That's the fate of drug-addicted Hollywood stars and grumpy millionaires — not exactly role models of flourishing and happiness.

More importantly, though, the formula is broken because it's backwards. As you've just learned, happiness fuels performance like nothing else. By sacrificing happiness, we limit our own potential for success.

Happiness leads to success much more than success leads to happiness.

A leading happiness researcher, describes the relationship between happiness and success:

"It turns out that our brains are literally hardwired to perform at their best not when they are negative or even neutral, but when they are positive. Yet in today's world, we ironically sacrifice happiness for success only to lower our brain's success rates...

When we are happy — when our mindset and mood are positive — we are smarter, more motivated, and thus more successful. Happiness is the centre, and success revolves around it."

It's an odd situation — the less happy we are, the less likely we are to get the thing (success) we expect to bring us happiness.

Let's assume you want to be happy. And let's assume you want to be successful too. Your best bet to achieve both of these goals is to double down on becoming happier.

Obviously, that achieves your first goal. And because happiness is a sort of precursor to success, you'll also be more likely to achieve the second goal.

Happiness brings you everything you want.

The point is, stop delaying happiness. Actively and deliberately work on becoming happier now. Not only will it make you happy, but it will make you a success too. Last but not the least, it will make everyone happy among your family, friends and colleagues. As emphasized in this book, happiness is contagious. So, let everyone be happy.

Bibliography

Al-Ghazzali, Imam, "The Alchemy of Happiness", Translated by Clau Field, 1910. Available online http://nasc.org.np, 2016.Nepal Administrative Staff College.

Blum, Kenneth. "Genes and Happiness", In Gene Therapy & Molecular Biology · January 2009.

Curie, Adam (1998) Happiness as a right, The International Journal of Human Rights, 2:3, 77-83, DOI: 10.1080/13642989808406747

Deeg, Dorly J.H. and Robert J. van Zonneveld. "Does Happiness Lengthen Life?: The prediction of longevity in the elderly" In: Ruut Veenhoven (ed) (1989) How harmful is happiness? Consequences of enjoying life or not. Universitaire Pers Rotterdam, The Netherlands. ISBN nr. 90 257 22809. Chapter 5.

Diener, Ed, and Micaela Y. Chan. "Happy People Live Longer: Subjective Well-Being Contributes to Health and Longevity" Applied Psychology: Health and Well-Being, 3 (1), 1–43, 2011. doi:10.1111/j.1758-0854.2010.01045.x

Dudeja, Jai Paul, "Happiness explained by the ancient Hindu Scriptures and the temporal nonlocality in Quantum Entanglement", https://www.researchgate.net/publication/333817144

Einstein's Formula for a Happy Life: There's a science to everything, Genius Turner, Dec 27, 2020.

Fisher, Cynthia D. " Happiness at Work", International Journal of Management Reviews · December 2010. DOI: 10.1111/j.1468 2370.2009.00270.x · https://www.researchgate.net/publication/227533694

Gada, Manila. "Jaina Religion and Psychiatry", Mens Sana Monogr. 2015 Jan-Dec; 13(1): 70–81. doi: 10.4103/0973-1229.153306

Garcia, Hector and Francesc Miralles. "IKIGAI: The Japanese Secret to a Long and Happy Life", Penguin Books, 2016.

Great Dream: Ten keys to happier livening , www.actionforhappiness.org, ADB South Asia Working Series, No. 42, Dec 2015.

Heap, Dr. Kris. "Happiness is a Habit", Successify.net

Helliwell, John F. et al. "Happiness and Community: An Overview", World Happiness Report, 2019, Chapter 1.

Hem, Bal Br. Hemchand Jain. "The Way to Real Happiness", Priya Shree Kanjiswami Smarak Trust, 2001.

His Holiness, Dalai Lama and Howard C. Cutler, "The Art of Happiness: A Handbook for Living", Riverhead Books, 1998.

Joshanloo, Mohsen; "A Comparison of Western and Islamic Conceptions of Happiness", J Happiness Stud (2013) 14:1857–1874. DOI 10.1007/s10902-012-9406-7

Journal of Management and Development Studies Vol. 27:pp.1-15

Kaczmarek, Lukasz Dominik. "Happiness", Jan 2017, https://www.researchgate.net/publication/319287771.

Kalmijn, Wim. "Methods for Measurement of Happiness", World Database of Happiness Measures of happiness Introductory text.

Knight, John and Ramani Gunatilaka, "Is Happiness Infectious?" Scottish Journal of Political Economy, DOI: 10.1111/sjpe.12105, Vol. 64, No. 1, February 2017

Lombrozo, Tania. "Is Happiness A Universal Human Right?", March 20, 2017, 9:03 AM, ET

Martela, Frank, et. al. "The Nordic Exceptionalism: What Explains Why the Nordic Countries are Constantly Among the Happiest in the World", World Happiness Report 2020, Chapter 7.

McCrae, Gemma. "The Happiness Revolution: Instant Happiness Volume", Prosperity Kitchen Publication, 2017.

Mihr, Imam Iskender Ali, "Islam Happiness Sufism", The Mihr Publications.

Monaco, Edoardo. "Notes on Bhutan's Gross National Happiness and its Measurement",

Norren, Dorine van, et al. "The Right to Happiness in three traditions of the global south: Buddhist Happiness, African Ubuntu, and indigenous American BuenVivir", dorinevannorren@yahoo.com

Radhika P et. al. "Happiness - The Role of Neurochemicals" , Volume 9 Issue 9, September 2020. www.ijsr.net

Ricard, Matthieu, "Happiness: A Guide to Developing Life's Most Important Skill", Little, Brown and Company, 2003.

Seethalakshmi, "Neurotransmitters and their Impact on Mental Illness", International Journal of Science and Research (IJSR), Volume 6 Issue 5, May 2017, 2319-7064.

Sheikh, Bisma Farooq. "Happiness Revolution: A Research transition from Illness to Wellness", Apr 2020, https://www.researchgate.net/publication/340399337

Sirshree. "The Secret of Happiness: Instant Happiness- Here and Now", Tej Gyan Foundation, 2007.

Stevens, Tom G. " You can choose to be Happy: Rise above Anxiety, Anger, and Depression", Wheeler-Sutton Publishing Co., Second Edition, 2010.

Stieg, Cory. "Work-life balance secrets from the happiest countries in the world", "Health and Wellness", Oct 16 2020.

Sud, Le Droit Au Bonheur Dans Trois Traditions. "The Right to Happiness in three traditions of the global south: Buddhist Happiness, African Ubuntu, and indigenous American BuenVivir", dorinevannorren@yahoo.com

Tan, Chade-Meing. "Joy on Demand: The Art of Discovering the Happiness Within", HarperOne, 2016.

Tay, Ed Diener and Louis. "A Scientific Review of the Remarkable Benefits of Happiness for Successful and Healthy Living", Chapter 6.

Thinley, Jigmi Y. "What is Gross National Happiness?", Centre for Bhutan Studies, Proceedings of Second International Conference on Gross National Happiness, 2007.

Tideman, Sander G. "Gross National Happiness", January 2011 DOI:10.1007/978-90-481-9310-3_7, In book: Ethical Principles and Economic Transformation - A Buddhist Approach (pp.133-153).

Tiliouine, Habib, " Happiness in Islam", January 2014, DOI:10.1007/978-94-007-0753-5_1544. In book: Encyclopedia of Quality of Life and Well-Being Research (pp.2662-2667), Springer Netherlands, Editors: Alex C. Michalos.

Ura, Karma. "The Experience of Gross National Happiness as Development Framework",

Veenhoven, Ruut. "Measures of Happiness: Which to Choose?", https://www.researchgate.net/publication/318857438

Veeraiah, Chandrasekaran, "The pursuit of happiness: An Advaita Vedanta perspective", https://www.researchgate.net/publication/305703294.

www.ingramcontent.com/pod-product-compliance
Ingram Content Group UK Ltd.
Pitfield, Milton Keynes, MK11 3LW, UK
UKHW041858190726
13854UKWH00002B/959

9 798885 461986